Murder

in the

Dollhouse

Murder in the Dollhouse

THE **JENNIFER DULOS** STORY

Rich Cohen

 FARRAR, STRAUS AND GIROUX   NEW YORK

Farrar, Straus and Giroux
120 Broadway, New York 10271

Printed in the United States of America
First edition, 2025

Frontispiece photograph: ZUMA Press, Inc. / Alamy Stock Photo

Library of Congress Cataloging-in-Publication Data
Names: Cohen, Rich, author.
Title: Murder in the dollhouse : the Jennifer Dulos story / Rich Cohen.
Description: First edition. | New York : Farrar, Straus and Giroux,
    [2025] | Includes bibliographical references.
Identifiers: LCCN 2024049209 | ISBN 9780374608064 (hardcover)
Subjects: LCSH: Dulos, Jennifer, 1968–2019. | Murder—Connecticut—
    New Canaan—Case studies. | Murder—Investigation—Connecticut—
    New Canaan—Case studies.
Classification: LCC HV6534.N379 C64 2025 | DDC 364.152/3097469—
    dc23/eng/20250122
LC record available at https://lccn.loc.gov/2024049209

Our books may be purchased in bulk for promotional, educational, or
business use. Please contact your local bookseller or the Macmillan
Corporate and Premium Sales Department at 1-800-221-7945, extension
5442, or by email at MacmillanSpecialMarkets@macmillan.com.

www.fsgbooks.com
Follow us on social media at @fsgbooks

10 9 8 7 6 5 4 3 2 1

To

Jonathan Galassi

and

Jessica Medoff

Life must be understood backwards. But . . . it must be lived forwards.

—SØREN KIERKEGAARD

Contents

~

Murder
in the
Dollhouse

INTRODUCTION

AT FIRST, IT seemed less terrifying than uncanny: on a typical suburban morning, a fifty-year-old New Canaan, Connecticut, mother dropped her kids off at the elite New Canaan Country School, then disappeared. How can a person as scheduled as Jennifer Dulos, a rich woman in one of the richest towns in America, simply vanish?

The details were filled in via the gossip network that connects parents across Fairfield County: there was a handsome husband, a family fortune, a contentious divorce. It was about money—it's always about money—but also about class, status, and children. Two sets of twins and the baby. In 2012, Jennifer started writing short articles about family life for the news website *Patch* and a blog called "Five Plus Two Equals Seven."

The story reached *The New York Times* on May 31, 2019: "Mystery in a Wealthy Town: She Dropped Off Her Children, Then Went Missing." The piece opened with Jennifer in her Chevy Suburban amid a line of cars outside the New Canaan Country School, the BMWs and Range Rovers, the nannies and lacrosse sticks.

Fotis Dulos was in the story, too. In a case like this, the cops always start by taking the husband aside and asking, "How is your marriage?"

The Duloses' marriage was not good; it had in fact been coming apart for months. At one point, Jennifer actually seemed to predict her own demise. "I know that filing for divorce, and filing this motion will enrage him," she wrote in a request for legal custody of the children. "I know he will retaliate by trying to harm me in some way."

Fotis Dulos was Greek, born in Turkey and raised in Athens before moving to the United States to attend Brown, where he met Jennifer Farber. That was in 1986—autumn, when fallen leaves cover the picturesque campus in Providence. They met, forgot each other, met again, married. Now Jennifer was missing, and Fotis—a fifty-two-year-old builder of luxury homes, suburban monstrosities with outdoor pizza ovens—was the primary suspect.

His nose was straight, his eyes were brown, and his motives were clear.

See the dashing man drinking Scotch by the fireplace in the ski lodge? That lady he's with is not his wife.

The mystery woman soon had a name: Michelle Troconis, known to friends as Michi, a kind of international party girl. Raised in Argentina, Venezuela, Chile, and Miami, she was the daughter of a heart surgeon, the oldest of several beautiful sisters. She had spent much of her adult life on the high-end resort circuit, either lounging or working at spas and hotels that catered to the superrich. She wrangled horses and taught skiing. She had a daughter from her brief marriage to Gaston Begue, a member of Argentina's Olympic ski team and a manager of the Cerro Castor ski resort in Tierra del Fuego, where Michelle had worked in marketing and public relations. She had golden cat-eyes, long auburn hair, and a sharp, angular face. Her visage could be unsettling. There was a mean, teasing quality in the way she looked at people. To some, she seemed like Lady Macbeth, pressuring her lover to do what she wanted done.

Many have pointed out Michelle's resemblance to Jennifer. Fotis clearly had a type—long-haired, elegant, and thin. A friend of Jennifer's described Michelle as "Bizarro Jennifer, similar but different, an evil twin, the surface beauty without the inner light."

Before she became Jennifer Dulos, Jennifer Farber was a sought-after beauty, a New York "it girl": smart, talented, connected. For the literary men who attended downtown parties in the 1990s, making a play for Jen Farber, and failing, was a rite of passage. Her father was rich, her mother was brilliant, and her uncle ran the multimillion-dollar apparel company he'd founded with his wife, Jennifer's aunt Liz Claiborne. In trying to describe Jennifer as she was in the 1990s, people resort to celebrity comparisons—she looked like Stephanie Seymour, Julia Roberts, Mia Sara—which is the ultimate compliment in a society where the famous seem more alive than everyone else. It told you that Jennifer was luminescent. With long hair framing her face, she was nearly six feet tall in heels, graceful, and slender (she was neurotic about keeping her weight below 116 pounds). While doing on-the-side fashion modeling during college, posing mostly for catalogs, she had used the name Jennifer Bey. It was an alias that grew into an alter ego, the person she became when she wanted to be someone else, but she could never really slip away.

Jennifer Farber was a star on the New York scene that included people who went to private schools, had trust funds, and attended parties at the Plaza and Pierre hotels where everyone knows everyone. She was the point and pride of a generation, the peak of a hierarchy, the product of decades of assimilation. She was like an orchid, so carefully sheltered that she seemed fragile. If you won her, it was not just a bride you won, but an entire world.

There is a picture of Jennifer taken five years before her disappearance. The wind blows her hair across her face. She looks happy, healthy. People who knew her in New Canaan say she looked different by the end. The interminable divorce, the custody battle, the presence of Michelle Troconis and her daughter (and the betrayal they represented) had taken a toll. Jennifer had become brittle and gaunt. Hollow, gutted, frail. "She did not look like the woman in the newspaper," one of her attorneys told me. "She looked scared, and vulnerable, and small."

Some criticized the dozens of national news stories about the case as overkill, saying they were published only because Jennifer was beautiful, wealthy, white. They even had a name for the phenomenon: "missing white woman syndrome." But it was more than just the surface details that made the story mesmerizing. It was the horror, the universal nightmare, the way death arrived amid the quotidian details of an ordinary American morning. Jennifer had restraining orders, bodyguards, and every possible resource, but when someone is determined to do you real harm, no amount of money can protect you.

According to police, Fotis was waiting for Jennifer when she returned home after dropping the kids off at school on May 24, 2019. He ambushed her in the garage—an encounter that ended with Jennifer losing more blood than any person could survive. The story riveted attention because it spoke a general truth: we all live on a razor's edge.

A week later, the Connecticut State Police arrested Fotis Dulos for tampering with evidence. He'd been caught on camera disposing of the remnants of what had clearly been a violent act. One item in particular—an extra-small Vineyard Vines T-shirt, Jennifer's favorite, covered in blood—made it all seem so terribly real.

At the time of the arrest, the police released the first of what turned out to be several warrants. Only by reading these warrants, hundreds of detail-crammed pages, would you realize just how much was left out of the news coverage. But the overlooked, seemingly unimportant details—the names of places and products, streets, towns, area codes—show what the people involved wanted, where they came from, and who they were. The big story is in the minutiae. It's in the makes of their cars—the Ford Raptor, the Chevy Suburban, the Porsche Cayenne. It's in the brochure-like descriptions of their houses—manicured lawns and security systems, mudrooms and bedroom suites. It's in the names of their private schools—Saint Ann's, New Canaan Country, Brown. It's in their private tutors and private coaches, their nannies and maids. It's in their trips to Aspen, London, South Beach. It's in the way that everything was ranked.

A particular detail jumped out from the warrants: according to Fotis, Jennifer, who had moved with her children from Farmington, outside Hartford, to New Canaan, had insulted him by telling the kids, "Successful people don't live in Farmington. They live in New Canaan."

While Farmington is merely rich, New Canaan is uber wealthy, a refuge for the 1 percent. In relocating there, Jennifer—a woman with a multimillion-dollar trust fund—was at once returning to the world of her origins and leaving her husband where she'd found him, among the striving class. It told the kids a truth about their father: he'd dwelled among the upper strata for a time, but only as a guest of the Farbers.

The more I learned, the more I felt as if I knew Jennifer, as if her world and mine were contiguous. We traveled in the same circles, were both writers, and had both made the bewildering journey from city to suburbs. It gave the story an electric charge: the closer the comet, the louder the blast.

I live a few miles from where the most tragic events in this story occurred. My kids went to the same theaters, were seen by the same doctors, and played on the same fields and in the same hockey rinks as the Dulos children, just as I attended the same parties and knew the same people as Jennifer in the 1990s, when we were both young writers in New York. The first meaningful write-up of one of her shows—she was a playwright—ran in *The New York Observer*, the small but influential salmon-colored weekly where I had my first real job. Later, when reading the legal documents and notes that accumulated in the course of Jennifer's divorce, I realized that at least two of the doctors she came to rely on were friends of mine, as were her old boyfriend and the guru who had shaped her artistic life.

Though the world is big, the world is also small, and while reporting this story, I kept running into reflections of my own experience. Maybe that's why I became so fixated not only on Jennifer's disappearance and death but also on her life. In reading about her, in visiting the places she had been and talking to the people she had known, I felt like I was seeing the story of my own generation in a convex mirror—distorted but recognizable.

For me, this project, which began with supermarket gossip, turned into a mission. After writing seven stories about the case as it unfolded for Graydon Carter's *Air Mail*, I began this book with the intention of going deeper and learning more. I tracked down and interviewed every member of Jennifer's circle I could reach: friends from high school, college, and graduate school; New York friends, writing friends, and friends from Farmington and New Canaan; detectives, private eyes, prosecutors, and defense attorneys. Some of the lawyers I interviewed, horrified by the case and wanting the divorce system reformed, showed me the police files, motions, depositions, transcripts, and legal notes, which I have relied on for factual information and for direct quotes.

Searching the places you work and live for a secret history is unsettling. It turns the familiar world ghostly. This is a story of love and hate, money, debt, and status, but it's also about the lives of people you only think you know. There is the world we live in, but there's another world below, where a subterranean river rushes by in darkness. Once you've learned to see that world, nothing ever looks the same.

Part
ONE

NEW CANAAN, CONNECTICUT, covers twenty-two square miles in the rolling hills north of Long Island Sound—five miles to the beach, fifty to New York City. It's one of America's old places, a town that grew rich with the nation, where clapboard gave way to red brick and country estate to subdivision, where builders, who followed the money, covered the inclines with split-level houses after the Second World War. Then came the hedge fund, the billionaire, the McMansion.

The lawns are lush and suspiciously green in New Canaan. The driveways ramble through groves of sugar maple and white pine. Locals point out the houses of robber barons and the houses designed by visionaries. In the 1940s, New Canaan served as a lab for a group of architects known as the Harvard Five: Marcel Breuer, Eliot Noyes, John Johansen, Landis Gores, and Philip Johnson, the latter of whom built his famous Glass House on Ponus Ridge Road in 1949. The town was notorious for its exclusivity. No Jews in New Canaan, no Catholics, no Blacks—that was the gentleman's agreement that gave name to the 1947 Gregory Peck movie. ("It's even worse in New Canaan," says a character in the book that became the movie. "There, nobody can sell or rent to a Jew.") New Canaan finally opened up in the age of Reagan. That's when the big money flowed in, and, as every American knows, big money soothes even the oldest prejudices.

With just over twenty thousand residents, New Canaan is currently ranked among the richest towns in America. The average income is $215,000, the average home price $2.3 million. Today, New Canaan's main street is less old New England than deciduous Rodeo Drive. There are high-end chain stores, designer shops, a movie theater, a bookstore, a toy store, a Ralph Lauren shop, a J.Crew. Though not on Long Island Sound itself, New Canaan is grouped with Fairfield, Westport, Darien, and Greenwich as part of Connecticut's Gold Coast. Most of the money derives from finance: the angel investor, the hedge fund manager, the short seller, and the breakup artist—the Medicis of the modern economy. There is a Metro-North station in downtown New Canaan—it's an hour and ten minutes by train to Grand Central—but the richest New Canaanites travel by hired car and private jet.

Even though New Canaan has diversified since *Gentleman's Agreement* days, it can still feel unwelcoming. Entire neighborhoods have been carved out of the woods and worked into terraces and courts and lanes lined with mansions, the smallest of which clock in at ten thousand square feet and the simplest of which feature wine cellars, fire pits, and hot tubs. The town is more eclectic than it used to be, but is still a monoculture, uniform and unvarying—only instead of race, color, or creed, the red lines mark out areas of wealth. Many of the residents have second homes in Vermont, the Berkshires, the Hamptons, or Maine. The men wear hard shoes on weekdays and soft shoes on weekends—a light sweater, chinos, glasses with tortoiseshell frames, the *Financial Times* tucked under the lavender button-down purchased by their wife—Midge or Geri—at the J.McLaughlin on Elm Street. If these people seem chilly, clipped, or superior, blame the landscape. The rolling hills of Fairfield County, combined with the vast plots that surround even the relatively modest houses, make the residents feel like other people are an intrusion that does not have to be tolerated. The town's famous historical aversion to Hebrews might make it seem a strange place for Jewish Jennifer Dulos to seek refuge from a collapsing marriage, but she'd always valued societies so exclusive they would have shut the door on her own grandparents. She exhibited signs of the Groucho Marx syndrome: she'd never want to belong to a club that would have someone like her as a member. To Jennifer, a triumphant phrase, spoken after an application has finally been accepted, was "We were the only Jews ever admitted."

The New Canaan Country School, a campus of bright white buildings on bright green lawns, was what brought her to New Canaan instead of to one of the other ritzy towns nearby. It was seemingly less about the curriculum, or the generations of successful alumni, than about the other parents: millionaires, billionaires, celebrities. The mountain is tiny at its apex; if you start there, you'll probably stay there.

The New Canaan Country School, which runs from preschool to ninth grade, is more expensive than most universities—the first-grade tuition is over $45,000 a year. Tuition for the Dulos kids was covered by Jennifer's eighty-two-year-old mother, Gloria Farber, who kept an eye on Jennifer and the divorce from her aerie high above Fifth Avenue in Manhattan.

Jennifer wanted the same sort of sheltered upbringing for her kids that she'd experienced herself, which kept her at a safe remove from the world. She grew up in a prewar redbrick apartment house at 115 Willow Street in Brooklyn Heights, within walking distance of the progressive private school she attended at the corner of Pierrepont and Clinton Streets.

Some of Jennifer's friends believe she was a victim of her own naïveté. In her adolescence, as her classmates navigated the city by subway or bus, she made use of the car and driver provided by her father, Hilliard Farber. Hilliard did not want to worry about his daughter on the F train or the 8th Avenue express, and because he was rich, he did not have to. Jennifer flew first class when necessary, private when possible. Hilliard had placed her on a greased rail that went straight from Saint Ann's to the Ivy League. "Vulnerable" is the word that kept coming up in interviews. She never learned about bad people.

"What breaks my heart, Jennifer is the person the least capable of defending herself against an attack," said Colette Burson, who founded a playwright-based theater company called the Playwrights Collective with Jennifer in the 1990s.

"Jennifer occupied her own realm," Burson added. "There was a car service—it followed her everywhere. Her dad was always protecting her. The car was always waiting right outside."

By the spring of 2019, Jennifer was finally beginning to feel at home in New Canaan. She had moved from a rental property to the $4 million house at 69 Welles Lane she'd purchased with the help of her mother. Six bedrooms, six bathrooms, 9,800 square feet—a house on a cul-de-sac. Built in 2016, it had been made to look timeless. There were two acres of land, some of it cleared, some of it wooded, places to barbecue and places to hide. There was a three-car garage, the floor of which was as pristine as the floor of an auto showroom. It was less than a mile from the New Canaan Country School.

Most mornings began the same way, with Jennifer moving from room to room, waking her kids and sending them down to the kitchen, where the family of six (two plus five minus one) gathered for breakfast with their nanny, Lauren Almeida, a University of Connecticut graduate who'd worked for Fotis and Jennifer before siding with Jennifer in the divorce. But Lauren, who'd become a kind of surrogate parent (two plus five minus one plus one) did not arrive until after eleven on Friday, May 24, 2019, which left Jennifer to handle the morning rush alone. Jennifer planned to drop the kids off at school, go home for breakfast, then drive to a doctor's appointment in the city. Lauren was to pick up the kids after school and take them into Manhattan to meet their mom. There were two cars in the garage, a Chevy Suburban and a Range Rover. Jennifer told Lauren she would take the kids to school in the Suburban, then drive the Range Rover, which was easier to park, into the city. Jennifer was very clear about that.

Many of the houses on Welles Lane are monitored by security cameras, high-tech fisheyes mounted above the doors. The view from these cameras is cambered—deep, detailed, and surprisingly clear. The New Canaan police gathered footage from every one of those fisheyes. Edited together, the videos created a nearly complete record of the comings and goings that day. In one sequence, recorded at 7:58 a.m., Jennifer is seen at the wheel of her Chevy Suburban. The car is full of kids. She sits upright, staring straight ahead. Her face looks washed out in the cold digital light. She resembles a ghost. A few minutes later, she is seen returning to her house. The kids have been dropped off. For a moment, she is blissfully alone.

Gloria Farber grew up in Newark, New Jersey. She went to Weequahic High School, graduating three years after the novelist Philip Roth. Weequahic opened in 1933 as if for the sole purpose of educating and assimilating the children of the Jewish immigrants who'd recently arrived from Eastern Europe. The redbrick building occupied the corner of Chancellor Avenue and Aldine Street in drowsy prewar, pre-riot, pre-fire Newark. Most of its students were first-generation Americans who spoke Yiddish with their parents at home. To them an idiot was a "schmuck," a thug was a "gonif," a person of quality was a "mensch." In such communities, it was the New World in the street but still the Old World at home.

There was a sameness to the mothers and fathers of Jewish Newark. The mothers were short and stout. The fathers had hunched shoulders and melancholy eyes, which were blue, brown, black, or that shade of green that looks like money. Most of the men still practiced the trades they'd learned in Europe before the Flood. There were doctors among them, accountants, rabbis, butchers, bakers, loan sharks, gamblers, mobsters. Many worked in the garment industry, the rag trade, either in a big factory across the river in Manhattan or in a small shop on Prince Street in Newark, where the tin roofs of the storage sheds ticked in the evening sun.

These parents had tremendous ambition, but not for themselves. Their goal was to earn enough money to educate their children. They sublimated their dreams, which were also the dreams of their parents and their parents' parents, the thwarted generations of ghetto and shtetl dwellers, into their progeny, who would burst from Newark and Bergen and Passaic like flames from an oven. The parents understood their place in what amounted to a multigenerational project. They understood they might not make it into the Land of (New?) Canaan, but they had faith that the crossing would one day be accomplished, that houses would be purchased, country clubs joined.

Gloria's maiden name was Ortenberg. Her father, an upholsterer, was a Russian immigrant. After years of subsisting on piecemeal jobs, he managed to open his own store in Newark. Her mother, who'd come from Poland, was a seamstress. Gloria's childhood would've been filled with measuring tapes, sewing needles, pinking shears, and fabric swatches. When hung before the windows to dry in the dusty rooms, the swatches would tint the light purple, green, orange, and blue.

Gloria's brother Arthur, born in 1926, was a dozen years older. The family lived across the street from a branch of the Newark Public Library, where first Arthur and then Gloria spent many hours a week, reading their way out of New Jersey. Arthur won a scholarship to the University of Wisconsin. He left with plans of becoming a doctor or lawyer, forwarding the generational progress, but, caught in the orbit of his roommate, whose father was a big shot in the rag trade, he went into the garment industry instead. It was while working for a company owned by his roommate's father that Arthur Ortenberg met Liz Claiborne. She was in her thirties then, a dark-haired heir to a prominent southern family—Liz's ancestor William C. C. Claiborne was the first governor of Louisiana; in New Orleans, you see his name everywhere. She'd studied art and design in Paris, then got her break in 1949, winning a national design contest sponsored by *Harper's Bazaar*. She was working in the Seventh Avenue Garment District in the late 1950s, walking in and out of meetings with a portfolio case, delivering designs the bosses ordered while pitching designs she wanted to make. One afternoon, she found herself across a table from Arthur Ortenberg. Liz had an idea for an inexpensive bathing suit to be followed by a line of moderately priced outfits for working women. Arthur was enraptured. Finding that his enchantment—with the designs and the designer—was not shared by his superiors, he married Liz and together they started a company of their own.

The connection between Jennifer Dulos and Liz Claiborne has been played up in the press to lend glamour to what can seem a noir-ish tale. Liz Claiborne Inc. (now Kate Spade & Company) is valued at $2.5 billion. Liz and Arthur, who was born into garments and stayed in garments, revolutionized fashion. She had the vision, and he handled the money end of the business.

But Gloria Ortenberg was at least as successful as her brother. She was better educated than Arthur and went further on her own at a time when it was twice as hard for a woman to go half the distance. She earned a bachelor's degree at Rutgers, a master's in education at Bank Street, and a PhD at Columbia. She became a leading expert on early childhood education, and the director of education at the Columbia

University Head Start Program. Years later, when Fotis Dulos decided to tangle with Gloria, he probably expected an easy fight with an elderly lady. But he made a classic mistake: he picked on exactly the wrong person.

For purposes of this story, the big moment in Gloria's life came on the Rutgers campus in New Brunswick, New Jersey, in 1957. Gloria Ortenberg's first meeting with Hilliard Farber was turned into a family myth: it stood as a perfect example of romantic love, love at first sight, and falling so fast and so hard it seems like fate. It became a fixation for Jennifer, a legendary affair that consumed her with dreams of matrimony. If she seemed restless in romance, never content with a suitor, always looking over the shoulder of life to see if someone better was coming through the door, blame the fable of Hilliard and Gloria, Adam and Eve without the Fall. Jennifer characterized her search for a partner as ideal for her as Hilliard had been for her mother as a "personal holy grail."

"'I saw your mother and I knew, just knew' is my father's mantra," Jennifer wrote in 1998. "My mother says, 'He was wearing that navy shetland sweater and when I said, "I guess I should be going," he said, "No, stay." I knew, I just knew.' It never occurred to me that people might fall in love in any other way."

Hilliard Farber, who would become big and thick, was big and thin when Gloria met him in 1957. He'd been raised in Rahway, New Jersey, a factory town. At twenty-one, he left for the military. He spent two years as a navigator at an air-to-air refueling station in Anchorage, Alaska. He enrolled at New York University when he returned. The GI Bill paid for his MBA. He was one of the only Jews in the executive ranks when he started at Chase Manhattan Bank. He figured out how to blend in by way of professional necessity. On the way to becoming the first Jew to run Chase Manhattan's bond division, he learned to dress, talk, walk, and shake hands like a white Anglo-Saxon Protestant. He brought these habits home, unintentionally expressing a set of values to Jennifer—that the Wasp is the ideal, that a Jew who can pass for a Wasp is the best kind of Jew, that there is something shameful about Jews who cling to the old ways and seem a little *too* Jewish.

Jennifer did not hate her background—she was not a self-hating Jew—but she did not love it, either. She did not go to temple or visit Israel. She believed blond was the best color for hair, and Christmas the best holiday. "I wanted to be the pure, fresh Ivory girl," she wrote of her childhood, "perfectly coiffed, smiling in a demure yet low-cut outfit with a single strand of pearls. Grace Kelly of the Ivy League, looking for an American prince, a corporate lawyer, an oil trader, a real life dream."

Yet Hilliard Farber never forgot who he was or where he came from. He might have looked like a Park Avenue banker, but at heart he remained a New Jersey Jew. The fact that he was without religious faith did not stop him from contributing annually to Temple Emanu-El. He also gave to progressive causes and to Jewish groups. It was not the deity he worried about, but the people. He knew the history of the Jews and hoped knowing it would offer a kind of protection. He was living proof of the old axiom "There is no one more Jewish than a Jewish atheist." And yet this message, if he tried to pass it down, was lost in transmission. If he sent the signal to Jennifer, it was not received. The only vision more powerful than Jerusalem is Candy Land.

Jennifer continued to prize the Wasp ideal even after that ideal—in the form of Chase's top brass, the embodiment of establishment power—betrayed her father. The Dunhill suits and Tiffany cuff links, the Lapidus over-the-calf socks and Top-Siders, the house on Fire Island—none of it protected Hilliard when the weather changed. As in the book of Jonah, the other passengers tossed the Israelite overboard to placate the angry sea, a.k.a. the U.S. Securities and Exchange Commission, which, in 1974, accused Chase of overvaluing assets to pump up its stock price. That Hilliard was seemingly a member of the club did not help him when David Rockefeller, the chairman of the bank, needed a scapegoat. Hilliard was asked to apologize and take the blame. Believing he'd done nothing wrong, he quit instead. "Hilliard Farber, a former senior vice president and a respected man in the bond market community, resigned last week as the overvaluation was disclosed," *The New York Times* reported on October 7, 1974.

Hilliard went on to found his own firm, Hilliard Farber & Co., which made him rich in a way that only an owner can be rich, but he never forgot the betrayal. You catch its echo in the wisdom he shared with Jennifer: You're never safe in America; you've got to have cash.

The fact that he'd been knocked down and survived gave Hilliard a certain aura. He was a big man who radiated the wisdom of experience, the confidence of the tested. People who knew Hilliard still speak of him with awe. (Gloria's brother Arthur described Hilliard as "a large man, once slim, tall and dark-haired . . . grown wealthy in the investment banking business.") If anything, people say, Hilliard was too good, too strong. Jennifer sheltered in his power, and it was the resulting sense of protection that later left her exposed. "'Hilliard must be dead'—that's the first thing I thought when I heard about Jennifer," said Colette Burson. "Jennifer would be safe as long as Hilliard was alive, but no one lasts forever."

From the windows in their apartment in Brooklyn Heights, Hilliard and Gloria could see Manhattan, the hurly-burly of towers gathered like a thunderhead in the distance. Their first child, Melissa, was born in 1965. Jennifer was born three years later. Melissa graduated from Saint Ann's ahead of Jennifer, and went on to study at the University of Pennsylvania. She struggled with her mental health in childhood and suffered a crisis in her late teens. She was put on medication that dropped a veil between her and the world. As an adult, she worked at Hilliard's company and lived in Hilliard's shadow, a responsibility for her aging parents. Fotis Dulos mentioned Melissa's condition repeatedly in the run-up to the divorce, citing a Farber family history of "mental illness" to argue his case for custody of the children.

Jennifer was born on September 27, 1968, a Libra, the doted-on baby of the family. She was close to her father in that special way of the youngest daughter. Asked many years later to describe her childhood, she lingered on a single memory: every night, without fail, her father tucked her in for bed. That was their time. Her mother's influence was more distant. It was in the glamour of Gloria dressing for a night in the city, the laughter and pearls, which led Jennifer to fetishize adult life. She enacted her fantasies with her dollhouses, which became an obsession, exquisite re-creations of period rooms, with wallpaper, fixtures, four-poster beds, antique wardrobes, and scaled-down walk-in closets filled with scaled-down period outfits. A good dollhouse, which can cost many thousands of dollars, was a place to arrange a perfect life and play God, a house without strife, arguments, or thrown crockery. At twelve, Jennifer became fixated on a Victorian dollhouse she'd seen in Manhattan. It came complete with a perfect little dollhouse family.

Gloria at first refused to buy the perfect little dollhouse with its perfect little family because, to her, they looked like perfect little Nazis—it had been made in West Germany—but she eventually relented. Hilliard would watch Jennifer from the doorway as she played with the dollhouse, then, referring to a particular doll, ask, "How's Rolf?"

"Playing behind my doll house, I created a family's perfect life, and it required only the slightest switching of gears to imagine and map out my own," Jennifer wrote in an essay titled "Window-Shopping for a Life," which was published in the collection *Personals: Dreams and Nightmares from the Lives of 20 Young Writers* in 1998. She went on to imagine her future in great detail: married by twenty-five, first kid by twenty-eight, second and third kids by thirty. Two boys—James and William, or Silas and Sebastian—and a girl—Samantha or Sophia. She would raise the kids with her left hand while penning plays with her right in the maid's room she'd converted into an office in her Classic Eight (with working fireplace!) on Park Avenue.

She based her fantasy of adulthood on the novels of Edith Wharton, the short stories of John Cheever, and the theatrical work of A. R. Gurney, whose play *The Dining Room* hit her hard when she saw it in 1982. It made her want to be both dramatist and Wasp. Jennifer could still quote dialogue from it decades later: "I'd like Scotch, sweetheart. Make it reasonably strong"; "You'll find the silver measuring gizmo in the drawer by the trays." Cheever, Wharton, Gurney—all portrayed Protestants, not Jews. Though not being a Wasp was an obstacle to Jennifer, she believed she could manage.

She was a product of her neighborhood as well as her dream. To her, it was simply "the Heights," a hermetically sealed land of privilege. When old-timers speak of Brooklyn, it's usually not Brooklyn Heights they have in mind. Since the 1800s, when the waterfront boomed and the city became a metropolis, the Heights has been a refuge, an escape from the rest of the borough with its patchwork of ethnic neighborhoods, seedy barrooms, underworld clubhouses, and endless avenues. The neighborhood sits above the harbor and has the best views in the city. If you see New York in a movie at the golden hour of sunset, the shot was probably taken from the Brooklyn Heights Promenade. It's always been a mythical place. Walt Whitman lived there, as did Thomas Wolfe, Hart Crane, Truman Capote, Benjamin Britten, and Norman Mailer. When Jennifer told people she grew up in Brooklyn, she did not mean the Brooklyn of *The Warriors* or *Welcome Back, Kotter,* or the hipster Brooklyn of today, but a neighborhood as old and established as any in New York.

The Farbers belonged to several private organizations, including the Brooklyn Heights Casino, which Jennifer described as "an exclusive racquet club the [well-to-do] joined so their children could play squash and take ballroom dancing—children who then went off to boarding school at Groton, Milton Academy, and Choate."

The Heights Casino, which accepted very few Jews, was a preserve of a certain type of wealthy New Yorker. Hilliard characterized these people with a single word: "Bank." They did not hustle, grasp, or climb. Jennifer explained the term in her essay:

> Bank was the furthest thing from new eighties money, for which students [from the University of Pennsylvania's Wharton School] came to Wall Street in droves. Bank was the old money mystique of firms like Brown Brothers Harriman, Scudder Stevens and Clark, money managers known primarily for handling trust accounts. The gentlemen at these investment banks (which did not hire Jews) spent their off-hours sipping Dickel Old-Fashioneds at the University Club, the all-male, all Wasp bastion on 54th and Fifth. They were the red nose crowd who came back from bona fide three martini lunches with red noses.

She added, "When I was young, the notion of Bank turned me on as much as Christmas trees."

Hilliard and Gloria's membership at the Heights Casino meant no small amount of schmoozing and making nice at the insistence of Jennifer. "My parents endured the harsh, almost reprimanding interview process so we could become the second Jewish family the Heights Casino had ever let in," wrote Jennifer. "[I then] spent every afternoon taking tennis or squash lessons there, or just hanging out with [my friend] Margot in our mandatory identical whites, me studying the two small boat barrettes clipped in Margot's dirty blonde hair." There were in fact several other Jewish members of the Casino, but it was apparently important for Jennifer, who seemed to assign an institution's value in inverse proportion to the number of Jews who belonged, to believe that her family was among the first and only.

Jennifer attended Saint Ann's, a private school at the corner of Pierrepont and Clinton Streets. Once religiously affiliated, Saint Ann's had become a secular, liberal-minded bastion by the 1980s. Its headmaster, an educational guru named Stanley Bosworth—his parents, Jewish immigrants from Russia, changed their name from Boscovitz—had created a pedagogical style that imprinted everyone who attended. Jennifer described Saint Ann's as "my progressive school, where children were taught to be creative and individualistic." There were few requirements—no standard curriculum, no traditional marks. ("How do you give a grade on an oboe's sweet, beautiful sound? Or how do you give a grade on a painting?" Bosworth asked a journalist.) Bosworth said Saint Ann's had been designed as "an amusement park in which the amusements would include Aristophanes, Darwin and Baudelaire." In 2004, *New York* magazine's Ariel Levy called the school "a cult of personality, but a cult that works," and backed up that conclusion with some numbers: "The ten most selective colleges in the country accepted 41 percent of the class of '03. Ten children apply for each spot at Saint Ann's, and that spot goes for $20,500 annually." (Yearly tuition is closer to $60,000 today.)

Writing in *The New York Times* in the summer of 2023, several decades after Jennifer graduated, John Leland described Saint Ann's as "a proud outlier among New York's private schools," adding: "It does not give students grades, and it promises parents and students, 'We celebrate each child's attributes—talented musician, gifted reader, remarkable artist—while encouraging all of our students to believe that they can excel in myriad pursuits.'" Leland quoted Stanley Bosworth as telling teachers, "If the student learns best under the table, you'd better get under the table with him."

"The school has balanced this loosey-goosey, no-grades ethos with a no-nonsense record of placing graduates into elite colleges," Leland continued. "In 2004, *The Wall Street Journal* named it as the nation's top private school in the percentage of graduates it sent to the most selective colleges."

Hilliard Farber donated large sums to Saint Ann's, as he did to just about every school that Jennifer or her kids attended.

Jennifer met Tom Beller when she was a freshman. Beller, who'd been taken in by Saint Ann's after being expelled from Riverdale Country School in the Bronx, was a senior, tall and handsome, already on his way to a writing career. Beller played basketball in high school and college—if Vassar counts. At fifty-five, he could still dunk. He was a senior when Jennifer met him, and one of the few Jews she'd ever fall for. Beller became the hub of a New York literary community in the 1990s—he co-founded the journal *Open City*, which is remembered as much for its parties as for its editorial content—but was still searching when he met Jennifer in 1986. If I mention him here, it's only because he became important to her later. He was one of Jennifer's many romantic partners, but he stands out as a kind of landmark.

"I tried on a series of men," Jennifer wrote long after high school, "figuring out how their lives would look on me."

Jennifer loved *The New York Times* weddings section, turning to it each Sunday "the way men turn to the Sports Page." To check the score, to separate the winners from the losers. The stories were filled with status markers only a select population could recognize and understand. It was a matter of titles and names—the names of schools, firms, and banks; the names of families, Jewish and Anglo, arriviste and ancient; the names of towns, Southampton, Westport, Edgartown, Brookline, Winnetka, Montclair. The section held hypnotic sway over Jennifer from the day she first came upon it at eleven. Studying the pictures, foreground and background, she felt she was "window-shopping for a life." She wanted to become one of those perfectly blond American girls.

Jennifer's high school résumé, built with the Ivy League in mind, was jammed with honors and extracurriculars. She was a member of the math team, the stock market team, and the squash team. Classmates remember her for her intelligence and looks, but also for her privilege. Her chauffeur would double as a spy, briefing Hilliard Farber on his daughter's activities, demeanor, and friends. A black town car waiting at the curb meant Jennifer was inside the restaurant, theater, club. People mention it whenever they talk about Jennifer's New York years. The black town car protected her, and she was defined by this protection.

Colette Burson and Kate Robin, playwriting friends, included Jennifer's car and driver in their 1999 movie *Coming Soon*, which starred Ryan Reynolds, Yasmine Bleeth, and Mia Farrow and follows several students at a school not unlike Saint Ann's as they approach high school graduation. The princess of this story, the dark-haired beauty fixated on marriage, is named Jenny Simon. When one character says Jenny does not have the scores for Brown, another says, "Jenny's father can always donate a library . . . She'll get in." Like Jennifer Farber, Jenny Simon is never far from her car and driver, waiting at the curb like chariot and charioteer. When a thick envelope arrives in the mail from Brown, Jenny kisses it and says, "My daddy finally found the right person to bribe."

Others counter this depiction. To old friends like Carrie Luft and D. J. Paul, Jennifer Farber was a funny, sensitive, poetic, seriously intelligent person whose life was complicated by her beauty and her childhood dream of perfect matrimony, which she could never quite shake. In pursuit of this dream, she sometimes pretended she was not as smart as she actually was and did not understand as much as she actually did.

Brown was the oddball of the Ivy League. It had gone full hippie in the 1970s, ditching the core curriculum and the literary canon of dead white males. There were neither grades nor requirements at Brown, making it a favored destination of New York's private schoolers. Students from Riverdale, Horace Mann, Dalton, Brearley, Trinity, and Saint Ann's, who'd met at bar and bat mitzvahs, sweet sixteens, and debutante balls at the Plaza and Pierre hotels in Manhattan, met again at Brown, where they formed an exclusive, nearly impenetrable clique. They gathered together on the quads and in the old ivy-covered buildings to talk about the city. They got drunk on the Amtrak to Manhattan, then lingered for one more pop at Penn Station before vanishing into their separate New York lives.

There were other cliques at Brown, too: scholarship kids, science kids, celebrity kids. "Ringo Starr's daughter was in my comp lit freshman year," said Maxim Shrayer, who was at college with Jennifer—he came to Brown directly from Moscow, where his father was a refusenik. "I had several classes with Roberta Civita, whose father was Brazil's big media mogul." The musician Lisa Loeb was in the same class (1990), as were David Rohde, Michael Costigan, Sam Lipsyte, A. J. Jacobs, Dan Maffei, and Rory Kennedy. "Everywhere you looked, it was these kind of people," said Shrayer.

Brown did in fact seem to have a special relationship with New York's most expensive private schools, where guidance counselors earning in the mid-six figures were on the phone with the admissions department in Providence several times a week, recommending this one, securing a spot for that one. It was as if they were connected to Brown by pneumatic tube.

Yet the foreign students—the monied sons and daughters of France, Germany, Greece, Abu Dhabi, Saudi Arabia, England, and Spain who paid the full freight and whose parents financed field houses, flower beds, and dining halls—were the school's real bread and butter. Brown was packed with international students in the 1980s, a population that could be further divided into two subgroups: the extraordinarily rich (which included the scions of European nobility) and the brilliant scholarship kids who were sometimes confused with the extraordinarily rich. Though his soft European accent, good manners, good looks, and detachment led many to believe Fotis Dulos was among the superrich, he was in fact solidly middle class. If he did not correct people who mistook him for a Greek shipping heir, maybe it was because he figured it was the only way that he'd ever get a shot at someone like Jen Farber. ("She was not just out of my league," A. J. Jacobs told me. "She was out of everyone's league.") Jennifer said she liked Fotis okay when she met him in 1986, but not in *that* way. For one thing, he was short. For another, he was "a bit boring."

Jennifer Farber was a book person. There are two kinds of book people: those who surround themselves with books and those who actually read them. Jennifer, who majored in literature and art history at Brown, devoured the books she collected. You could tell by looking at the margins, which were crowded with asterisks and exclamation points, or the spines, which were broken. She read in search of usable facts. She was after what Hemingway called "the true gen" (genuine information) and wanted to experience the same things as the heroines of her favorite novels, namely sex. Her first college boyfriend was a guy named Rich Yelland. They met in September of freshman year and were dating before Thanksgiving. I'm not sure what Rich looked like then, but I can tell you what he looks like now: tall, sporty, and handsome. He's a documentary filmmaker whose titles include *Birth of the Endless Summer* and *Sine Qua Non: The Psychology of Big Wave Surfing with Greg Long.* Jennifer did not date ugly men. Good looks were part of the fantasy.

Jennifer's relationship with Rich followed a trajectory that became a pattern. She fell fast, became consumed, then lost interest. Instead of ending in some epic fight, these affairs tended to peter out. They were like pencil lines that start dark, then fade. First she's in love, then her boyfriend is more like a brother, then they've stopped talking.

It was over with Rich by Christmas, which is why Rich's friend Hugh Warrender felt it was kosher to invite Jennifer to visit his family in England. Hugh was shocked when Jennifer accepted—the invitation had been aspirational. When I asked him about the visit, Hugh responded with a letter that reads like a sepia-toned memoir of Jen Farber at nineteen:

Next thing I know, my dad is getting letters from Hilly Farber, her sweet Dad, with extensive arrangements for her trip that involved flying her over on the Concorde and him hiring a Rolls Royce and driver for the entirety of her trip. I think she had bigged up our circumstances and was under the impression she was spending Christmas at Balmoral with the Queen. The reality was rather more modest and my father, at a loss as to where the hapless driver would stay when with us, did everything he could to talk Hilly down from the idea, but he would not be put off. In the event the driver was dispatched after dropping her off from Heathrow, and we drove down to our house in Bath in my Mum's old Honda Accord.

She came laden with hugely expensive gifts for everyone in our family, unaware that we had a policy of finding creative ways to give each other presents that should cost no more than £5 each. I think Scully & Scully paid a special dividend that year after her shopping spree, and she was a bit nonplussed by the few eccentric trinkets she got from us in return!

The other thing she had taken a bit too seriously was a day of shooting I'd told her about. I'd explained that my dad was a member of a local shooting syndicate that always had a "family day out" on Boxing Day and she should come prepared for a single cold and wet Cotswold winter day. Upon her arrival in London, she took off to the Holland & Holland gun shop armed with Hilly's Amex Card and kitted herself out with a spanking new set of tweeds, Wellington boots and a glamourous cocked hat for the occasion. She looked gorgeous. Little did she know that everyone else would be shivering in motheaten outfits created circa 1940 during rationing.

Either way, when the day came we got up at the crack of dawn, with even more cracking post-Christmas hangovers, to venture out into the freezing rain and mud and wander around with men bearing antique firearms hoping to take the lives away from some poor unsuspecting pheasants who were still perplexed as to how they ended up being shot at with 12 bores in a Gloucestershire copse when they should have been regaled as prizes by Chinese Mandarins.

Tatty clothes apart, the gathered company for the day of sport was a mixed bag of rosy-cheeked aristocracy, scions of British banking dynasties and assorted local eccentrics. By 10 a.m., Jen had quite enough of getting rained on amid deafening gun-blasts whilst being told to keep quiet, and made a bee-line for the nearest Land Rover. She fired up the engine, somehow got the AM radio to blast out Rod Stewart tunes that echoed up the valley ensuring that all wildlife with a heartbeat within half a mile went off in the other direction, not popular as you can imagine.

Boxing Day lunch, which punctuated the shooting, was a modest but boozy and hearty meal in the village pub's private room. I think all of us at some point have been in a noisy room when one voice stands out amid the roar of conversation and leaves everyone speechless. On this occasion it was Jen's, unmistakable given it being female and American. A few shandies down herself, she was sitting between two old half-cut roués, well past their 60th birthdays, when she came out with the line 'I'm not ashamed to admit that I masturbate at least twice a day' . . . Silence reigned, only broken by the creaking of the old chairs in the room as a dozen old men felt a tightening of the groin. The Chairman of the bank, our host, looked down the table and simply said "Gentlemen—what did we miss out on in the sixties?"

She never stopped looking for a boyfriend Hilliard would recognize as Bank. For a time, she thought she found him in a Brown lacrosse player she called "Gunnar Graham" in her writing. He had a crooked nose and clear blue eyes, and he'd gone to the exclusive all-male St. Bernard's School in New York, then Collegiate, then Brown. She figured he'd work at Merrill or McKinsey while living on Fifth Avenue in the 70s, then make the move to a hedge fund in Greenwich. His wardrobe would be dominated by Hermès ties. "Gunnar embodied a New York myth I knew by heart," Jennifer wrote in "Window-Shopping for a Life."

So why did she break up with Gunnar, who seemingly represented everything she'd ever wanted? Because he bored her. Because she had a side that Gunnar could never reach. Because she could not be her true and complete self with him. Because with him she was always acting. Because there were only so many hours in a day that she could talk about golf, and what happened on the back nine, and the water hazard near the fifteenth at Quaker Ridge, a private club in Scarsdale, New York. But she never forgot Gunnar Graham, who turned up in various guises in much of her writing. He was the road not taken. "I should have married him," Jennifer wrote near the end of her life. "That was the big mistake. I did not know I had the right thing until I had the wrong thing."

After graduating from Brown, Jennifer moved to Manhattan to study dramatic writing at New York University. The city was perfect in the early 1990s, a tidal flow of music, drugs, late dinners, multiday debauches, and burning visions of sex and fame. It was the Odeon and Nell's and Avenue A at four in the morning. It was Deee-Lite singing "Groove Is in the Heart" on a taxicab radio. It was the back entrance to Chumley's and cheeseburgers at the Corner Bistro. It was the Spin Doctors at Wetlands and Darryl Strawberry at Shea Stadium. It was the Mercury Lounge and the Limelight and Webster Hall. It was Pax Americana, U.S. soldiers at sea and in the air. It was the last good time, the last great party, the last decent meal, the last glimpse of paradise.

Most of the people enrolled in NYU's graduate dramatic writing program came from some other town, city, or country. They relied on financial aid and odd jobs, scratching to pay for tuition and housing in what had become maybe the most expensive city in the world. If they did not live in a dorm, they shared a small apartment in a generic postwar tower or in a prewar walk-up with other students near Washington Square.

The people who went to graduate school with Jennifer speak of these as their adventurous days. The fact of not having money was as much a part of the experience as the classes and the workshops. Not having money shaped the city into a crucible that burned off impurities. It made you hungry, and that hunger made you see and understand New York for the first time. The avenues at dusk when they are full of cars heading to the suburbs. The avenues at daybreak when they are desolate and steam rises from the manholes and the falcon is perched on the cornice of the Schickel & Ditmars building at Eighty-Third and Park. The bars at night when they smoke and roar. The same bars at noon when it is just you with a newspaper and the jukebox playing Hank Snow.

Jennifer's grad school classmates quickly became aware of her wealth. "I told her to break free from her family and go live in the East

Village and be a bartender and forget the money for a while, and the people telling her what to do," said Colette Burson, who met Jennifer in her first year at NYU. But Jennifer made a face and said, "Then I'd have to sweep up cigarette butts."

Jennifer did not live in a studio apartment with a bathtub in the kitchen like many of the others. Nor did she live in a concrete box in the sky. Nor did she stumble home with a single crumpled dollar in her pocket trying to remember what she had said and done. When I asked a friend from Jennifer's downtown days where Jennifer had lived in Manhattan, he said, "Go to the arch of Washington Square Park and look north. Pick out the building that you imagine would be most suitable for Jen Farber. That's where she lived!"

One Fifth Avenue is a 350-foot art deco tower at the corner of Fifth Avenue and Washington Mews. A riot of setbacks and cupolas, shaped like a brick and colored like café au lait, *The New Yorker* called it a pompous shaft when it opened in 1927. It started as an apartment-hotel, an ideal spot for the wealthy gentleman whose marriage was on the rocks. By Jennifer's time, it was known for its celebrity residents. Blythe Danner lived there, as did Brian De Palma, Helena Bonham Carter, Tim Burton—fitting, as it cut the jagged profile of a haunted house—Jessica Lange, Sam Shepard, Patti Smith (Robert Mapplethorpe photographed Smith for the cover of her album *Horses* there), Patti Hansen, and Keith Richards, who told the co-op board that with such a simple address (One Fifth) he'd never fail to find his way home.

Occupants of the building, those with a sense of history, have always considered themselves inhabitants of a neighborhood set apart from the rest of Greenwich Village. As the streets to the north and south have shifted like a phantasmagoria, the blocks around One Fifth have remained unchanged, a slice of old Manhattan that's always been a magnet for artists and the millionaires who chase after them. Writing in *The New York Times* in 2014, C. J. Hughes called these blocks, known as Lower Fifth, a "neighborhood-within-a-neighborhood, whose residents tend to cite the avenue as their address rather than the encompassing Greenwich Village. Nicknamed the Gold Coast, and perhaps the inspiration for the many others that have followed, the strip has also retained its ambience of exclusivity."

Jennifer frequented the restaurant on the ground floor of One Fifth, which appeared in several classic New York movies, including Woody Allen's *Crimes and Misdemeanors* and Paul Mazursky's *An Unmarried Woman*. Her friends might be living in New York, but Jennifer was living on a film set, a postcard fantasy. The lobby is huge, well-appointed, and manned by uniformed doormen. The lobby light, as golden as single-malt Scotch, makes you think of debutantes, robber barons, tycoons. While her theater friends were waking in the East Village of Joey Ramone, Jennifer was asleep in the land of John D. Rockefeller.

Hilliard Farber got her the apartment, a one-bedroom on a high floor. She could see Washington Square Park from the window, the towers of Lower Manhattan, the sky over Brooklyn. Jennifer was fastidious, the apartment sparsely furnished. She disdained clutter for the same reason she paid careful attention to her weight: she could not stand waste, excess, or any of kind of disorder. Everything had to be perfect.

There was a big bed with a down comforter in the bedroom, a table in the kitchen, a desk with a laptop computer, an answering machine, a TV, and two items that seemed as symbolic as they were functional: a Stairmaster, which filled the living room ("Every time you talked to Jennifer on the phone she was out of breath because she was on that Stairmaster," said Colette Burson), and, weirdly, a baby crib. This stood for the life Jennifer wanted: three kids, a husband returning from work at Brown Brothers Harriman.

"We hung out in that apartment a lot," Steve Garbarino, a *New York Post* editor and once a member of Jennifer's circle, told me. "It was spare and a little strange. The Stairmaster, okay, I get that, but who has a baby crib and no baby and no plans to have a baby?"

"What did she do with the crib?" I asked.

"Nothing," said Garbarino. "She just liked to look at it. She talked about wanting kids all the time."

Several of Jennifer's NYU classmates would go on to successful careers in the entertainment business. Colette Burson, from Virginia, created the HBO show *Hung*. Dmitry Lipkin, from Russia, has written movies and shows, including *The Wild Oats* and *The Riches*. Dan Rybicky, from upstate New York, is a documentary filmmaker. Kate Robin, from New York, has worked for, written, and produced several television shows, including *Six Feet Under*, *The Affair*, and *One Mississippi*. Carrie Luft, the friend from Dartmouth by way of Indiana who would stick by Jennifer through it all, is a playwright, a private tutor, and a freelance book editor.

These people met and bonded in the classroom of a first-time teacher, a charismatic young gay playwright named Eduardo Machado, who would become guru and guide as much as instructor. Eduardo, whose family had been chased out of Cuba by Fidel Castro, had written and produced a handful of plays by the time he reached NYU.

I worked with Eduardo on the Starz show *Magic City*, which was loosely based on the saga of Miami's Fontainebleau hotel. Eduardo was brought in to lend the Cuban characters authenticity. (The show was set immediately after Batista's fall, when the Cuban elite, including Eduardo and his family, fled the island for Florida.) I was tapped for my Jewish gangster knowledge. Meyer Lansky, the model for *The Godfather*'s Hyman Roth, was a presence at the Fontainebleau.

Eduardo was middle-aged when we met, gray-haired, paunchy,

sharp-tongued, sarcastic, gossipy, and occasionally mean. Also brilliant. You could be caught in the sparkling glare of his eyes. He wore button-down cotton shirts and tilted his head back when he laughed. I was in my forties and found him occasionally intimidating. He challenged every idea, poked, second-guessed, mocked. I could only imagine his impact on a workshop of writing students in their early twenties. He was the kind of teacher who becomes a guru, and his presence became a cause of concern at NYU. To some, the group of students assembled at his feet seemed disturbingly cult-like. There was in fact an effort to remove him, but his disciples rose up in protest, winning him a reprieve.

Because he'd never taught at the graduate level before, Eduardo invented a playwriting program on the fly. It was based on the acting method pioneered by Konstantin Stanislavski. Eduardo did not call it Method Writing, but he might as well have. He led students through each chapter of Stanislavski's guide *An Actor Prepares*, remaking the exercises for the writer. He asked his students to tap into their own experiences and emotions while creating characters and dialogue. You're not acting, but reacting from your own experience—that's the key to the Method. In Eduardo's class, this became "You're not writing, but remembering." Eduardo was less interested in plot points and character arcs than in honesty. "We were supposed to use our own memories and experiences to figure out what was important to us emotionally," said Colette Burson, "then use that as a launching pad into the psyche to create characters fueled by an emotional truth."

In her 1998 essay "I Didn't Always Think They Were Assholes," in which Eduardo appears as "Armando," Carrie Luft wrote:

> Armando was on to something real. He suspected that Stanislavski's method for the actor could be applied to the

playwright. We navigated through *An Actor Prepares* lesson by lesson, with Armando translating each section into a writing exercise, which he administered, part attending physician, part guru, while we scribbled away. It worked. By tapping an emotional state and letting it bleed into imagination, one could write something honest and alive. Rather than contriving to make characters say something preconceived we asked, "What *are* they saying?" and listened, writing down the results without censoring. Aloud in class we read our exercises, and Armando delineated that which was honest from that which hedged the truth. What ran out of the pen was scary. Real lives were revealed, both as fictionalized personal history and as fantastic desires, obsessions, and fears.

Some students bought in, others didn't. The believers convened after hours and out of school, where readings turned personal, raw. "It was for you, or it wasn't," said Kate Robin. "Many people who were just freaked out and felt it was too aggressive. It made them uncomfortable. They dropped Eduardo's class. Those who remained became the core. We had faith. We believed. And for us, it worked. In every class, someone would make a breakthrough. Even if you thought that your writing was fine before, even if you thought it was terrible, you would do an exercise and suddenly you would feel you were in the truth of that writer's voice. It was exciting."

When I asked another classmate if Jennifer ever had that kind of breakthrough in Eduardo's class, she paused, then said, "No, I don't think so. You had to be willing to tell the truth, which means burning your bridges and killing your family, and I don't think Jennifer was willing to do that. I've never met anyone who loved their family more, or who was that impressed by their own father."

"There was a spareness to Jen's dialogue," Kate Robin told me. "I always sensed a deep sadness and aloneness, an intense longing for love and connection, but there were fewer words on the page, so it had a poetic quality."

Colette Burson summarized Jennifer's writing with the phrase "frosty paws." She explained it to me as follows: "Jennifer read us a scene in which she was a little girl riding on her father's shoulders, and he takes her hands in his hands, and says, 'Oh, you have frosty paws.' It's her hands. They were cold. I was shocked when she first read her work out loud. I couldn't make heads or tails of it. It was the world seen through pink glasses. She wanted pretty pictures, idealized things like frosty paws."

Eduardo told Jennifer she needed to go deeper, and he pushed her in ways that made her uncomfortable. "He made her write a play about being trapped in a vault," said Dan Rybicky. "That's how Eduardo saw her: locked in a vault. 'You're a woman in a vault and all you can eat is cat food.' It had Nazi Germany connotations. It was weird. I don't know. Eduardo was an incredible teacher, but there was a cruel streak."

One day, Eduardo told the core group that the only way they could become "real" playwrights was to stage their work. "If you want to do it," he explained, "you have to do it."

And so several of Eduardo's students—including Colette Burson, Kate Robin, Dan Rybicky, Dmitry Lipkin, Carrie Luft, and Jennifer Farber—formed the Playwrights Collective, with Eduardo serving as leader, adviser, and guiding spirit. The aim was to produce original work while keeping the playwright at the center of a process that was usually dominated by the producer, the director, and the actors.

February 1991. They introduced themselves with a manifesto: "The Playwrights Collective is a democratic, nonhierarchical, not-for-profit company of twelve young writers who are committed to preserving the theater as the final refuge for the dramatic writers' voice."

Most of the members were in their second year of the graduate program. They met twice a week—at NYU, in apartments, coffee shops, bars. They read their work in progress aloud. When a play was deemed as close to finished as possible, the company began production. The job was broken into pieces and shared. If your play was not being staged, you might serve as director, set builder, head of wardrobe, press officer, ticket seller, or fundraiser. In this way, everyone would learn everything.

At the beginning, shows were staged in whatever space the company could get—an NYU student center, a Second Avenue theater— small rooms fitted with a riser and a few dozen seats, most of them filled by friends and family, cigarette smoke pooling along the ceiling.

The Playwrights Collective mounted an astonishing seventeen plays in its first two years. *Virus* by Keith Tadrowski was followed by Colette Burson's *Madra with Child*, Dan Rybicky's *Youth Is Wasted*, Eduardo Machado's *Three Ways to Go Blind*, and Kate Robin's *Given Away*.

The group was soon getting attention from the downtown press. It was considered an important new entry in the city's booming youth art scene. *Her New York* ran its December 20, 1993, story under the hyperbolic headline "The Women of the Playwrights Collective Wake Us Up to American Nightmare." *The Villager* described the collective as "a group of 24–27 year old disgruntled New York University graduates who are impassioned with theater and with bringing their work to the stage." To *The Village Voice*, Eduardo Machado was a "charismatic Cuban American playwright [who] has become both friendly guru and professional muse to the Collective, holding sessions that are one part support group, two parts creative hypnosis."

"With no money, and little institutional interest, we had to rely on our outrage," Colette Burson told the *Voice* reporter.

"The theatre has turned a deaf ear to the dramatist's voice," Jennifer Farber was quoted as saying, "but together we found we can scream really loud."

The *Voice* sent a photographer to take a picture of the group: nine playwrights in a row. There's evidence of happiness in the picture, the joy of a Little League team on the first day of practice. Jennifer stands out even here, at the dawn of things. Eight playwrights dressed like downtown bohemians. The ninth (Jennifer) wears a business suit. They resemble a mime troop. She looks like their manager, the only adult present. Some friends got on Jennifer for this—*dress for the life you want!*—but it actually speaks well of her. She was a serious person with her mind fixed on a serious and somewhat conventional family-filled future. She did not have a single bohemian inclination. That was the truth of her life and the subject of her work, and she never tried to pretend otherwise.

The Playwrights Collective took up residence on the ground floor of an office building at 74 Varick Street in Soho. They called it the Gold Room, but it was really just a boxy space lent to them by a friend. It could seat maybe fifty. A typical production ran six to eight shows. These plays were not recorded, nor the scripts saved. If any of this work survives, it's only in the minds of a few dozen people.

Jennifer's early plays included *Eclipsed*, *Glenda's Vault*, and *I Could Write a Book*—titles I gleaned from production notes and flyers archived at the Rose Collection of the New York Public Library. That's seemingly all that remains: detritus, ripples left in the wake of their own vanishing. The worlds built by the collective were like bubbles in the sea foam—they existed for a moment, then went *pop*. The Japanese have a term for this: *wabi-sabi*. It was transience that made them beautiful.

Everyone had their specialty at the collective. For Jennifer, it was fundraising. It was her job to keep the operation solvent, a task achieved with contributions and promotions as well as galas. When all else failed, she'd simply ask her parents and their friends to kick in. Hilliard Farber bought every unsold ticket for most shows, handing them out to Farber & Co. employees, who felt obligated to attend.

Hilliard and Gloria always appeared at the top rung of the collective's donor list: $1,000 and up. Liz Claiborne and Arthur Ortenberg were usually listed in tier two: $500–$999. Stephen Sondheim and Terrence McNally were listed in tier three: $100–$499. Jennifer's childhood friend Laurel Watts was in tier five ($25–$49), along with the actor Eric Bogosian. Tom Beller appeared in tier six (under $25), as did the writers Sam Lipsyte and Nick Davis.

The members of the group got to know the Farbers as a result of their patronage. Jennifer's sister, Melissa, was at every opening and party, always third in line when the Farbers arrived. Hilliard, then Gloria, then Melissa—that's how it sorted out, in the way of a single multicell organism. "They were a presence throughout my time at the collective," Dan Rybicky told me. "They were lovely, loving benefactors. Hilliard was wonderful. He seemed like a man who had truly won in life. He had an exuberance that was contagious. He had a joy about him that he wanted to share. It came off as generosity of spirit. He made me feel almost like a son. I acted in a lot of the collective's productions, and I was kind of fat, and I played fat. Not chunky. Fat. I lost weight later, but, back then . . . Well, Hilliard was a big guy, too. I think he just loved seeing me perform and took a shine. Maybe he was like that with everybody, but I really think he was more like that with me. Because he knew I needed it more. My dad died when I was ten. I was from a small town. And I was fat. And he saw all that and was wonderful. Jen had the same exuberance. She was a frail wisp, but she had a hearty sense of humor and life."

To some, Hilliard's presence could seem less a matter of love than of surveillance—just like the car and driver. Hilliard did not approve of Jen's downtown friends or see a future for his daughter in show business, and so he kept an eye on the situation. He was wary of Eduardo's technique, which shaded toward public exposure. Hilliard Farber was a private man. Each time Jennifer tapped into her past to create a character, she threatened his sense of decorum.

To Hilliard, Jennifer's passion for playwriting would have been a kind of sideline, a glorified hobby, something to broaden and enrich his younger daughter while she waited for her real life—as philanthropist, socialite, wife, mother, and possible employee of Farber & Co.—to begin.

"The collective was Jennifer's rebellion," Colette Burson explained. "Hilliard knew that, and wanted to keep us close. Yes, he was generous, but how generous? He gave a few thousand bucks a year and bought tickets. So what? By the end, he'd put maybe ten thousand dollars in the collective. How many millions did he give Fotis Dulos? What does that tell you?"

Hilliard and Gloria hosted a dinner for the Playwrights Collective shortly after its founding. It's a night that members of the group vividly recall. It was a glimpse into an alternate reality, a different New York. It was at Le Bernardin on West Fifty-First Street between Sixth and Seventh, the most expensive restaurant in the city at the time. It was a genie's bottle inside, velvet seats and walls coated in shimmering steel.

"The Farbers stood in a line to greet us," said Colette. "They were so beautiful you could not believe it, but Jennifer was the most beautiful of all. It might have been her birthday. Maybe that was the occasion. It was late summer, and Jen was born on September 27. Dan, Carrie, Kate, Eduardo, and myself were all invited. And we had the best time. The food was the most delicious food I have ever eaten, and the surroundings were the most luxurious. It was lovely. Hilliard gave a speech. He was like Father Christmas, super tall and bald and big and smiley in glasses. Kind of humble, but the humble brag, a powerful guy aware of his power. With humility. Or no, not humility: humanness. He was approachable, friendly, not intimidating at all. Jennifer was always there at his side. It was like Ivanka and Donald. I think that was very important to her, being next to him. You can't overestimate Hilliard's influence, or what his absence would mean later."

That was the first time the other members of the collective understood the nature of Jennifer's wealth. It was big banking money, a milieu they knew only from television shows and magazines.

The Playwrights Collective staged two major Jennifer Farber plays. Taken together, these works, the culmination of her theatrical career, illustrate the promise and the demise of her life as an artist.

The first was called *The Red Doors*. It dealt with Jennifer's obsessions: marriage with and without love, the pressure to settle, the illusiveness of true affection. Also parents, children, real boyfriends, and fantasy lovers. Hilliard was in it, as was Gunnar Graham and a handful of well-known people, including Bill Clinton; Charlie Rose, whom Jennifer knew from the charity circuit; and Matt Lauer, whom Jennifer had fixated on from afar. If she knew Matt sexually, it was only in dreams. Various other men appear, speak their piece, and then vanish in the hours before the protagonist is to be married.

The stage bill took the form of an invitation: "Mr. and Mrs. Daddy Cohen request the honour of your presence at the marriage of their daughter Bunny to Mr. Lawrence Hurschowitz or Mr. Charlie Rose or her ex-boyfriend Zuke or Bill, etc." The name "Cohen" tells you these people are Jews; the name "Bunny" tells you they are of the country club set; the word "etc." tells you the suitors are types and, as such, are interchangeable; the letter "u" in the word "honour" tells you they have Anglo pretensions. *The Red Doors* in the title refers to the entrance of Elizabeth Arden's Red Door salon, which, for generations of New Yorkers, was a symbol of upper-class pampering. The invitation was fronted by red doorlike flaps that opened onto a cast list.

Gloria used to take the preteen Jennifer on shopping sprees that ended at the Red Door. Jennifer tapped those memories to give the play resonance. Actual red doors dominated the set, but Bunny Cohen did not step through them until the end of the show. Most of the action took place at their threshold, which, like the door in the Kafka parable "Before the Law," stands as a barrier as much as a gateway. On this side, indecision. On that side, certainty. On this side, the fallen world. On that side, matrimonial bliss.

Tim Cunningham, who joined the collective in its second year, was tapped to direct *The Red Doors*. "I always thought of it as a twisted version of *Alice in Wonderland*," he told me. "There's a young woman, it's her wedding day, and she falls into a reverie. She has fantasy episodes. Charlie Rose is in one. Kathie Lee Gifford is another. There are ex-boyfriends. She has scenes with all of them. She is worried that she has made a mistake, and is about to marry the wrong person. None of us really thought about marriage at the time—we were in our twenties—but it was Jen's play, and she never stopped thinking about it."

Cunningham went on: "She could have written about these things in a facile way, and it would have been very commercial. But with the pressure of Eduardo's process, these darker elements crept in."

"That play was about the fear of marrying the wrong person," said Dan Rybicky. "The protagonist is having all these conversations with old boyfriends, real and fantasy. She wants to get married and doesn't want to get married and her father keeps tapping his watch and saying, 'Hurry up. We've got a wedding to do.' The most powerful line in the play, a line that's stayed with me, comes from the father, who looks around with disapproval and says, 'What is this? This isn't perfect. I paid for perfect.'"

Dan then added, "Jen's best work is almost surreal. It's funny but also incredibly serious. She was a woman, standing onstage, asking herself, 'Can I be happy and be alone? Do I have to get married? Does not having children in some sense mean saying no to life?'"

Because it seemed so personal, *The Red Doors* provoked speculation about Jennifer's private life and decisions. "She was very much someone upon whom other people projected their fantasies," said Kate Robin. "I'm sure that her beauty had something to do with it. There was also an element of mystery. She had a kind of reserve. Maybe that comes with great wealth. When I talk to friends from the collective about what happened to Jen later, each of us has a different opinion, and I feel like we're really expressing something about ourselves. To me, Jen was a person who had a habit of falling in love with unavailable men. She was drawn to men who were inevitably going to hurt her. I saw it play out multiple times. Many of them were just these banker douches. Maybe she felt she had to repeat the magic of her parents'

marriage and find someone like Hilliard. She had a very, very, very, very close relationship with her father. That's the key."

"Jen carried a list of the qualities she was looking for in a husband in her pocket," Eduardo Machado told me. "I'd see her sitting alone in the theater, looking at it."

Here's the crux: Jennifer Farber lived in two different worlds. There was the downtown world of her playwriting friends, small apartments, dingy bars. There was the uptown world of society galas, charity balls, and properly eligible men. She was careful to keep the salt and the fresh water apart. "We were never invited to those uptown parties," said Kate Robin. "She would simply say goodbye, get in the town car, and drive away."

The collective's calendar was crowded with opening nights and parties. The best started at the Gold Room and spilled across the street to a loft on White Street owned by Robert Worth Bingham IV. Rob was like Jay Gatsby in that you occasionally found yourself at one of his parties but might not be exactly sure who he was. (I went to at least two of those parties.) Rob was twenty-seven when Jennifer began to frequent the loft, which became a common space for the downtown scene.

Rob, a member of the Brown class of 1988, had the air of a person mourning his own future, which had been snatched away. He was the scion of one of the most powerful families in the South—*The Binghams of Louisville* is the title of a book by David Leon Chandler. Rob's great-grandfather Robert Worth Bingham Sr. built a media empire centered on *The Louisville Courier-Journal*, which his father was in line to inherit when he was killed in a freak accident while driving a convertible to the beach on Nantucket. Without a ready heir (Rob was only three months old when his father died), the business became an object of interne-cine warfare that the family settled only by selling out to Gannett when Rob was in college, leaving him with money—his share amounted to around $100 million—but without a mission. And so he drifted, first to Cambodia, where he worked as a reporter and began using heroin, then to New York, where he bought the loft and wrote short stories. His breakthrough came in 1995, when *New Yorker* fiction editor Deb Garri-son found one of his pieces in the slush pile. The stories in Rob's collec-tion *Pure Slaughter Value*, which was published in 1997, were compared to the work of Graham Greene and Robert Stone.

The writer Strawberry Saroyan—granddaughter of William—described Rob and the loft in her essay "12th, between a and b," which appears in *Personals: Dreams and Nightmares from the Lives of 20 Young Writers.*

> He had a drug problem and could often be found at the end of the evening after the party was over, in a semiconscious stupor. Then one of the others would take it upon himself to make sure he made it home safely. His apartment was massive. The first time I went to a party there, I described it to people afterward as being the size of an airport hangar. I had never seen any-thing like it in the city, except in museums. Fascinated by who he might be, I ducked into his office one night and came upon a piece of his writing. Of course, I immediately recognized it as a work of brilliance. He was the real writer of them all, I thought to myself. And gradually, without my even speaking to him really, the combination of his tremendous wealth yet obvious unhappiness, his need for help, his distractedness . . . his talent, his prep school clothes even, began to work on me until they coalesced into a fantasy of our ending up together.

Though Jennifer had met Rob at Brown, she only got to know him in New York. In some ways, they were similar—both rich, both pressed by familial expectations, both waiting for their lives to begin. The fact that they were gifted by circumstance, rich and talented, carriers of a family legacy and a tribal dream yet cursed by fate, had to mean something. It was the pull and push of magnetism that brought them together and kept them apart, that had them whispering to each other in a corner of Rob's loft. They entangled like photons. Whatever happened to one would happen to the other, no matter where life took them.

Rob's biggest parties were those announcing the publication of a new issue of *Open City*, the downtown journal he had taken on as publisher. *Open City* was the creation of Daniel Pinchbeck (the only child of Joyce Johnson, who was dating Jack Kerouac when *The New York Times* published its career-making review of *On the Road*) and Tom Beller, who met Daniel when he showed up at a party Tom was hosting at Verkhovyna, a bar on East Seventh Street.

Open City was seemingly Daniel and Tom's attempt to tap the literary genius of their generation, to do for Gen X what George Plimpton had done for the postwar generation with *The Paris Review*, or what Harold Ross had done for the Lost Generation with *The New Yorker*. Though *Open City* did indeed "discover" several talented young writers, it may be best remembered for the parties on White Street. The smoke and music, the hookups and blackouts, the downtown gossip. Eric Stoltz was there, as were Noah Baumbach, Peter Dinklage (later known for his star turn as Tyrion Lannister in *Game of Thrones*), Bret Easton Ellis, Fran Lebowitz, Hilton Als, Jonathan Franzen, et al.

This is when Tom and Jennifer reconnected. Beller had walked into the loft on White Street, where the Playwrights Collective had gathered to rehearse. If this were a movie, you'd cut directly from Saint Ann's, where Tom, a six-foot-five senior, is chatting up freshman Jen Farber, to White Street, where Tom bends down so that Jennifer can shout into his ear. "She had gone to the high school that had taken him in for his senior year, and they had talked in the school's lobby," Beller wrote in his short story "Caller ID," a fictionalized chronicle of the relationship that appears in Tom's 2000 short-story collection, *The Sleep-Over Artist*. "She had been a freshman. One faintly memorable conversation, interrupted for about a decade and picked up again at a party. Senior/freshman. The dynamic still percolated."

Tom was twenty-nine. Jennifer was twenty-five. They would be together for less than two years, but it was a relationship that mattered. Tom was a future that might have been. He was also about as close as Jennifer ever got to finding a romantic crossover, a partner who could play uptown and downtown. He was tall and handsome, athletic and brainy, a private schooler but not rich, artistic, ambitious, smart and Jewish, but not *too* Jewish.

It happened fast. First talking, then dating, then a standout couple on the scene. "They seemed like they'd been made for each other," said Lee Smith, a writer from Illinois and one of Rob Bingham's close friends. "Both of them were tall and brilliant and kind, but not too kind, and of course beautiful." Lee remembers Tom and Jennifer walking into Rob's parties side by side, king and queen. "It was a real entrance," Lee told me. "It was the peak of a certain moment, which I guess you'd call our twenties downtown."

Jennifer offered Tom a door into a kind of luxurious New York life he'd heard about but never truly experienced. Tom's father died when Tom was young. His mother, a modern dancer and choreographer, raised Tom by herself in a modest Upper West Side apartment. The atmosphere was Manhattan bohemia circa *Panic in Needle Park*. When

Tom was kicked out of Riverdale before his senior year for a transgression made in conspiracy with two other kids who got off with mere admonishment, he was scooped up by Saint Ann's.

He was already succeeding in literary New York when he reunited with Jennifer. After graduating from Vassar, he earned an MFA in fiction writing from Columbia University. He sold his first short story to *The New Yorker* in 1992, while still in graduate school. That piece, "A Different Kind of Imperfection," was selected for *Best American Short Stories* when he was twenty-seven. He continued to publish in *The New Yorker*, where, for a time, he was mentored by Roger Angell and employed by Talk of the Town. His collections—*Seduction Theory, The Sleep-Over Artist, How to Be a Man: Scenes from a Protracted Boyhood*—began to appear soon after.

And yet, despite his success in the 1990s, Tom Beller's life in New York never stopped being a financial struggle. Jennifer must have entered it like a reprieve. For Tom, being with Jennifer was like getting in out of the rain. "I was suddenly sleeping on the softest sheets," he told me. "We got tickets to everything and never had to worry about getting a taxi or squeezing into the subway at rush hour."

Life was *too* easy with Jennifer, explained Tom, who believes in the upside of the downside. Discomfort builds character, giving you the needed material to write. There was no grit with Jennifer, no sand in the gears. That bothered Beller; the relationship felt like a trap, like a feather bed he couldn't escape.

He began to look for a way out of the Farbers' snow-globe New York. For a time, he seemed to find it on the road. Get in the car with Jennifer and drive—away from the cocoon of city and family, away from Eduardo Machado and the grind of the Playwrights Collective, away from Hilliard and One Fifth Avenue. These trips were augmented by stimulants. The couple imbibed and watched the colors bleed. Maine, Colorado, Florida. At times, it felt like it was the country and not the car that was moving, towns and rest stops streaming past.

Tom writes about these trips in his story "The Breakup," which appears in his 2005 collection *How to Be a Man.* They would drive the car around Jennifer's neighborhood on their way out, loading up on provisions. They'd ghost through Manhattan as if for the last time, as if saying goodbye, then exit through the Lincoln, Holland, or Midtown Tunnel, or over the Queensboro or George Washington Bridge. Once they were out, it was as if the city never existed.

Returning was even better. Your knees hurt and your neck aches and you have listened to every compact disc twice, and then, there it is, Manhattan, at first just the tops of the tallest buildings, then the entire city stretched across the horizon like laundry drying on a line.

The trip out west was a high point for Jennifer. They left at dusk and drove all night, from western Pennsylvania to the Ohio flatness. The steel mills south of Chicago went by in the dark—the stacks belching flames as in a vision of Sodom and Gomorrah. Iowa, Nebraska, Kansas. Then the Rockies in the West, first the foothills, then the mountains, then the mountains behind the mountains.

Jennifer later said she loved the Rockies because the country was beautiful, and because she'd been happy there with Tom. Such a trip is like a nap taken in the middle of your life—there is before and after. As for Tom, he does not even remember going out West. "[But] we went everywhere," he told me. "We went just to go."

Tom was happy, too. Just not as happy as Jennifer. In "The Breakup," Tom wrote:

> We'd taken road trips like this before. A year earlier, we'd
> taken a trip through the South in her old college car . . . Even

then, certain nagging questions about where we were going were starting to surface like alligators in a pond. I could just see their eyes, peering above the surface and posing the question, "What are you going to do next?" . . .

In some ways I felt my love for her most intensely when I was driving and she was sleeping, beautifully at rest and safe by my side . . . In hindsight, I would say that, however much you are overcome with tenderness at such moments, it's probably a bad sign if your favorite time with your girlfriend occurs when she is sleeping.

Jennifer wanted to get married. Tom didn't—at least not to Jennifer. That was the fundamental problem. When Jennifer pressed, Tom made excuses. He said he was too young to settle down. As a writer, he said, he would never make the kind of money necessary to support her in her accustomed manner. She wanted to live in New York. His career might take him far from the city. She wanted to have three kids. He said he was not sure he wanted to have even one.

Jennifer chronicled this period of argument and negotiation in "Window-Shopping for a Life," in which Tom appeared as "Jake." "The issue of our suitability again trips me up," she wrote. "We are both Jewish, from New York, from good schools, he too is a writer. We are at the same level of attractiveness. We feel so close, have such similar paths, that it's sometimes more as if we're brother and sister than lovers from separate homes . . . I tell him I'll go anywhere, live at any level, that if the institution of marriage will keep us apart, I will ignore that it exists, I can still be with him."

"We are at the same level of attractiveness"—think about that. It's as if she was playing dress-up, seeking a perfect match for her doll in the dollhouse.

The relationship ended on one of those road trips. Tom had been steeling himself for the moment, which he knew would come. He recounted it in "The Breakup," in which Jennifer appears as "Jill":

> Jill and I had been going out for two years. Courage in relationships is often seen in terms of having the strength to walk away from a bad situation. But it's much harder to walk away from a good situation, one in which the current moment is sweet, and yet you never let go of the feeling that this is just a visit, temporary. Courage is being willing to be the bad guy, as opposed to the victim. After a year or so, in your thirties as I was, or approaching it, as Jill was, you simply have to own up to your ambivalence and raise the stakes on the matter. At a certain point, you can't think of ambivalence as being some mysterious shackle on your life; you have to acknowledge that the nature of your love isn't strong enough to overcome your ambivalence. Whose fault is that? The fault—my fault, in this case—is not coming clean. Why—besides the sheer inconvenience—don't people come clean? Maybe you just think you're in love because it's a necessary myth. If you're not, what the hell are you doing here, other than being an example of how being comfortable is not sufficient? Being comfortable is not enough! Comfort, as a relationship's greatest virtue, eventually becomes uncomfortable.

They had driven Hilliard's Jeep Cherokee down to the Florida Keys. Hilliard "had the tires checked before we left," writes Beller, continuing:

I respected the tenderness of this gesture, even as I knew we would more or less nullify all safety concerns with whatever recreational drugs we were bringing along. I was glad for the sturdy vehicle, but it also seemed confining. Its reliability was annoying. I resisted this bland vehicle and what it stood for in my life. Looking back, I think the brave thing to do would have been to acknowledge that feeling and end the whole thing right there. Instead, I took the Jeep, and its owner's daughter, for a ride.

Tom was on a collision course with Jennifer, a typical *her-*and-*him-*in-early-adulthood situation. While she was fixated on the horizon, he was focused on the ground beneath his wheels—writing, publishing, and drifting from obstacle to obstacle, going just to go, riding just to ride. Something had to give.

The decisive break came on the side of the road near Islamorada Key. Beller shifts his account to the third person, as if to remove himself from the discomfort. He has said something inconsiderate. She has made him pull over. They get out of the car. There is an exchange. They go off in different directions:

> Then the man stops, turns around, starts walking back to the car, then passes it; he breaks into a trot, then a run, and catches up to the woman. She keeps walking. He reaches for her elbow . . . You will have recognized that moment, a universal moment in the choreography of fights between men and women, when the man reaches for the woman's elbow and she, in fury, yanks it away. That gesture says: Get off me. It says: Leave me alone. And it says, more than anything: I can't believe that of all the men in the world it's you who I'm stuck with by the side of the road.

The woman is furious, hysterical, grieving, crying, unforgiving. About what? That day's original sin is long out of sight, forgotten, a tiny banana peel that led to a slip that led to a swerve, and shortly a world war has broken out that is out of proportion with its origins. She's lashing out violently, but the object of wrath—to his amazement and horror—is herself. She bangs herself on her head. Hard blows to the head. Self-inflicted wounds. The man watches this for a moment in shock and then begins gushing apologies. He reaches for her wrists to stop her. He grovels. He begs . . .

"I hate myself for loving you," she blurts out.

Holy shit! Thinks the man. She's quoting Joan Jett! Does she know that?

Such are the internal monologues of a man standing amid a ruin of old lobster traps behind the roadside brush off Route 1, as his girlfriend of two years beats herself and has a nervous breakdown because their relationship is clearly going down the tubes for the simple reason that he doesn't love her, or love her enough to marry her. Which is not really a simple reason.

Jennifer's second major production with the Playwrights Collective was called *What Party?* She put everything she knew into the play, which read like a companion to *The Red Doors*. It was the same material and the same world, only she tried to go deeper, to paint a more sympathetic picture. In an interview with *The New York Observer*, Jennifer called it a romantic comedy. "It's about a single woman in New York looking for her dream groom," she told the reporter, according to whom the "comely," "pert" Jennifer Farber had a "debutante gone wrong quality." "She finally meets this Fortune 500, wealthy Jewish guy, who she thinks is her ultimate suitor, but it turns out he's her worst nightmare because all he offers is this Park Avenue party life. In the end she gives up love and her entire emotional life to have that world."

Asked if the work was autobiographical, Jennifer said, "Well, there was a time in my life where I seriously considered whether I was in love with a certain person, the one person I had ever been with who had an insane amount of money. When I was done with the relationship, I explored what I hated most in myself, and I kept saying, 'I'm going to write a play about this. I can't waste all this good material.'"

"There is a marriage in this one, too," said Tim Cunningham, who acted in *What Party?* "But it's about more than that. It's about a world Jennifer knew to the bone, about the demimonde of globetrotting Eurotrash, and a young woman trying to navigate it. It's more sophisticated than *The Red Doors*. There are old boyfriends in it, and a wedding that she's trying to avoid, and a wedding dress, and there is a lot on her feelings about marriage in general. Artistically, it was a big advance for Jen."

After the group sessions and table reads, when the consensus said the play was never going to get any better, the decision was made to produce it. Eduardo Machado volunteered to direct. Jennifer quickly accepted. Several people urged her to choose someone else. They were all a little scared of Eduardo, who had, if such a thing is possible, too much artistic integrity. He did whatever he thought the show called for, regardless of the feelings of the playwright. Jennifer took the suggestions to choose a different director as a slight. She thought her colleagues were saying she was not good or mature enough to work with the maestro.

"We tried to talk her out of Eduardo," Tim Cunningham told me.

"We were worried that he was going to do something she wasn't going to like. Eduardo doesn't fool around. He does exactly what he wants artistically. And so, we're like, 'Are you sure you want Eduardo?' But she was adamant. I understand why she might have taken our advice as an insult, but it was Eduardo—not Jennifer—we were worried about."

Eduardo started with casting. He wanted an actress who could become Jennifer Farber. He scored a coup by landing Tatyana Yassukovich, whom Eduardo calls "a truly great actress."

Tatyana was born and raised in England. She moved to the United States in 1982 when she was twenty, studied at the Lee Strasberg Theatre & Film Institute in New York, and became a member of the Actors Studio. She has written and appeared in dozens of plays but is probably best known for her voice-over work. She is beautiful and blond, and was in the mood to try something challenging when Eduardo approached.

"He sent me Jennifer's play and I sat down and read it straight through," Tatyana told me. "Then I read it again, and knew, after that second reading, this was a role I could play and wanted to play, because, though it was New York, it was very much the world I grew up in. It's the world of the very wealthy, the very privileged—so privileged it's absurd. I came from the same world, but, unlike Jennifer, I escaped, so I felt tremendous sympathy. Jennifer was still young and this play seemed like the start of her escape. As an artist, you *must* break from your parents."

Tatyana continued, "Jennifer had the kind of beauty I always wished I had, tall and thin, that classical American look." She studied Jennifer to become Jennifer onstage. "In playing the part, I wanted to tap into my own experience, so I searched for places our stories overlapped. My first marriage had been a society wedding. I did not want to get married, but I thought it was what I was supposed to do. Then I ran away. That's where I found the parallel. I thought that Jennifer would run away, too. So, as I was rehearsing, feeling more and more like Jennifer, I decided that I had to wear my actual wedding dress in the play. My God! I was such a Method actor! I needed the real dress so I could embody the character. It was a very 1940s sort of dress, very elaborate. I wrote my parents and had them ship it. That's the dress I was shoved into onstage. In the play, these men pick me off the ground and shove me into the dress. I was naked when they did it! Completely nude!"

"The play was supposed to show how people in this *White Lotus* world are real and have real concerns and real problems, but, bit by bit, Eduardo made it into a satire," Tim Cunningham told me. "He just couldn't take the concerns of these people seriously, so he didn't. By the end, it was not the situations that gave rise to the humor, but the people themselves. It worked so well as a satire, as hard satire, that I thought that at some subconscious level that's how Jen had always wanted it."

"By the way," said Eduardo, "she's called Jennifer in the press, but to us she was always Jen."

"I was there during every rehearsal and I watched the play change," Tim Cunningham went on. "It started as a warmhearted comedy about the rich, but, within a few weeks of Eduardo's direction, it had become a vicious satire. When we realized just how much the tone had changed—I mean, it *really* changed—we tried to reach out and make sure Jen was okay and happy with it. And she indeed appeared to be very happy, laughing along during the rehearsals."

"She seemed to think that what Eduardo was doing was brilliant," said Tatyana Yassukovich. "I remember thinking, 'Oh, she's enjoying this so much. I am so happy we are able to give her what she needs,' but of course later the whole thing backfired."

What Party? opened in March 1997. The reviews were laudatory. Every account noted the quality of the writing and the ingenuity of the stagecraft. ("Machado keeps pushing the sudsy action into humorous tableaux of conspicuous junior league consumption," wrote Charles McNulty in *The Village Voice*.) In one scene, a dozen male actors advance on the lone woman—now nude, now being slammed into a wedding dress. In another, the same men roll across the floor in office chairs. In a third, they form a conga line, each singing a bit of dialogue in turn. Under the headline "Park Avenue Princess Writes Play," *The New York Observer* tagged it "social farce" and described Jennifer as a "media society mover." To *The Village Voice, What Party?* was "a lively soap opera spoof of the New York twentysomething jet set that could have been called, 'Lifestyles of the Rich and Ditzy.'" The *Voice* continues: "In this cordoned-off world of cell phones, limos, and anorexic glamour, Bergdorf-bred Alison (Tatyana Yassukovich) meets her match in Roger (Ed Vassalo), a Donald Trump in the making, who cockily challenges her to break his heart. Their narcissistic courtship moves between 4-star New York restaurants and Monte Carlo discos, where the huge tab is dwarfed only by the unmentionable emotional cost."

The run sold out, and the collective made plans to add an additional week of shows, something they'd never done. But the moment was double-edged for Jennifer. Success, but at what price? The theater was filled with laughter, but what kind of laughs were these? Was Jennifer subjecting her family to mockery? "We weren't making fun of Jennifer, but we *were* making fun of her kind," said Tatyana Yassukovich. "And they were sort of ridiculous, to be quite frank, these people and their status obsessions. What can you do but make fun of them? I think Jennifer thought the play was about something deep, but we made it seem shallow. I get how it could upset her, when it's your own story up there and everyone is laughing."

"I thought it was a funny play and, at first, so did Jen," Eduardo told me. "I got a bunch of amazing people to be in it, and it got rave reviews, then everything got strange."

The turning point, a pivot not only in her career but in her life, came a week into the run, when Hilliard and Gloria saw the play with several Farber & Co. employees. Hilliard exited while the actors were taking their bows. He'd offered to throw a cast party after the show and was standing at the bar when the cast and crew came in. "That was the first time I'd ever met a really big-time business guy," said Eduardo, who described Hilliard as tall, taciturn, and judgmental. "He was a powerful man who wanted to protect his daughters. They were the princesses, but he was in control."

Eduardo explained what happened next with shocking succinctness: "Jen went to the bar to hug her father, but he stepped away and said, 'You're a whore. You've made yourself and your family look like prostitutes.' That was it. We never saw Jen again."

"I don't know if it was quite that harsh," said Colette Burson. "We love Eduardo, but he has his own way of remembering. Hilliard did not like the play. That's absolutely true. He hated the way it made his family look, and all those people from his office were there. He told Jennifer he hated the play and said it made her look like a fool. That's what I heard."

"When I close my eyes, I can still see the scene," said Tatyana Yassukovich. "We had come in together for the party, and there was Hilliard waiting at the bar. We were hanging out, having a great time, happy the show had gone well, when Jennifer went over. We knew something bad was happening without having to be told. You could sense it like a change in the weather. You know that feeling, when the wind shifts and you can smell that snow is coming?

"I wasn't trying to make her character shallow," Yassukovich went on. "I don't believe any character, when you really get into it, can be shallow."

"Jen had been at every rehearsal and was involved in every

decision," said Tim Cunningham. "When the audiences loved it, she loved it. Then her family came. Maybe she didn't even know what she was writing. You don't always realize what you're getting on the page. I think she was upset that other people were upset. And we were all like, 'So what if you're upsetting people? That's good theater.' But she couldn't take it. And suddenly there was this crazy flip-flop. The show, which she'd considered such a success, she decided was a failure. We did not see Jen again. We just got a note. The next day. It said that she did not agree to extend the run, that the play was finished. We never heard from her again; this was after seven years of working together in the most intimate of circumstances."

To Tatyana, it seemed like a failure of nerve. Jennifer Farber was an artist. As an artist, she had the obligation to sack the temple and destroy the idols. She went right up to the altar, then chickened out. "You have to let go of that fear of what people will think," Tatyana said. "Most people can't. They get halfway and turn back. Jen turned back, and it sent her down a different path. When I read about what happened in Connecticut, I thought, 'Oh no, she never found the strength.' I felt so sad. Not just about her death. Also about her life. She never found the power to make the break. Maybe that in itself made her feel powerless. She had one kind of power—beauty and wealth. But never developed the other, more important kind of power, the power to express herself, break away, and be free."

What does a person do when her first dream dies?

Does she start over and try again? Or does she get in bed and stay there? In such a case, having money can be less blessing than curse.

If Jennifer Farber had had no money when she quit the Playwrights Collective, she would've been forced to work and in the process might have found another project, a mission, a way to live. But Jennifer did not have to work, so she turned inward instead. Having given up the theater, she focused on the old fantasy: a dream man who would love her in a Classic Eight on Park Avenue. It put her back on the party circuit—fundraisers, openings, society balls, media shindigs—where the eligible eligibles swim by in great trout-like schools. "She was always going to a fancy party with [André] Leon Talley or a person like that," said Lee Smith. "And she never did it casually."

She was courted by a plethora of men. But no matter how promising, each of them turned out to have some flaw, at least from Jennifer's point of view. Too short or too grasping, too big or too old, too Jewish or too dumb, too gentle or too rough, too nice or too mean. Like Penelope's suitors in *The Odyssey*, these men lingered in the royal court, drinking wine as Jennifer wove and unwove her tapestry. Like the princes in *Rapunzel*, they stood beneath the tower, calling for Jennifer to throw down her long, magnificent hair. Each of them came away with a story, and each was a story of failure. One said he proceeded far enough to be invited to the Farbers' house on Fire Island, where he was stung by a wasp and whimpered and cried, disqualifying himself as too unmanly. "She looked at me with pity," he said. "That's when I knew it was over."

"We loved her," said Lee Smith, speaking for the downtown literary crowd, "but deep down we knew she was never going to marry one of us."

The names of the men she dated or hung with read like a roster of American media at the turn of the century: Toby Young, the famous *Vanity Fair* flameout; Lee Smith, who worked at *Open City*; Steve

Garbarino, who worked at the *Post*, the *Voice*, *New York*, and *Vanity Fair*. And others who do not want to be named.

"Her chauffeur drove a Fleetwood Brougham, one of those big old black cars," Steve Garbarino told me. "He would take us up to Elaine's so we could look for Kurt Vonnegut and Norman Mailer. Then over to the 21 Club to grab a cocktail with George Plimpton. Then down to the Baby Doll Lounge, a strip club with a go-go bar, then to Café Loup or Nell's or wherever. There was lot of drinking, and Jennifer was very chic. She was one of those girls who wears riding boots and faded jeans. But she always seemed to be looking for something better."

Jennifer began to panic as she got deeper into her thirties. Where was the man? She feared that she would never meet him, or had met him but did not recognize him, that she was fated to spend her life childless and alone. Hilliard counseled patience. "The person you are looking for is probably someone you already know," he told her. "You will not meet him at a party or in a bar. It will happen when you are sitting by yourself at home."

In 1994, Jennifer purchased a dog, a Cavalier King Charles Spaniel. She drove to a breeder in Hopewell, New Jersey, and took away a six-week-old puppy she named Sophie. She chose Sophie for her beauty and her scrap—she was the pick of the litter, "always being pushed out of the fray, yet getting right back in there with her siblings."

She treated the dog like a baby. This should usually be taken as a warning sign—a person who overly anthropomorphizes a pet, no matter how adorable, demonstrates a need for affection. Sophie slept in Jennifer's bed, which probably resulted in the eye infection that landed

Jennifer at St. Vincent's Hospital, where she showed up with Sophie in her crate. "I could not part from her for one minute. Much like a newborn," Jennifer explained. Describing a cross-country trip she took in October 1999, she wrote, "Sophie . . . slept on my lap all across flat Kansas, where the cruise control was on 70, and my legs were up and across to the passenger seat."

With Sophie at her side, Jennifer finally found the strength to leave New York. "She moved out west with me in 2000, to Colorado, when I moved there, knowing no one, but knowing it was where I needed to be," Jennifer wrote. "But I was not alone. I had Sophie . . . She loved men. She wanted me to find someone so she could love him as intensely too."

Jennifer went to Aspen, where she rented a condo across from Red Mountain. Often referred to as "Billionaire Mountain" for its wealthy inhabitants, the land is green in summer, white in winter, and blanketed by new growth in spring. Aspen was a nineteenth-century boomtown muscled from Ute Indians by frontier settlers and fortune hunters. In 1870, the name was officially changed from Ute City to Aspen. It followed a classic arc from there. By 1895, its summits— Highland Peak tops twelve thousand feet, high enough to make your nose bleed—were riddled with silver mines. The town grew fat on mineral wealth, becoming a tiny metropolis, its twenty thousand residents filling the velvet seats of the Wheeler Opera House, and the spittoons at the Isis Theatre. They raced horses, started fights, and drank Old Forester bourbon in the saloon at the Hotel Jerome, which later became the haunt of the king of gonzo journalism, Hunter S. Thompson.

By 1900, after the repeal of the Sherman Silver Purchase Act and the ensuing panic, the population had halved and halved again. Aspen became a ghost town, its grand hotels empty, its stately mansions fallen to ruin. The population had dropped to 705 when the town was rediscovered by veterans back from the Second World War, specifically members of the army's fabled 10th Mountain Division, an alpine unit that fought the Germans in the Dolomites on skis. Many of these men arrived in a state we might recognize as scrambled, not yet ready to conform to the rules of polite society. In the early 1950s, several of them lived in the way of modern surf bums, sleeping in abandoned miner shacks, hiking up to ski down, as free as Jim Bridger, the most famous of the old mountain men. It was a way of life that attracted attention first from adventure seekers, then from celebrities, then from entrepreneurs. The Aspen Skiing Company, which operates the lifts and maintains the trails, is currently owned by the Crown family of Chicago, who hold stakes in General Dynamics and JPMorgan Chase. In a good year, Aspen Mountain generates $100 million, making human diversion even more lucrative than silver.

Jennifer worked on a novel in Aspen. The town still had the rugged beauty of old western America, but none of the hardship. The entire valley would have been visible from her windows. In the afternoon, looking up from the desk where she'd been writing a scene about a rich man and his anxious daughter, say, she would've seen the skiers taking their last runs of the day. The trails empty. The Jacuzzis fill. The saloons roar to life. Snowcats, flurries caught in their powerful lamps, crisscross the mountain. The alpine world at night, the stars wheeling above, is woodsmoke and pine.

Jennifer's novel was about her life as a story of romantic misadventures. According to the journalist Vanessa Grigoriadis, who reported on the Dulos case for *Vanity Fair*, Jennifer finished the manuscript, then "put it in a drawer."

"The book kind of was a garden, something that was alive," a friend of Jennifer's told Grigoriadis. "She knew that she wanted to go back and tend that garden. Sorry to be that hokey, but that would be the metaphor that I would use for it. So, for her, it was like, 'I don't know when I'll get to that, but I know that I want to. And I know that it's there.'"

Aspen was a strange choice for Jennifer. Despite the inflow and outflow of the uber rich, it's a small town with just a handful of restaurants and stores. It's dead in the spring and the fall, and half alive in the summer. The town is truly itself only in the winter, when the peaks are buried in more than two hundred inches of snow, but Jennifer Farber did not like to ski.

So why Aspen?

Possibly because she'd been happy in the mountains with Tom Beller. To her, the region would represent a time as well as a place. Maybe that's why she went back. Or maybe because it was so far from home. Jennifer loved Hilliard, and loved his love, but it could be suffocating. Maybe she had to get away—geographically, physically, emotionally—to live.

It was Hilliard who encouraged in Jennifer tastes that were not just Waspy, and not just non-Jewish, but seemingly hostile to Judaism, at least as it was practiced in New York. Hilliard gave money to the expected causes and served on the board of his synagogue, yet he allowed his daughter to believe that the best club was the club that did not take too many Jews, that the best school was the school that had its roots in Christianity, that the best money and the best people, those he called Bank, were partly defined by their non-Jewishness. And so, when Jennifer went to Aspen, in addition to a place where she could write and a place where she'd been happy, she was searching for a place where she could stop being Jewish, which, ironically, would make her even more attractive to Hilliard, whose influence she was trying to escape. It seemed that only by becoming a gentile could Jennifer be Hilliard's ideal, at least as she imagined it.

Jennifer had used an alias while modeling at Brown. She'd supposedly done it to protect her privacy, but it also involved an element of role-play. A new name is a new life. Jen Farber is a Jewish girl from Brooklyn. Jennifer Bey is someone else. Jen Farber is hemmed in by codes, expectations, traditions. Jennifer Bey is a tabula rasa.

When she lived in Aspen, Jennifer broke off relations with her parents and began calling herself Jennifer Bey. Then—and this was the killer, the shank in the Jewish heart—she converted to Christianity and started wearing a cross. This was not about belief. In none of Jennifer's letters or other writing is there any mention of Jesus, faith, or religion. It was about identity—shedding her past. Jennifer was not Simone Weil praying in a convent. She was Issur Danielovitch changing his name to Kirk Douglas because he wanted to be a real American.

It's unclear how much Hilliard and Gloria even knew about the conversion. (According to Fotis, Jennifer never told her parents.) They'd stopped communicating. "Estranged" is the word that comes to mind. The fact that Jennifer was still being bankrolled by her family—she never had a paying job—highlights two fundamental truths: first, Hilliard would never cut off Jennifer, no matter what she did; second, Jennifer wanted to be free but was not willing to be poor—to "sweep up cigarette butts."

Jennifer didn't tell her New York friends about the conversion, either. "I know about it only because I saw the cross around her neck when I visited Aspen," Lee Smith told me. "We argued about it. She told me she'd been converted by an Episcopalian minister, so was now Episcopalian. I'm a Catholic. To me, Episcopalian seems like Catholic lite. I said to her, 'If you are going to do it, at least do it for real.'"

Perhaps being able to call herself Episcopalian mattered as much as anything.

After spending not quite a year in Aspen, Jennifer took Sophie to

Los Angeles. Friends refer to this as her period of "bopping around." Though she was now Episcopalian, her life made no more sense to her than before. She went to L.A. because that's where her playwriting friends had gone. The city was booming at the turn of the millennium. The initial gold rush of long-form cable TV that followed in the wake of *The Sopranos* flooded Hollywood writer rooms with the sort of novelists and playwrights who would've once stayed in New York. They revitalized dilapidated streets in Hermosa Beach and Venice, doing to the rickety bungalows and diners what the veterans of the 10th Mountain Division had done to Aspen. New restaurants opened, fern bars that appeared like mushrooms after a storm. Rents skyrocketed.

Most of Jennifer's friends lived in suburban-style houses near the beach. Jennifer preferred to replicate her full-service New York lifestyle. "I saw Jen when she'd moved to L.A., which would've been in 2000," said Dan Rybicky. "We went to the movies. We'd been close friends, connected at so many levels. I think I knew Jen in a way that other people did not because we were so much alike. There was a queerness to her that was not easy to see through the drop-dead beauty, but it came out in her writing. But she never really went with it. Like in L.A. She could have lived anywhere but ended up in an apartment in a big, bland doorman building in Westwood, a weirdly anonymous part of Hollywood. We were thirty-two or thirty-three, both a little lost, both trying to find our footing. Jen was writing, and trying to figure out if Los Angeles was a place she was going to stay."

"I think I'm the only person who knew her in all three places—New York, Aspen, and L.A.," said Lee Smith, who was living in Los Angeles when Jennifer arrived. "She had a place in a strange doorman building on Lower Wilshire, an area where absolutely no one lives. It was as not-L.A. as you could get in L.A. I told her I hated going there, so we would meet at the bar at the Four Seasons for drinks. Or, not just drinks, but to get drunk. We'd talk about her parents and family. Jennifer said there was no wellspring of goodwill in her family growing up. That's why she changed her name and her email to Jennifer Bey . . . her fantasy name . . . her modeling name. She stayed in L.A. for less than a year. She was just roaming around, searching. She still didn't know what she wanted to do."

Part
TWO

THE WORLD TRADE Center and the Pentagon were attacked on a Tuesday. Jennifer was on a plane, returning to L.A. after a visit to New York. The pilot came on the PA system to say that all commercial air traffic was being grounded. Jennifer's flight landed in Cincinnati. She spent two days alone in an airport hotel. She lay on the king-sized bed, staring out the window at the parking lot and the semi-urban sprawl. "She was freaked out when she called me," said Lee Smith. "She was watching the news and wondering if the world had come to an end. She said, 'You're a midwesterner. What the hell should I do here?' I said, 'One, I'm from Illinois, not Ohio. And two, stay in your hotel, order room service, and watch HBO like everyone else.'"

It was an interesting interlude for Jennifer, confined to a room in the middle of the country, in the middle of her life. America was one kind of place when she checked in, and another kind when she checked out. She knew she was through with L.A. even before she'd rebooked her flight.

She went back to Aspen instead, determined to get on with her quest. "It's like she planned to camp outside the Aspen airport and stay there till the right sort of man finally stepped off the right sort of plane," said Smith.

December 2003. The ski season begins in December—after Thanksgiving, before Christmas. When the first big storms blanket the mountains, the hotels fill with families, the runways with private jets.

Fotis Dulos spotted Jennifer as he walked to baggage claim. He recognized her from college. She'd been the pinnacle at Brown. She did not recognize him, not at first. She had not been attracted to him in school. She felt differently that day at the airport. That's thirty-five compared to nineteen. That's what time and desperation can do to perception. An unremarkable city in the morning becomes fascinating when you're alone at night.

They talked. Fotis was short but very handsome. Vanessa Grigoriadis described him as an "Adonis" in *Vanity Fair*, "a beautiful creature, with extraordinarily fine, delicate features, saucer-size brown eyes, and a fastidious appearance."

Fotis was traveling with his oldest friend, Andreas Toutziaridis. The two had known each other since childhood. Andreas was Fotis's closest connection to his youth in Athens. He was nearly as good-looking as Fotis, and, though he never moved away from Greece, he visited Fotis in America often. Again and again, he appears at Fotis's side at some crucial moment. It was Andreas who would offer the key advice, make the suggestion that changed everything. It was Andreas who told Fotis to pursue Jennifer. He said it as you might encourage a friend to pursue a good business opportunity.

Jennifer handed Fotis her phone number, but he didn't call. Several weeks passed.

Giving up on her years in Aspen, Jennifer moved back to New York and considered contingencies. At thirty-five, single motherhood seemed like an option. She'd begun to consider using a sperm donor when an email with an unfamiliar address appeared in her inbox. The message consisted of just four words: "Test—Are you there?" Fotis had accidentally deleted Jennifer's phone number. He'd been searching for her contact information ever since.

Hilliard had told Jennifer that the right person was probably someone she already knew. Well, she already knew Fotis Dulos. Hilliard had told Jennifer that she would be sitting at home alone when it happened. She was at home alone when the email arrived. Jennifer believed in symbols and signs. Taken together, they can read like fate. Fotis's "test" email reached Jennifer on January 13, 2004. It was a date the couple would celebrate as their anniversary.

Lee Smith—who told me that Jennifer wrote "long, beautifully intricate letters; she gave good email"—remembers the moment Fotis entered the picture. "It was new and exciting," he said. "He checked off so many of Jennifer's boxes—Ivy League, handsome, athletic. He actually sounded too perfect."

The fact that Jennifer had met Fotis at Brown, that they had friends in common, would have made him seem safe even though she did not really know him. Jennifer was usually careful with strangers, suspecting they were interested in her for the wrong reasons. In this case, she lowered her Rapunzel-like hair without a second thought. It was only when Jennifer finally got around to doing some due diligence—she googled him after their third date—that she learned that Fotis was already married.

Hilary Aldama graduated from Brown nearly a decade later than Jennifer and Fotis. She studied prelaw and public policy. After college, she worked for Accenture and Ernst & Young, where, according to the website of a foundation for which she serves, she "managed a business team on a billion dollar enterprise-wide business process redesign for Cigna Health Care, led the organizational design for Ford Motor

Company, and managed a seven-year plan to improve sales for JPMorgan Chase & Co."

In short, Fotis was apparently attracted not only to a certain physical type—like Jennifer Farber and Michelle Troconis, Hilary Aldama, in pictures anyway, is a tall, thin brunette with a narrow face, a broad smile, and big dark eyes—but also to accomplished, educated, career-oriented women.

I tried and failed to get in touch with Hilary in the course of my reporting. She got a law degree at the University of Texas in 2008, then worked at major firms and as in-house counsel for large corporations. She practices law in Shreveport, Louisiana, where she serves as corporate counsel for a biomedical research foundation. "In 2013, she was appointed Board Chair for March of Dimes—Northwest Louisiana Chapter," according to the foundation's website, "and is very active in the Shreveport-Bossier Junior League where she currently serves as a Nominating Advisor." In 2015, the Greater Shreveport Chamber of Commerce honored her as "A Woman of Greatness." She remarried, divorced, then married a third time. She has become something of an advocate for women who find themselves partnered to men she describes as "high level dreamer" personalities. She currently goes by Hilary Aldama Wooley. She has two children.

For Hilary, it must be chilling to read about her first husband, Fotis, and the life he went on to lead after he married a wealthier woman.

Jennifer confronted Fotis. He apologized, saying he hadn't told her about Hilary because the marriage was basically over. "She's too young for me," he explained. "We're at different stages in life, and want different things." The implication was parenthood. Fotis was ready. Hilary was not. A moment that could have disqualified Fotis made him seem more eligible instead.

Jennifer told Fotis that, regardless of the reason, she could not date a married man. He nodded, then went away. He disappeared, then reappeared. On March 1, 2004, he called to tell Jennifer that he had filed for divorce. She met him in Aspen less than a week later.

A psychopath is a chameleon. He sees what you want, then becomes that thing. It's unfortunate that Jennifer Farber met Fotis Dulos when she was vulnerable, when she feared her window on motherhood was closing. Fotis's talent was to recognize Jennifer's problem and turn himself into the solution.

Fotis Dulos was born in Turkey on August 6, 1967. His first years were spent as a member of Istanbul's oppressed Greek minority. Hellenes and Turks—the enmity is ancient. Fotis was told to be alert whenever he left the house: never trust the Turk; be prepared to fight. When his parents moved to Athens in 1974, Fotis's mother, Kleopatra, said it was so she could "feel safe sending her little boy outside to play."

Fotis's father, Petros, was a small-time merchant. He felt he'd been mistreated in Turkey, which fostered a militant sense of Greek pride that he passed on to his son. Business failures broadened the grudge until it took in the world. This, too, was passed on to Fotis: the fury, the rage, the sensitivity to slight, the inability to let it go. In their sense of persecution and pride, in their belief that anything of value, including civilization itself, has its roots in their history, the Greeks are like the Jews.

Petros Dulos had been born in 1912. He was three years old when British soldiers were dying on Gallipoli, and twenty-nine when the Nazis occupied Greece. His sensibility was antediluvian. He believed in the old values, the traditional roles. A man could do what he wanted as long as he provided for his family. A man stepping out on his wife is not cheating. He is being a man. Marriage is an institution designed to produce progeny, not to contain a healthy libidinous nature. A man did not *have* children with his wife. He *gave* his wife children, as he gave his wife a house. A woman would be cared for and protected as long as she met the needs of her husband. This is what Fotis learned in the house of his parents.

Kleopatra Dulos was twenty-one years younger than her husband, an age difference that would give Fotis the sense that the man is the adult in the relationship. Kleopatra met Petros on an airplane. They were Greeks, returning from abroad to Istanbul, which they still called by its ancient name, Constantinople. They fell into conversation. A second meeting was arranged. Within a year, they were married. Unlike the Farber family legend, the Dulos story does not mention love at first sight. It happened because it made sense. Unmarried Christians in Muslim Turkey, male and female, with a desire to procreate, found each other at thirty thousand feet. They wed in 1952. Petros was forty. Kleopatra was nineteen. Rena, their first child, was born soon after. Thirteen more years passed before Fotis arrived. He was named for Photios I, a ninth-century patriarch of Constantinople who reigned before the coming of the Turks.

Fotis recorded these details in testimony and interviews given during the divorce and custody hearings. He spent most of his childhood in Athens. When he was eleven, his mother, worried he was becoming a hoodlum, doing nothing but "running around in the street," enrolled him in a waterskiing school. The coach of the local team spotted him right away. He was a natural partly because he loved it. The first trip around the bay was maybe the first time he felt truly free. The power of the boat, how it pulled you up and out of the sea. The wind and the sun. The spray. The crystalline water outside the wake. The triumphant feeling of returning to the beach with a ski over your shoulder.

For most Americans, waterskiing seems less sport than activity, a diversion, something you do at summer camp, but it's a way of life in the Greek archipelago. There are waterskiing schools and waterskiing scholarships, national rankings, and tournaments that end with one person kissing a trophy. Fotis had the ideal build for a skier—compact, perfectly proportioned, surprisingly strong. He was selected as an alternate on the Greek national team in 1980. He lived with sixteen other skiers. Their routine was Spartan. They woke at dawn, ran, and lifted weights. They skied before school, when the sun was a red ball on the horizon, and skied again after, when Venus was rising in the west.

Fotis excelled at the slalom, where competitors navigate the course on one ski. He earned a starting spot on the national team in 1981 and held it until 1985. He was a student athlete. When not training, he was studying. At fourteen, he tested into Athens College, the city's top high school—only 10 percent of applicants are accepted. By the time he arrived at the campus in Psychiko, a suburb of Athens, he'd begun to tire of his sport. Having spent his childhood on a few small islands, he craved experience, travel. "I wanted to get exposed to societies and cultures beyond my own," Fotis wrote in a personal essay. "Greece, which is demographically a very homogenous country, was my home, but I felt an overwhelming need to be immersed in an environment with more cultural diversity."

He applied to Brown because it was a favored destination of the elite—the children of industrialists and shipping tycoons. For Fotis, college was not just a way out, but a way up. Brown was as much about status as education. He arrived in Providence in the autumn of 1986.

Though Fotis was a scholarship student, the wealthy Greeks accepted him because he was well-spoken, handsome, and had been a member of the national waterskiing team. But he never forgot his position, which meant pain and longing. When he met Jennifer, she stood out for her beauty but also for her pedigree—she looked like a golden road to the upper air. Years later, when asked to state the qualities that drew him to Jennifer, Fotis cited "the totality of her." Asked how many times he'd socialized with Jennifer at Brown, he said, "Not many. Maybe five." There'd been "chemistry," he claimed, but the timing wasn't right.

Fotis amassed enough credits to graduate after three years, then returned to Greece to help his father, who, at seventy-three, had opened a store. In the spring of 1990, when Jennifer was in her last semester of college, Fotis was working in a shop in Athens. He tried to use what he'd learned at Brown—he'd majored in economics and applied mathematics—to expand the business, but Petros wasn't interested. This frustrated Fotis, who worried he was wasting time, watching his best years fall like dead leaves. He hinted at his restlessness, but Petros, who was like Geppetto behind the counter of his Florentine toy shop, refused to accept the hint, shaking his head and saying, "No, I need you here."

Fotis took the GMAT and quietly applied to business schools in the United States—quietly because he did not want his family to know he was rejecting his father's path. Fotis was not content to be a shopkeeper in a small country. He wanted the most and the best: big houses, luxury travel, power boats, yachts. He later said he applied only to New York schools because New York was closely connected—via regular flights and a large Greek community—to Athens. But the truth was probably simpler: New York is the capital of finance, glitz, cash. In short, he aimed for the bright lights. Accepted by NYU and Columbia, he chose Columbia because Columbia is Ivy League. Then, one afternoon, he told his father he was knocking off early, went to the airport, and flew to America.

Fotis was twenty-eight when he arrived at Columbia University. He was interviewing for jobs before he'd finished his first year in the business program. A soon-to-be multiple-degreed Ivy Leaguer, he was an incredibly appealing applicant: presentable, well-spoken, bilingual. His timing was good, too. The mid-1990s were a financial boom time. The GDP was high, unemployment was low, the stock market ran like a stallion. He took a position at the multinational consulting firm Capgemini. He was an analyst, visiting companies around the world, touring facilities, meeting workers and executives, creating growth plans that made use of the newest technology. The job paid well—in 2023, a Capgemini business analyst started at around $85,000 a year—and he loved the travel. "I met people from every corner of the globe," Fotis said later, "and that excited me beyond belief."

Fotis met Hilary Aldama through a friend in 1998. They married in June 2000. The relationship soured when Hilary decided to move to Texas for law school. By then, Fotis was already planning his next step. He wanted to quit Capgemini and go into home construction. He credited this dream to his sister, Rena Dulos Kyrimi, now married and working as an architect in Athens. Watching her canvass a site, draw up a blueprint, hire workers, and oversee a job made Fotis want to build. But to do it, he needed money. For a contractor, as for a movie producer, securing financing is not merely what you do so you can do the thing. It *is* the thing. "Where will I get the money?" is a question that Fotis never stopped asking. Then, one afternoon, just as his first marriage was coming apart, he stepped off a plane in Aspen, Colorado.

~

The timeline is important:

> September 2003: Jennifer's dog, Sophie, dies.
>
> December 2003: Jennifer meets Fotis at the Aspen airport.
>
> January 2004: Fotis emails Jennifer. ("Test—Are you there?")
>
> March 2004: Fotis files for divorce.
>
> July 2004: Fotis signs the divorce papers.
>
> August 2004: Fotis marries Jennifer.

"It happened very, very fast, and that seemed out of character for Jennifer," Carrie Luft said in an interview. "Jennifer's very measured. She's not a rash, impulsive person. She's pretty much anti-impulsive."

Every study I've read about homicidal husbands suggests that speed—the need to get hitched right away, before the other person realizes you're crazy—is characteristic of psychopathy.

Why did Jennifer, who'd waited years for Mr. Perfect, suddenly move with such haste? And why did she settle on Fotis, a mismatch in many ways? He was superficial, did not care about art, did not read novels, was neither Jew nor Wasp, and was definitely not Bank.

A half dozen friends offer a half dozen reasons. Some say it's because Fotis was the first suitor with the strength and tenacity to get by Hilliard, who guarded his daughter like the Star of Artaban. If true, it means Hilliard had built obstacles guaranteed to deliver a psychopath, as only a psychopath could breach them. Some say it's because Jennifer turned desperate in her midthirties. A man she'd hardly noticed in 1986 looked like the last train to Memphis in 2004. "It happened so fast because it happened so late," said Colette Burson. "Jennifer could see forty right over the hill, and here comes a good-looking guy she'd known at Brown. She felt like she knew him because he'd been with her at school and her father had said, 'It'll be someone you already know.'"

"If you look at it from Jen's perspective, it makes perfect sense," said Dan Rybicky. "There's something she wanted her whole life and she was just about out of time. Then here is a man straight from central casting who arrives just before midnight, which makes for a great story. Jen is someone who loved great stories. If it happened to me like that, I would have married Fotis, too."

"Jen was quirky and smart but had a bit of that beautiful-girl thing," said D. J. Paul, who fell for Jennifer when they met on vacation in the Caribbean after college. They'd been at Brown at the same time, but never really knew each other. Jennifer liked D.J., but not in a romantic way. "She was superficial in certain regards, especially with men," D.J. explained. "She wanted somebody pretty. And Fotis was pretty. And there was something exotic about him. Greek, European. And he really put himself together. It's easy to see why she fell for him."

Jennifer had waited for a storybook proposal all her life, but when the moment came, Fotis made it seem more like business than romance—an arrangement among royals. There was no great ceremony or fanfare. "I'm Greek," Fotis explained. "We don't get on one knee."

Hilliard Farber was seventy-one when Jennifer announced her engagement. He was at the peak of his power but smart enough to know there's only one direction from the peak. He was already battling some of the health issues that would be his undoing. It was time to plan. He must've been disappointed with Fotis. Not a Wasp, not a Jew, not even an American. Neither rich nor especially successful. Divorced. Smart but not *that* smart—it'd probably have been better if he were just plain dumb. Half-intelligent is worse than dumb. If you're dumb, at least you know you can't get away with certain things. Best to work out the arrangements in advance in such a case—be clear, get him to commit, tie him up in string. Hence, Hilliard agreed to bankroll Fotis, putting up the millions he would need to buy land and build houses. According to several friends of the couple, Fotis had, in essence, promised to be a good husband to Jennifer, to be a good father, and, crucially, to raise the children as Jews. Fotis denied this during the divorce proceedings, citing the fact that Jennifer had converted to Christianity before they started dating.

While Hilliard and Gloria would surely have preferred a traditional wedding, Fotis and Jennifer decided to get married immediately. Jennifer, who was nearly thirty-six, wanted not one, not two, but three children—and there was no time to waste. Fotis rushed for a different a reason. "I don't care if we have kids," he told Jennifer. "I just want to be with you"—which makes sense only when you realize that for Fotis the home-building business was the baby.

They wed in a civil ceremony in the Farbers' Brooklyn Heights apartment on August 28, 2004. Jennifer told a friend she'd been truly amped to change her name. "[She] went out immediately after the ceremony to get a new social security card and a new driver's license. She did not want to be Farber anymore," the friend told me. "She was so excited to become Jennifer Dulos."

Hilliard and Gloria threw a wedding party in February 2005, at the Metropolitan Club on East Sixtieth Street between Fifth and Madison Avenues. Founded in 1891 by disgruntled New York oligarchs—Cornelius Vanderbilt, J. Pierpont Morgan, Frank Sturgis—who'd been rejected by older clubs, it reeked of Bank. It was built on land purchased from Consuelo Vanderbilt, the Duchess of Marlborough, who signed over the deed at the U.S. consulate in London. The four-story building was designed by Stanford White in imitation of the opulent style of the Italian Renaissance. Thus, three flags hang over the Fifth Avenue façade.

The town cars and limousines began to arrive at sundown. Central Park glittered with snow. It was twenty-four degrees at 5:00 p.m., which would allow guests to wear their fur coats and stoles. Cocktails were served in the foyer, followed by a ceremony in the West Lounge and dinner in the Presidents' Ballroom.

Jennifer's college friends dominated the dance floor. "It was like a class reunion," said D. J. Paul. "All the pretty people I knew but did not necessarily like at Brown—the Dalton, Saint Ann's, Horace Mann, and Riverdale kids—were in attendance."

As notable as those who were invited were those who were not, including nearly every member of the Playwrights Collective. Perhaps Jennifer was still embarrassed by the unintentional self-exposure of *What Party?* Perhaps she did not want her downtown friends to see what she was about to become—a suburban housewife. Though he had in fact been invited, collective veteran Dan Rybicky refused to attend. "I don't go to weddings that don't have my approval," he explained. "And that one, the speed of it, everything, did not seem right to me."

"There was something about the wedding that felt very Waspy, which I found ironic," said D. J. Paul. "Because Fotis was not a Wasp, and neither was Jen, but this was not really Jen's party. It was Hilliard's party. And Hilliard made it seem downright goyish—not your bubbie's wedding. Or maybe it was just 'the right kind of Jews'—German Jews, the old families. It was also one hell of a night, because, like I said, it was Hilliard's party, and Hilliard was larger than life, and larger-than-life people throw larger-than-life parties."

You went in the front door at dusk, and when you came out what felt like ten minutes later it was dawn. Everyone was sober, then everyone was drunk. The dancing went on and on. Jennifer's friends gossiped about Fotis in the bathrooms: Who is he? What does he want? "The guy was pretty, but left zero impression," said D. J. Paul. "I didn't dislike him. I didn't think about him either way. Or, if I did, it was as a pretty boy, Jennifer's prize, her trophy husband. She wanted somebody she would look great dancing with at her wedding. And she got it—they did look beautiful together on the dance floor."

Watching Jennifer, her dress hiked above her knees, her hair down in her face, friends had the sense that she was going away. She'd be moving to Connecticut after the honeymoon, leaving the city and the streets that had been the focus of her dreams.

Guests were handed a gift on the way out, a sterling silver pill case. D. J. Paul called it "a perfect keepsake for the moment, because it was such a druggy time, and here finally was a container for my benzos." He added, "I thought it a bizarrely wonderful way to mark the wedding, classic Hilliard, but now, looking back, it seems symbolic in the worst possible way."

Canton, Connecticut, was small and rural, less suburb of Hartford than suburb of West Hartford, poor neighbor to Simsbury and Avon. It was filled with people who dreamed of living not at One Fifth Avenue, but in Farmington, ten miles southeast. There were neither playwrights nor theatrical productions in Canton in 2004. The local paper, the *Valley Press*, featured stories about selectmen, spelling bees, and the Canton Cougars high school football team. When Jennifer, who'd moved to Canton with Fotis that fall, walked the town's nineteenth-century

Main Street, which, with its mansard roofs and gabled windows, seemed as ramshackle as a Hollywood mockup of a frontier town, she must have felt like an emissary from a more sophisticated world.

Canton sprawls across twenty-five square miles. It's twelve miles northwest of Hartford and twenty miles south of the Massachusetts state line. There were around ten thousand residents when Jennifer arrived. The town was founded in 1806, but the area was settled much earlier. Some of its streets were laid atop ancient trails that were traversed by Native Americans centuries before the arrival of the *Mayflower*. No one is sure why it's called Canton. Some say the name came from the word "canton," a Swiss territorial division, because the valleys and streams were reminiscent of those in Switzerland. Some say it was named for the region in China that gives us so much delicious food.

The town is on the west branch of the Farmington River, a tributary of the Connecticut River. Parts of the west branch are as drowsy as an August afternoon, parts break over rocks and are thrashed to white water, parts run clear and cold and reflect the sky. A defunct factory spans the river in the center of town, where the water drops like a sheet over a ten-foot dam, sending up a spray that puts the world behind a mist.

Canton was once a manufacturing town known for mass-producing axes and for saw and grist mills that drew farmers from the countryside and immigrants from Massachusetts cities like Lowell and Lawrence to the north. America's shift from building to consuming had, over the centuries, turned Canton into a bedroom community, a suburb in the outer settlement ring. People have long loved the area for its beauty. There are streams in Canton, and lakes and trails that seem nearly alpine. For Jennifer, a creature of cocktail parties—the great indoors!—it must have come as a shock. In the city, she'd been surrounded by streets (and streets intersecting streets), signals, signs, symbols, crowds, conversations, and bodegas that never close. Canton was nothing but hills, ramshackle houses tucked into valleys deep as Appalachian hollows. Many of those houses were dilapidated colonials, the most expensive of which cost around $400,000 in 2004, half the price of a five-hundred-square-foot studio in Manhattan. Being pressed between hills made them feel even more isolated. Looking out a window in the summer, when the trees were in leaf, you'd have trouble finding evidence of other human life—an ideal landscape for misanthropes, nature lovers, and criminals on the lam.

Jennifer didn't even get to choose her own home, but instead moved into the place Fotis had lived with Hilary Aldama: 10 Sunrise Drive. Big, featureless, perched on the lip of a ravine. One wrong step and it's goodbye. There were five bedrooms, which, to Jennifer, would have looked like one master and four empties awaiting children. (That was the work to be done.) The ground-floor in-law suite was occupied by an actual in-law. For Jennifer, moving to Canton also meant moving in with Fotis's mother, Kleopatra. She had come to America with Fotis's father, Petros, who passed away in September 2004, shortly after Fotis and Jennifer got married. Fotis insisted Jennifer co-sign the mortgage, meaning the extended Dulos family was partially supported by Hilliard Farber thereafter.

Jennifer must have experienced marriage as exile. She spent much of her time helping Fotis build his business, which her parents bankrolled. Her entire life had been curated by taste. Every scene had been carefully selected and perfectly arranged. Now she was here, in Canton, Connecticut, a thousand rungs down the social ladder. But if it was a demotion, she accepted it joyfully. She'd switched trains, left the city, and plunged into the provinces.

It seems like happenstance. She ended up in Canton because of Fotis, but Fotis got there by accident, too. He missed the water when he lived in Manhattan, and went in search of it as soon as he could convince his first wife to follow. In New York, when someone says they want to live by the water, they usually mean the ocean. If, on one of their early dates, Fotis had told Jennifer, "I'd like to live on the water," she would probably have assumed he meant Palm Beach or East Hampton. But to Fotis, the water meant a place where he could water-ski, and for that there was nowhere better than the small, teardrop-shaped lakes of central Connecticut.

In the early days of the marriage, Fotis split his time between recreation, which meant hiking, biking, snow skiing, mountain climbing, and waterskiing, and business, which meant real estate. He started his company with cash borrowed from Hilliard and bank loans guaranteed by Hilliard—secured, because of Hilliard's reputation and relationships, at the lowest possible interest rates. Hilliard also served as a backstop. If the books didn't balance and the loan officers began to call, Fotis could reach out to Hilliard, who would make the crooked straight. In short, in addition to buying a husband for Jennifer, Hilliard paid to make that husband appear successful. Fotis was a Potemkin son-in-law. He looked solid from a distance, but walk through the front door and you'd find yourself in an open field.

When people say that Fotis Dulos, no matter what else you might think, was at least a good businessman—his houses won awards—remember that Fotis did not have to raise money, which, in real estate, is more than half the job.

Fotis called his business the Fore Group. His financial plan was simple: buy land with Hilliard's money, pay an architect to draw a blueprint, hire contractors and acquire supplies with more of Hilliard's money, build the house, sell the house, bank the profit.

Fotis built most of these houses west of Hartford, with a focus on the affluent suburbs: Avon, Simsbury, Farmington. But the towns of

Fairfield County were the ultimate goal: Greenwich, Darien, New Canaan, Westport. That's where the real money was. "We typically work on homes that range from 4,000 square feet to 15,000 square feet and are priced between $1.5 million and $9 million," Dulos told *American Builders Quarterly* in 2014. The Fore Group built eight homes and sold four in its best year, clearing $8 million. There were also dry spells, months and even years when no ground was broken and no sales were made.

Fotis worked out of a home office in Canton. That's where he was living when he completed his first project: a spec house on a double lot in Avon purchased with a $400,000 loan from Hilliard Farber. "Handcrafted brick," "wrought iron pipes," "marble bathtubs," "wine cellar," "fire pit," "five car garage," and "media room," conveniently located in the "beautiful Farmington Valley." Fotis resorted to brand names when selling, catchphrases that appealed to the buyer's aspiration and status anxiety.

Jennifer served as an executive at the Fore Group. Her job involved taste decisions (burnt nickel or stainless steel?), copy writing ("beautiful Farmington Valley") and investor liaisons (call Hilliard). Having made the move to Canton, she committed all the way. Unlike Lot's wife, she did not look back. It was not just the city she left behind, but many friends. Break clean, cauterize the wound, move on as if her previous existence had been the childhood she needed to outgrow.

When I asked Dan Rybicky if he found it strange that Jennifer quit playwriting so abruptly, he said, "It was strange and also not strange, because, as long as I'd known her, Jen always had these conflicting desires which pulled her in opposite directions. She wanted to write plays and be an artist and be surrounded by art, but she also had a burning need to be a wife and a mother. That's the core of what makes this such a tragic story. That conflict. After graduate school Jen had trouble find-ing her footing in the right relationship, and balancing the desire to be both an independent person and a creative force, a wife and a mother. In a perfect world, she could have had both. But she felt she had to choose. And so, she chose."

Jennifer set up a studio in the Canton house where she wrote emails and filled journals. For her, writing a passage, any kind of passage, was like sinking a drill into an underground lake. It kept her in touch with her secret self and her strategic reserve. Even if no one read what she wrote, even if no one even knew that she was writing, it was essential for her survival.

What could not be processed in words, she burned off with ex-ercise. A common sight in Canton was Jennifer Dulos jogging the winding country roads in Nike shorts, Nike shoes, and a Vineyard Vines T-shirt. She listed running among the activities she described as a "sacred time" and a "pocket I retreat into." Best of all was "Day-break running. When it's still dewy and overcast as the sun has not yet burnt through the thick layer of dense fog in the sky, nor has the sun yet cleared the thick layer of heaviness in my mind." She added, "I often have elevated thoughts, or revelations, while running. Ones which may seem tiny to another, but not to me." At another point she wrote:

> Today while running and thinking of all my to-do's, my heart started to race. And I thought, What am I doing to myself? I push and push and push. But is this really the answer? More? Now! This way! Do it just right, right now?
>
> I am an overachiever. I am someone who gets things in before the deadline. I am someone for whom the word

perfectionism was invented just [to] get me revved to go for the impossible. I start to salivate at the thought of actually coming close to some flawless, sanitized ideal.

But wait. Breathe. Be alive. Slow down. Enjoy the run, enjoy the time. Do less, but live more fully.

Jennifer had kept in touch with a few old friends, but most of these people were driven away by Fotis, who could be obnoxiously aggressive. "He was typical of men who are cheaters, in that he imagined every other man was a rival," said D. J. Paul. "He was incredibly possessive, which made him awful to be around. Fotis and Jennifer came to L.A. and we went to dinner at the Fords' place. (I'm friends with Harrison Ford's son.) Jen and I were sitting there, talking. And, you know how a dog will instinctively get between a stranger and its owner? Fotis did that. No matter where I went—I kept moving because it was super annoying—he positioned himself between Jennifer and me."

Carrie Luft went with her husband to see Jennifer in Canton, where she witnessed a fight between Jennifer and Fotis, which in itself was no big deal. Everyone fights. It was the way that Fotis fought that got Carrie's attention. "He ranted at her for about ten minutes without allowing her to get a word in edgewise," Luft told *Greenwich* magazine. "I can't even remember what it was about, but it was so insignificant. Something very small. And he just laid into her verbally, cutting down her character: 'You're a terrible person! How dare you do this!' There was a warning sign in that. That's usually just the tip of the iceberg, right?"

Then there was his driving—an activity that tends to reveal character. "Fotis drove like an absolute maniac," said Luft. "He enjoyed scaring people. [My husband and I] were definitely not hothouse orchids, but we made a pact that we would never ride in a car with that man again. It was terrifying—wrong side of the road, crazy, breakneck speeds on winding Connecticut roads. Just unnecessarily show-offy and disturbing. Jennifer was in the passenger seat and could only laugh softly. Obviously, she was afraid to say anything to him. It spoke volumes that she couldn't intervene."

If Jennifer did not see the warning signs, it's because she was singularly fixated on her dream: happy marriage, beautiful children. They started trying for kids immediately. In too much of a hurry to play the averages—a thirty-six-year-old woman attempting for the first time—Jennifer went straight to the most expensive option: in vitro fertilization (IVF). She was pregnant with twins by August 2005.

The marital pressures worsened as the due date approached. That is not uncommon, according to Stephen Herman, who wrote the court-ordered psychiatric report on the Duloses and their relationship. Though he could not talk about the Dulos case specifically, he did tell me about his method in general, saying he focuses on just a handful of moments in a couple's life: "The period after the engagement but before the marriage—that's when people suddenly realize they're in it forever. The naming of the kids, the child's first illness, and what happened during that first pregnancy. That's telling. Did both parents want the kid? Was the pregnancy planned? Did they do what the doctor said regarding prenatal care? Did they both attend prenatal classes? Or did only the mother go? Did they fight about this? It's a gold mine of information."

Fotis later said he'd never really wanted children. He was apparently content with Jennifer and the money that came with Jennifer. Children were merely part of the deal.

Jennifer said Fotis changed during her first pregnancy. He spent more and more time away from home, at a "worksite" or "on the road for business." Maybe Fotis felt, having fulfilled his side of the bargain (getting Jennifer pregnant), he was free to do what he wanted.

Fotis had been on his best behavior since that meeting at the airport in Aspen. It's almost as if he'd been playing a character, being exactly what Jennifer wanted; now that she was expecting, he could stop pretending.

I think there was actually a moment when Jennifer realized she'd been fooled—that the man she'd married was not the man he'd seemed. It came later, as an epiphany, a flash in the dark. You hear it in the hysterical, nonsensical letter she wrote in 2007 at a moment of crisis—not to her mother, or to a friend, but to Rob Bingham, the writer who'd hosted the parties at his loft on White Street in the 1990s. Jen Farber, who'd drawn close to Rob in Manhattan, where they seemed to live mirror existences of wealth and disappointment, turned to him again as the nature of her marriage became clear, even though Rob had died of a heroin overdose in 1999. She appealed to him as you might appeal to a saint:

> Dear husband, best friend Rob,
> Is there a path for me and Fotis? Help me. I need to rely on You . . . It's best when I pretend with him. Okay. I can pretend. I've done it with [Gunnar Graham] . . . I believe in God and I also need him to help with the weight, be 116 . . . I pretend with Fotis, period. The best way. Time apart . . . I need to write, to read, to have an intelligent human conversation, a New York level conversation . . .
>
> Jennifer Bey

I've condensed this letter, but the tone and sentiment remain unchanged. If it sounds scattered and confused, it's because that was the state of Jennifer's mind. I do not know what everything in it means. Maybe she didn't know herself.

Jennifer's twin boys were born on April 20, 2006. Petros and Theodore. She later told a story so outlandish it has to be true. She was holding the babies when Fotis came in with a valise. He'd found his old stamp collection and wanted Jennifer to admire each collectible. Fotis exploded when his wife's attention seemed to drift. There was a fight; the bad mood lingered. Finally, disoriented by his new status—outranked by babies!—Fotis threatened to pack his bags and return to Greece— "vanish!"—a threat he'd make again and again.

The dynamics of the marriage, which was still new, had shifted. From here on, the children would take up most of Jennifer's time and affection, setting Fotis adrift. Motherhood was bliss for Jennifer—but maybe her bliss made Fotis feel as if he had lost his place in the center of her life. For Fotis, Jennifer's happiness felt like a downgrade. No longer the cornerstone, he seemingly thought, *If I'm not her number one, why should she be mine?*

Noah is the most popular name for Jewish babies in America, followed by David, Abraham, and Jacob. Hilliard Farber must have blanched when he learned his firstborn grandchildren were to be named Theodore (from the Greek Theodoros, "gift of God") and Petros (Greek for Peter, Christ's first disciple). Then came the invitation to the christening. The christening? Hilliard was apoplectic. He'd believed Fotis had agreed to raise the children as Jews. The first sign that his son-in-law didn't intend to honor that agreement came with the invitation. This required more than a phone call. The Farbers got in the car and headed north.

Hilliard and Gloria, Fotis and Jennifer—they all sat in the dining room to talk. Hilliard reminded Fotis of his promise. Fotis said there had been no promise, nor could there be, as he would never raise his children as anything but Greek Orthodox.

It was a discussion that started badly, then deteriorated. Hilliard called Fotis an abuser and a liar. Fotis told Hilliard to blame Jennifer, as it was she who'd been dishonest by failing to tell them that she'd converted to Christianity. Hilliard threatened to call off the deal—no more money, no more loans.

"Why do you care?" asked Fotis. "You aren't even religious. What do you care about religion?"

Hilliard called Fotis an antisemite.

"Fine," said Fotis, jumping up. "I'll liquidate the business, take the money, take Jennifer and the kids back to Greece. You'll never see any of us again. We'll vanish!"

There's that word again.

"My in-laws were very upset the kids were Christian and they were going to be christened," Fotis explained in a calmer moment. "They objected and came to the house and created a scene. To back them off I said I had contingency plans in Greece and said Jennifer and I would liquidate the business, sell our two properties, pay the investors, pay the taxes, and go to Athens. Her dad was a wonderful man, but a very powerful man and because the children were not Jewish, he was threatening to pull his investment out of the business. He called me a loser and antisemitic and other names."

Fotis picked up a chair and threw it at Hilliard. It missed. But still.

Gloria, though a doting mother close to both her daughters and a hands-on grandmother, stayed out of the teeth of the battle, apparently less concerned with the fate of the Jews, or the continuation of a family tradition, than with her relationship with her husband and child. Fotis, who disparaged his mother-in-law in court as an "old lady," would have her trust only until he lost it, which would happen soon enough.

What about Melissa Farber?

She seems like the sister in the shadows. She supported Jennifer as best she could, but there was a sense of melancholy in her presence. Jennifer's theater friends, who, by the nature of their trade, have a keen sense of irony, told me they found it surreal that in the end Melissa would be the last surviving member of the immediate family, left to carry on the legacy.

In the end, Melissa was the only Farber to attend the christening.

It's a mystery for those who knew Jen Farber at the Playwrights Collective. If Hilliard's disapproval had been important enough to get Jennifer to quit theater—she loved her father with filial intensity—how was it that she just sat there as Fotis disrespected Hilliard, and even threw a chair at him?

Why didn't she walk out, scream, do something?

Perhaps because, as much as she loved her parents, she loved her children more. Perhaps she said to herself, 'This is the bed I have made, and now I must lie in it." Perhaps because Fotis was the first man she knew with the strength to stand up to Hilliard, whom she had not been able to stand up to herself. That's why she'd gone to Aspen, changed her name and religion. It was not being a Jew she was escaping. It was Hilliard.

As close as she'd been to her father, Jennifer had always felt a little distant from her mother. This was possibly due to her intense connection with her father, Hilliard, who picked her up and carried her around like a prize won at the county fair, cast every other relationship in the shade. Gloria Farber was an incredibly accomplished professional, which was a great feat for a woman born in the 1930s and raised in pre–Betty Friedan America. She should have been an inspiring role model for Jennifer, a hero, but Jennifer's attachment to her all-powerful father left little room.

In choosing Fotis over Hilliard, Jennifer was making the great stand of her life. It was the first time she'd ever openly defied her father. It was also the most Jewish thing she could do. Genesis 2:24 talks about a man leaving his father and mother, and holding fast to his wife, with the new couple becoming "one flesh." That implies that the wife will do the same.

Fotis said he was able to patch up his relationship with Hilliard, but it was never the same. The marriage, though it went on, never fully recovered from the scene in the dining room in Canton. How could it? With time, it became increasingly clear that Jennifer and Fotis did not value the same things. What did Fotis want? A worshipful wife, a business that gushed money, and freedom to wander. What did Jennifer want? A loving husband, a stable home, and more children. And so, as Fotis rollicked and roamed, Jennifer went for another round of IVF, resulting, on October 31, 2008, in the birth of her second set of twins, Christiane and Constantine. Fotis and Jennifer had gone from newlyweds to a family of six in just over four years.

Fotis had not wed an overburdened, sleep-deprived suburban mom, so how did he end up with one? It was with no small degree of self-pity that he began to seek diversion. He traveled with friends, and traveled alone. Jennifer never knew exactly where he was or what he was up to. He spent much of his time at the Avon ski club, Old Farms Skiers, where he found a community of like-minded sportsmen.

Dana Hinman is the club's presiding deity. His father helped design the man-made ski lake, known as the Pond at Avon, considered a premier venue in the Northeast. The fact that it's hard to find makes it magical. You see nothing but warehouses when you park beside Old Farms Road in Avon—the facility is tucked between the self-storage units of Extra Space Storage and the Farmington River—but, if it's summer, you will hear voices, cheers, and the chug of engines. You follow the noise down a dirt road to the clearing, and there it is: an inky-black pond framed by soft green hills. The shore is dotted with Adirondack chairs. There's a barbecue shed, the smell of hot dogs on the grill, Bob Marley on the radio.

When I asked Dana, himself a world-class skier, to describe life at the club, he laughed and said, "Oh brother, it's sweet! When you get to the heart of it, it's just a way to hang out with your buddies all summer long."

Dana had known Fotis from the waterskiing world. They became friends in the 1990s. When Dana went to Greece on his honeymoon, Fotis took him on a tour of Athens. After moving to Canton, Connecticut, Fotis got in touch, paid the dues, and joined the Old Farms Skiers.

"If you're really into skiing, Avon is the place," Dana said of the pond. "It was built in the seventies. The guy who owned the land had been mining gravel—the lake was once a gravel pit—but was a big-time skier, too, and dug it out determined to make it into *the* perfect waterski lake."

He noted the role of man-made lakes in competitive skiing. "People ski rivers, and people ski oceans, and some people even ski the intercoastal waterway—Florida is the mecca because you can ski year-round—but man-made lakes are the best because you can engineer the ideal conditions," he explained. "Avon is just big enough to fit the slalom course and the jump. The shorelines are super gentle, so there's no backwash from the boat, and, when you go down the lake, the waves dissipate into the banks. It's spring fed and freshened by overflows from the Farmington River."

He added that waterskiing isn't a cheap sport. "The equipment is expensive, and a club membership is expensive because we've got to buy and maintain boats," he said. Even so, Old Farms Skiers was a thriving club. "We have about three hundred members," Dana said, "and there's always a long waiting list to join."

Fotis began taking the older twins, Petros and Theodore, to the pond as soon as they could walk. Their serious training began at five, with Fotis instructing them from the back of a boat. By age seven, they were on the water six or seven hours a day most Saturdays and Sundays. Fotis was a lot like many other maniacal sports parents. The fact that he dreamed of his kids becoming champions not in soccer, baseball, football, ice hockey, or lacrosse but in waterskiing somehow illuminates the absurdity of all such parental ambition.

Fotis connected with his kids at the pond. He taught them how to swim out, get set with the tow rope, and rise up on their skis. He taught them how to jump their wake and glide into the summer glass.

He made videos to show them what they were doing wrong. If you search the internet, you can find some of these. In them, you see Petros, Theodore, Constantine, and Christiane skiing the churn behind the boat. You see white clouds and blue sky. You hear Fotis barking orders in his clipped, accented English.

He entered them in competitions. First locally—the Avon club hosts an annual tournament called King of the Pond—then nationally and internationally. "Christiane is ranked Number 3 in the U.S. in Slalom U-10 Women," he said in court in 2019, when Christiane was ten. "I believe she's a major contender for a U.S. title or at least a podium finish in the U.S. Nationals. Theodore, who is only eleven, can podium in overall and place highly in slalom, jump, and tricks. Petros and Constantine, while highly ranked, ski at their own pace and desire. If they decide to commit, they can also place well."

Jennifer thought Fotis pushed the kids too hard. Each year, he began them skiing in April, when the water barely reached sixty degrees. He made them do the same trick again and again until they got it "exactly right." In the week leading up to a competition, Fotis said, practice for Theodore and Petros consisted of "three days on, one day off, depending upon weather." Asked if she ever went to the pond, Jennifer said, "I normally do not because I feel [the children] are suffering."

Jennifer craved quiet interludes, rituals, holidays. Christmas was her favorite—cozy family time as she'd imagined it as a girl. The Duloses had one of those Santa sleighs on their front lawn. Candy-colored lights glittered from the eaves of the house. At times, it seemed as if the house itself was holding its breath, waiting for the children to come downstairs. "Fotis's mom dressed up as Santa every year," a Farmington friend told me. "Christmas morning was always a huge deal. Hilly was usually there. One year, Hilly gave them a check for nine thousand, nine hundred, ninety-nine dollars, as much as they could without having to report it to the government. Jennifer ran to show the check to Fotis. She said, 'Look at how generous! Don't you appreciate this gift?' And Fotis said, 'Oh great. We can use it for the new bathroom.'"

Fotis's father was ninety-two when he died in September 2004. The fact that Petros was old when he died, that he had seemed old even when Fotis was young, would not lessen the impact. The father had died and, in dying, afforded the son a glimpse of the abyss.

Kleopatra Dulos became the head of the family. She spent most of her time with Jennifer and her grandchildren, and never went far from her cat, Madonna.

Meanwhile, Fotis traveled as many as ten days a month and was in fact in Athens on September 20, 2010, when Kleopatra was in front of the family's new house at 585 Deercliff Road in Avon, helping the twenty-four-year-old Greek nanny, Evangelia Niora, maneuver the Land Rover in the driveway. Kleopatra, who was standing beside the car, told Evangelia to turn on the headlights. It was getting dark. The nanny searched for the switch—she had two of the kids in the car with her—then looked up. The way was clear. She started to drive. There was a sickening thump. She stopped, then pulled forward once more. There it was again: Thump. Then she saw Kleopatra on the ground.

Jennifer heard the commotion and ran outside. Kleopatra was sitting up by the time she got there. She said she'd been dizzy the day before. She must've fainted and fallen in front of the car, which was why Evangelia hadn't seen her. Jennifer called an ambulance. The police came and questioned everyone. According to the report, "The accident involving Kleopatra Dulos was not a criminal event and no arrests were made."

Kleopatra was seventy-seven. She had been raised in Turkey and had lived in Greece. She was admitted to Hartford's Saint Francis Hospital for observation. The doctors said she'd be okay and just needed rest. Jennifer passed this information on to Fotis in Athens, then sat with her mother-in-law. Kleopatra said she was cold. Jennifer called a nurse, who checked the patient's vitals and said everything looked fine. At some point, Jennifer went home to sleep. And, while Jennifer was sleeping, Kleopatra Dulos died.

Fotis was bewildered and angry when he got home. He did not blame the nanny, bad luck, or fate for the death. According to court testimony, he blamed Jennifer. If she'd been more attentive, if she'd not left the hospital when she did . . .

How this impacted the already troubled relationship is impossible to know. The fact that Fotis was in Greece when the tragedy struck, having left Jennifer—eight months pregnant—to care for the four young children, probably tells you what you need to know. In most of the ways that mattered, Jennifer was already alone.

When it came to child number five, Jennifer conceived without recourse to IVF. When asked how it happened, Fotis said, "Because we weren't trying." (Subtext: Because we didn't want another kid.) Fotis was forty-three and financially dependent on his father-in-law. His mother had just died. He had four children, the oldest not yet seven.

"I just got my wife back," he told Jennifer. "Now I am going to lose her all over again."

The word "abortion" does not appear in the court documents, but

Fotis's preference seemed clear. Jennifer had refused. There was a fight. The relationship had always been based on Fotis getting his way. For possibly the first time in their married life, Jennifer had said no. A natural pregnancy? After all these years? It was too miraculous to terminate. "All the other kids were for us together," Jennifer said in court. "This one is for me alone."

Fotis called it a turning point. Jennifer had defied him. He said she'd turned into a person he did not recognize.

The fifth child, a girl, was born on October 10, 2010. Fotis insisted on naming her after his mother. Jennifer did not like the name Kleopatra. They couldn't agree. According to Dr. Stephen Herman, the moment of choosing a name offers key insight into any marriage. "It shows you how these people negotiate," he said. "It tells you if this party or that party is willing to sacrifice for the greater good, if they are willing to take a small loss for a bigger win. It tells you if you are dealing with a reasonable or an obstinate person."

Jennifer wanted to name the baby Noelle—French for "Christmas." She said Cleopatra (with a "C") would be the middle name.

"If that's the case, I'll have nothing to do with her baptism or life," said Fotis. "If that's the case, I'll go back to Greece and you'll never see me again."

I'll vanish.

And so Jennifer gave in. Her fifth child was christened Cleopatra-Noelle. Jennifer never got used to the name and instead called her Clea, or Noelle, or Clea-Noelle.

"They let us out of the hospital after less than 24 hours," Jennifer wrote. "I had Clea up on the third floor with me as Christiane hovered about her new little sister. The first two weeks were the hardest thing I have ever done. Trying to feed her all through the night and her crying because she wasn't getting enough."

As mentioned, the Dulos family had moved—first to a house at 5 Charlotte Court in Avon, then to what amounted to a Fore Group model home at 585 Deercliff Road, also in Avon. Fotis planned to stay there only until a buyer could be found. Jennifer had an office on the second floor. She began working on a new book as soon as Clea settled into a routine. Said to be a thriller about a woman trapped in a loveless marriage, the manuscript has never been found. Fotis considered the many hours Jennifer spent writing in her office a sign of mental illness. *All she does is sit there with the door closed doing . . . what? Doing nothing.*

For Fotis, Avon was a step up from Canton—a step closer to Fairfield County and the rich seam of real estate to the south. The town, with nearly twenty thousand residents, is pocked by lakes and ribboned by streams, many flowing from the peak of Avon Mountain. Avon Old Farms, a prep school that turns out Ivy League athletes, is one of the town's largest private employers. When the founders of the Vineyard Vines clothing brand pictured their perfect consumer, they probably imagined him in Avon, amid its winding roads, broad porches, red-brick storefronts, and tree-lined streets. This is the land of autumn, where the leaves are always turning and never turned, and the wind is autumnal and sad, and it's always about to be Christmas. Jennifer's favorite outfit, which had been a black cocktail dress in Manhattan, was jeans and a Vineyard Vines T-shirt in Avon. That shirt was seen on the children's playdates, at pickups and drop-offs. Fotis was fueled by commercial ambition. Jennifer just wanted to lose herself in the quotidian details of domestic life.

"I think Jennifer came to see the real problem with her relationship as a problem of class," D. J. Paul told me. "He wanted to make money, be accepted, gain status. Jennifer, who was born with all those things, came to see Fotis's ambition as a little sad and pathetic. What he saw as her indolence—sitting in a room, staring at a screen—she considered the most important work a person can do. It made them incompatible."

Jennifer started writing for *Patch*, a community website that covers hyperlocal news. By studying her articles like a Kremlinologist, and reading between the lines, you can chart the decline of the Dulos marriage.

Fotis hated the articles. He hated that Jennifer, in his view, wasted so much time writing them. He hated that they were filled with personal information. These short pieces, the first of which appeared on January 9, 2012—"Carpool and Early Rising Musings"—are filled with subtextual warnings. Though Jennifer's tone is anesthetized throughout—she notes the passing of clouds and writes of how the shadows make her feel—she does not avoid the big subjects: Paternity. Commitment. Love. "I have been reading Erich Fromm's The Art of Loving," she reported in that first article. "I remember as a teenager my father had mentioned it and said, in some gruff sort of way, You can't love anyone until you love yourself first." From Fromm, she wrote, she has learned that love is less noun than verb, something you have to practice like an art, with effort and care every day. "We must love and continue to love through an active choice to love," she explained.

In her January 11, 2012, article ("New Year's Resolutions, How Am I Doing?"), Jennifer said she feared she was at fault for not giving Fotis enough attention. "Why do I always feel like a failure along these lines?" she said. "We did go to Miami for New Year's and I did water ski with him for a couple of days. But once back . . . I am a bit overwhelmed and outstretched, and it's him whom I shortchange first." She wrote about the workaday choices that make up the fabric of any domestic life: sleep or sex, now or tomorrow. As anyone with a house full of kids can tell you, sleep is actually more important than sex.

At times, the *Patch* articles read like Jennifer coaxing herself through life by trying to find transcendence in the mundane. On January 16, 2012, she devoted an entire article to her morning routine (as if she were preparing her face, as the poet said, "to meet the faces that you meet"). She spoke specifically of "a Zen-like state," a "blow-dryers high," that she achieved in the course of her morning ablutions. "I have the bathroom all to myself most mornings," she explained. "I stay far away from . . . Fotis's wake up point, so that I can have just this. I once mentioned, wouldn't it be nice to have separate bathrooms if he's building all these homes and we can potentially design anything we want. He looked at me and said that would be the end of our marriage, defeat."

In writing about the movie *Waitress* (in her January 20, 2012, article), she could have been writing about herself. The movie tells the story of a woman trapped in a bad marriage who finds comfort with another man. The woman feels lost when she gets pregnant but suddenly knows exactly who she is and what to do when the baby arrives. "Once they place her newborn daughter in her arms, everything else melts away," Jennifer explained, "and there is Absolute Foreground Clarity."

But if Jennifer ever did cheat on Fotis, it was only in her mind. Fantasies. Dreams of a different life. That's what my reporting tells me, plus common sense. Jennifer had five children in less than six years. She had a new dog, a golden retriever named Beckham. She was the caretaker of Kleopatra's cat, Madonna, after Kleopatra died. She had to adjust to a succession of new homes, new towns, and a husband whose mood was as capricious as the commodities market. She was too busy, too scheduled, and too nervous for extramarital romance. Besides, she still believed in the fantasy, the beautiful dolls in their perfect house. She turned to the past when she needed to escape, idyllic memories: the

Giants games her father took her to when she was small, the enormousness of the Meadowlands, the fans doing the wave, the snow coming down in the fourth quarter, the scoreboard a smear of color through the snow, the lights on the highway, the city rising in the distance.

Childhood.

A buyer made a satisfactory offer on the Avon house in the winter of 2012. As the deal neared closing, Jennifer and her kids boxed their stuff and prepared to move into yet another Fore Group property, a garish McMansion at 4 Jefferson Crossing, a private street in Farmington. There were six bedrooms in the ten-thousand-square-foot mansion, ten bathrooms, multiple rec rooms, an office suite, and a four-car garage. According to Zillow:

> The master bedroom suite features a wood-burning fireplace, a sitting room, a walk-in closet, marble slabbed shower walls, a soaking tub, and two marble vanities; [there is] a gourmet Christopher Peacock kitchen, Viking appliances, marble countertops, a butler's pantry, a six-burner stove with a grill, three ovens, a warming drawer, microwave, and a Subzero fridge; [there is] a second floor laundry room with marble countertops, two washing machines, and two dryers; [there is] a library complete with arched ceilings and custom butternut cabinets, a wine cellar, a furnished exercise room, and an elevator.

Hilliard had secured the bank loan Fotis used to build the house. When Fotis ran out of money halfway through, Hilliard made up the difference, which amounted to over $1 million. The house was valued at $4.2 million. It was another step up for Fotis, still closer to the dreamed-of destination. From a peak on the edge of Farmington, you can almost see it: Weston, Darien, New Canaan, the affluent towns of Fairfield County, the lights of the ships on the Long Island Sound.

It was a change for Jennifer, too. With twenty-five thousand residents and every sort of store and industry, Farmington was the biggest place she'd lived in since leaving New York—less village than town, less town than small city, the headquarters of Otis Elevator and United Technologies. It had cachet. Farmington is the home of Miss Porter's, the elite girls' school that educated Barbara Hutton, Gloria Vanderbilt, Jacqueline Bouvier, and Lilly Pulitzer. And it's beautiful. Once you exit the highway, it's easy to get lost on the narrow roads that meander through the trees—chestnut and sycamore and oak—that turn red and gold in October.

Lisa Nkonoki, a Farmington mother and grandmother and a member of the local Black power elite, worked in public relations before she found her calling as a kind of hired consigliere, problem solver, and friend, especially to Fairfield County's maritally challenged wealthy. In 2016, *Town & Country* called her a "no nonsense life coach"—she's founded at least two businesses, Live Your Dreams Life Coaching and Dads Do Make a Difference—"whose clients include Ray Charles Jr. (with whom she recently traveled to the White House for a celebration of his father's legacy) and a Greenwich finance executive named Jill Gilbert Callahan."

"I'm not your Junior League, ladies-who-lunch type," Lisa told the journalist Mickey Rapkin. "I obviously know decorum, but I can be straight-no-chaser, let's say."

Lisa met Jennifer at the private Renbrook School, where Jennifer's kids were in the same grades as Lisa's grandkids. If Lisa stood out among the other guardians, it's not only because she was a Black woman in a world dominated by white men. It's because she's flamboyant and fun and lives in a Poplar Drive mansion known as the Purple Palace. (The front doors are indeed purple.) And because she serves as an unofficial keeper of Farmington lore, an oral saga of fortunes, breakups, and busts.

Lisa—who goes by "G.G.," for "gorgeous grandma," and at sixty-five, tall with astonishing eyes, really is gorgeous—explained to me the significance of the Duloses' new address: "It's not so much that it was Farmington, but *where* in Farmington." Jefferson Crossing tops a hill where some of the richest people in town live. The CEO of United Technologies had a house there, as did Richard Gordon, the developer who owned the Hartford Whalers. Being on the hill amounts to status.

Jennifer had mixed emotions about the move to Farmington. Excited plus sad equals melancholy. So many landmark life events, good and bad, had happened at the house in Avon. It was where Petros and Theodore learned to ride their bikes. It was where Christiane and Constantine learned to walk. It was where Jennifer nursed Clea-Noelle. Leaving the house was like walking away from an epoch.

"Clea-Noelle was just put to bed, for the last time here before our move . . . We had the Last Dance Party, with all the furniture cleared from the living room and Fotis . . . playing Greek party hits," Jennifer wrote for *Patch* on February 17, 2012. She described the scene in lyrical detail: the baby clapping, Christiane leading in a dance that could've come from *Soul Train*, Theo moving like a robot as Petros wrestled Constantine to the floor.

In the articles that followed, you can sense that Jennifer was having trouble adjusting to the new house. There are intimations of misunderstandings and intimations of fights. "I wish I were a stronger person and that confrontation did not both scare and appall me," Jennifer wrote in March 2012. In a piece written the next month, she said she craved female companionship and then addressed her youngest child directly, telling her that she knew the bad times would cease but feared she—Jennifer—"may be in a body bag by then."

Time passed. The leaves on Jefferson Crossing flamed to red, then dropped. Clouds closed off the horizon. Everything turned gray. Snow came. The yards sparkled in the snow, and the snowblowers drowned out the cardinals, who'd stayed when all the other birds flew south. Then winter, grime and slush, bitter days. The first crocus, the first robin, the first peeper peeping in the first black pond of spring. Then summer. Pollen on the wind. The Dog Star in the west. September again, football weather, bonfires and spiked cider. Another turn around the sun, another crawl from equinox to equinox. And the children grow. And the days add to weeks, then years, which fall from the calendar: 2013, 2014, 2015. "My mother-in-law used to say that time speeds up the older you get," wrote Jennifer. "Another sad truth of staying on this planet year after year. That along with arm flab, considering tummy tucks, and seeing a seminar about menopause posted on the Avon *Patch* and wondering who would actually dare go."

Fotis's looks improved with age. His small, symmetrical features were suited for the middle years—years of wealth and discernment. He was a lothario with a touch of gray. There was something inscrutable about him, mysterious. At times, he seemed shuttered and empty, a person who cannot put himself in the position or behind the eyes of another, who does not care how anyone else feels. At times, he seemed insecure, a man driven mad by want for what he does not have, or by what he has and cannot handle.

There are those who murder, then everyone else. There are some lines even the unstable will not cross. Most people can't and don't. A few can and do. Fotis would end his life among the can and do, though it did not seem possible until the very end. Friends regarded him as a man of principles and codes. He believed in education, society, and sport; the superiority of Greek culture; the righteousness of the Orthodox church. All five Dulos children were christened. "She really did practice the faith," a friend of Jennifer's told me. "They had Cleo-Noelle's baptism in Greece. All the kids got a special box of Munson's chocolate on their name day. A tutor went to the Montessori to teach them all Greek."

Fotis believed in heritage, tradition, rituals, rules: one set for the husband, another for the wife; one set for the sons, another for the daughters. He did not seem to believe that God exists, or that each person carries a divine spark, or that if you kill someone you destroy a piece of the divine.

He'd been content to channel his ambition into business. The Fore Group built forty-five houses in its first decade. Most were in Farmington, Avon, West Hartford, Simsbury. The company was valued at $4.5 million in 2017, with gross sales totaling $37 million. The group often had four or five projects going at once—teardowns, gut renovations, and new construction, the latter of which tended to be opulent, houses with wine cellars, bedroom suites, media rooms, and so on. His preferred customers were newly minted members of the 1 percent, nouveau riche Baby Boomers, and Gen Xers who wanted to make it clear just how much they had and just how high they'd climbed. Many of the houses were on streets with fanciful names. Mountain Spring Road is not on a mountain, or atop a spring. Jefferson Crossing is not connected to this nation's third president, or at a crossing.

On a video introducing a property he'd refurbished at 80 Mountain Spring Road in Farmington, Fotis, fifty-one, trim and handsome in an oxford shirt and blazer, says, "Hi, I'm Fotis Dulos and I'm the owner of the Fore Group. We're custom builders working primarily in the Hartford and Fairfield counties. I'm here today to introduce you to a home that is historically important to Farmington because it's an excellent representation of the pewter style." By "pewter style," Dulos apparently meant the fixtures—pewter doorknobs, pewter chandeliers, pewter faucets and showerheads—pewter being a dull, brushed, silvery tin that radiates an aura of antiquity. Modern suburban Byzantium—that's what the Fore Group was after.

"Fotis Dulos was well-known for his lushly designed mansions," the *Hartford Courant* reported in 2019. "In development circles, he is known for a flashy, brazen style. He aggressively pursued the niche of mansions for the wealthy at a time when many builders were moving toward smaller, energy-efficient homes requiring less maintenance."

The Fore Group spent money and made money and won awards from realtors who enjoyed the outsized commissions. Fotis's houses were spectacles, but there was also something generic about them. That was the great innovation of the McMansion: its designers found a way to regear the middle-class cookie-cutter development for the superrich.

William Levitt, the developer who created Levittown, was derided in song for building "little boxes made of ticky tacky," but the Fore Group built the same way, only instead of little boxes, it was giant rectangles, and instead of ticky tacky it was Calacatta marble and burnt brick. It's strange that Jennifer Dulos, who valued the bespoke, spent so much of her adulthood in these indistinct cookie-cutter spaces.

There was something phony about the Fore Group, too. The houses were real, and the people who lived in them were real, but the numbers used to pitch the business to investors and banks were unreal. The developer's most important tool is debt. He is judged by his ability to raise, manage, and retire debt. But as long as Fotis had Hilliard, he did not have to worry about debt. According to Timothy Dumas's excellent piece about Jennifer in the September/October 2020 issue of *New Canaan–Darien & Rowayton* magazine, "Fotis built the Fore Group upon Farber largesse. Between 2004 and April 2016, he borrowed $10 million from Hilliard Farber, and at Fotis's death he owed Hilliard's estate $2.5 million, a sum he contested by calling it a 'gift.'" If left to live on its own credit and cash flow, the Fore Group would not have survived a year.

If Fotis had a long-term strategy, a path to self-sufficiency, it can be summed up in a word: expand. Get out of the Farmington Valley, away from the scrub between Boston and New York, away from customers who are rich only in comparison to other customers in the scrub, and start building in Greenwich, Darien, Westport, and New Canaan—the land of hedge fund managers and angel investors, helicopter pads and car elevators. Fotis was promoting himself as a Fairfield County builder long before he did any serious work there. It was not a lie; it was an aspiration. "He always said the goal is Fairfield," Jennifer explained. "He told everyone at the Fore Group that the goal is Fairfield County because that's where the money is."

The Fore Group built a guest house on a weekend property Gloria and Hilliard owned in Pound Ridge, New York, just across the border from New Canaan. The 1,800-square-foot structure, where Jennifer and her family could stay on visits, was to serve Fotis as a near-at-hand model home for potential customers. That was a first step into the lucrative market Fotis saw as his destiny.

Why did Hilliard Farber continue to subsidize the Fore Group? Why did he keep pouring money down the same drain? Why didn't he force Fotis to establish himself?

Two possible reasons.

One, Jennifer was accustomed to a certain lifestyle. She had grown up rich and, as far as Hilliard was concerned, could live no other way. She needed babysitters and nannies, first-class plane tickets and five-star hotels. The only way Hilliard could sustain her in that manner was by making her the wife of a wealthy man.

Two, Hilliard believed Fotis was dangerous. He'd thrown a chair at Hilliard when he was financially stable. What would he do if the Fore Group went bust?

Jennifer and Fotis were typical sports parents, but each was a different type. Jennifer got her kids involved in the sports favored by the New England gentry: horseback riding, polo, lacrosse, ice hockey. But for Fotis, there was only one sport that mattered: waterskiing. If his kids snow-skied in the winter, it was partly because snow-skiing built the skills they would need on the water. Waterskiing is a niche sport, but Fotis pushed his kids in the exact same way that Emmanuel Agassi pushed Andre in tennis and Earl Woods pushed Tiger in golf. Crazy sports parents are all the same. It's the mania, not the game, that characterizes them.

Jennifer worried that the children were suffering at the pond, but she usually let Fotis have his way. He was impossible to resist. When summer came, he simply carried the kids off to the club. Theodore was the standout, but Fotis pushed all five. If you were not skiing, you were watching the others ski. There was always something to be learned. Failure is an opportunity to improve. The last runs were made in the fading light. Crepuscular, the pond glassy at sundown. The best usually came when you were too tired to think, when you let your body find its own way. Fotis told his kids to watch carefully when he took his turn in the water. He said this was for the purposes of pedagogy, but, according to friends, he probably just wanted to be admired.

Jennifer went to the pond only for drop-offs or pickups. If Fotis needed help, he'd take the nanny, Lauren Almeida, who probably knows more about what happened in the Dulos marriage than any other living person. She was a student at the University of Connecticut in 2011 and working as a research assistant in the school's Child and Adolescent Anxiety Lab when a friend introduced her to the Dulos family, who were looking for a babysitter. Fotis offered her additional hours at the Fore Group. It's not hard to see why. If Fotis Dulos had a type, as the *New York Post* asserted, Lauren fit it perfectly. Tall and willowy, olive-skinned with dark hair and crescent-shaped eyes, she could have been Jennifer's little sister.

Lauren, who lived nearby in New Britain and was not yet twenty-five, spent her mornings working at the Fore Group office in the Dulos family mansion. Over time, her responsibilities grew. She took clients on property walk-throughs and met with disgruntled buyers. She spent afternoons and evenings—2:00 to 8:00 p.m.—with Jennifer and the kids.

Lauren spent many of her working hours at the pond, getting the kids ready to ski, then congratulating or consoling them depending on what happened in the water. "It's intense," she said in court. "In the summer, it's six days a week, we wake up at eight and go to the pond.

They're there all day, going back-and-forth for their sets. They have to do numerous sets, and there's nothing else to do, so if you're not skiing, you're just sitting around. We can be there until six or seven o'clock at night."

That his son Petros did not love waterskiing annoyed Fotis. Theodore did love it but was very tightly wound, which annoyed Fotis in a different way. "Theodore is the one out of the five that I think really does enjoy water skiing," Lauren Almeida said in court. "He's really good at it. And he can be really into it. But he does have his moments where if something doesn't go his way, he freaks out. He'll go off on anybody who is next to him and start yelling at them like No, no, no. He's thrown Petros's phone into the water because he got angry at something. He does these impulse things without thinking."

Almeida was especially concerned about Clea-Noelle, who was just five years old when Fotis began pushing her at the pond. He'd snap if she fell. He'd say, "If you continue eating Oreos, you're going to become fat and you're not going to waterski."

"I remember for a few months [after that], Clea-Noelle would constantly look at me and be like, 'Am I pretty? Do I look fat?'" said Lauren. "From a five-year-old! And then the same thing this year. Every time she gets in the water, she screams. She screams the whole time she's in the water and Fotis gets annoyed and says, 'You're eating too many Oreos—that's why you can't get [up on your skis] and out of the water.'"

Fotis entered the kids in competitions around the world. If there was a medal sitting on a table beside a pond in Spain or Greece, Fotis took them to get it. They climbed the international rankings. After Jennifer and Fotis separated in 2017, Fotis asked a famous waterskiing coach to write the Stamford judge, making the case that the Dulos children were special and needed to stick to their rigorous training program regardless of custody rights.

The ski season ended with the King of the Pond competition, in which members of the Avon ski club were grouped to compete by skill level. For Fotis, King of the Pond meant bragging rights. If his kids won, it proved the superiority of his method as a parent and coach.

One afternoon, when Jennifer went to the pond for pickup, she heard some kids taunting Theodore and Petros, calling them "sandbaggers."

"What's a sandbagger?" Jennifer asked in the car.

"They think we cheated in King of the Pond," said Petros.

"Is that what a sandbagger is? Someone who cheats?" asked Jennifer.

"It's someone who plays down," said Theodore. "Someone who lies about their rank so they can compete at a lower level, and ski against kids he knows he can beat."

"Is that what your father had you do?"

Theodore shrugged.

Fotis scoffed when confronted. "There is a thing called strategy," he said.

"Our children were labeled sandbaggers because you told them to sandbag," Jennifer told Fotis in court. "And so, every time I go to the pond, they are sandbaggers who cheated because they had to win King of the Pond."

Petros told Jennifer he was tired of waterskiing and spending all his time at the pond. He said he did not care about his rank and had no interest in being a world-class water-skier. He wanted to play ice hockey, soccer, and lacrosse. He wanted to be on a team. Jennifer argued Petros's case, but Fotis ignored her.

Jennifer went looking for a therapist to help Petros—he had made comments suggestive of suicide—a search that led her to Aaron Krasner, considered one of the nation's top child psychiatrists. She met him alone, in the manner of a scouting mission. She liked him. He agreed to see Petros, but could not do so without permission from the boy's father. Jennifer knew this would be a problem. Fotis loathed psychiatry. You caught a hint of antisemitism whenever he talked about psychiatrists. Jewish doctors. Jewish science. He believed it the provenance of the weak-minded and considered Jennifer's own years in therapy to be proof of mental illness. Told of his son's suicidal ideation, Fotis dismissed it as Petros being dramatic.

When Jennifer reported back to Dr. Krasner with dismay—*Fotis said no*—he suggested a workaround. He would treat Jennifer, teaching her strategies and skills she could then use to help her children. Explaining this, Dr. Krasner told Jennifer that she would be "the point of entry" for the family.

Dr. Krasner wrote Jennifer a prescription for an antidepressant called Pristiq, the use of which Fotis later cited as a reason to deny Jennifer custody. *There's something wrong with her! She's on drugs! She's depressed!* If Jennifer was indeed depressed, it's probably because her life had become depressing.

When Jennifer had played with her dollhouse in Brooklyn, she never wondered if Rolf was still sleeping with his wife, or if Rolf was traveling too much, or if Rolf had fallen out of love, or if Rolf had found some other doll to share his dollhouse bed.

With Fotis, it was different. He began traveling to Miami several times a year. He said he went to water-ski and to train his kids when the lakes in Connecticut were frozen. That he visited even when his children were in school was explained by his need to see friends or to simply get away.

He joined the Greater Miami Ski Club in Doral, a center of the waterskiing world a few dozen miles from South Beach. He purchased a boat—something he never did in Connecticut—an eighteen-footer he kept at the club. He bought it at a store called Miami Ski Nautique for $50,000.

It was probably the frequency of these trips that made Jennifer suspicious. Why is he going to Florida in September, when the Avon ski club is open? Why on days when he's supposed to be selling a house? Why is he distant and cold before he leaves and warm and chatty when he returns?

The sages had an expression: If you have to ask why three times, you are irredeemably lost.

Part
THREE

FOTIS DULOS MET Michelle Troconis at the Greater Miami Ski Club in 2016. He was with Theodore and Petros. Michelle, who lived at 7900 Harbor Island Drive in Miami Beach, was with her nine-year-old daughter, Nicole, a top-ranked snow-skier and water-skier.

Was it the kids who introduced the parents? Petros and Nicole meeting in the water, talking, then coming up the beach side by side? Fotis was immediately attracted to Michelle, who is tall and lissome. She looks like Jennifer, only not. Jennifer's friends say Jennifer was prettier because Jennifer radiated warmth, whereas Michelle seemed as cold as an outer planet. One friend described Michelle as a kind of bizarro Jennifer—Jennifer as she'd be in a world gone wrong.

Unlike Jennifer, Michelle Troconis is a jock, a snow-skier as besotted with competition as Fotis was. She speaks with an accent that shows the influence of the many places she has lived: Argentina, Venezuela, the United States. She comes from a family of professionals. Her father, Carlos Troconis, is a pediatric cardiologist. Her mother, Marisela Arreaza, is a mental health counselor. Michelle earned a degree in psychology at the Universidad Central de Venezuela, then worked with developmentally challenged children. She brought them together with animals, specifically horses, to put them in touch with the physical world. For many, the relationship Michelle Troconis helped forge between animal and child constituted the first emotional bond of their lives.

She worked at high-end resorts, catering to members of a luxury class willing to pay thousands an hour for a unique horseback riding experience. A regular gig at the Ghantoot Racing & Polo Club in Abu

Dhabi led to lucrative communications work for an Arabian sheikh. She moved among a community of jet-set princelings who lived beyond and above any particular nation, loyalty, or cause, who occupied a hidden stratosphere. She was hired as an on-air analyst for a program on ESPN Global called *Snow Time*; did public relations for Cerro Castor, a ski resort in Tierra del Fuego; and married the manager, Gaston Begue, a member of Argentina's Olympic ski team. They had a child, then divorced, but the child—Nicole—stayed close to both parents.

On August 28, 2023, Michelle posted a picture of her younger self on X, along with a press release–style summary of her background: "Michelle Troconis grew up in a loving family & had the privilege & honor of continuing the legacy of her family. She had the honor of studying at AVEPANE founded by her grandfather. From there her dreams began to come true & to this day she has never stopped working with children." And an Instagram post from the following day, including a clip of Michelle on *Snow Time*, read, "Michelle Troconis has always challenge [*sic*] herself into discovering new opportunities. While living in Argentina she saw an opportunity & opened her own TV production company & had her own shows. Among them she was also a producer & host for a snow sports show for ESPN South America."

After her divorce, Michelle moved to Miami, where most of her family was living, and started a business with her sister Daniela. They made waterproof shoe-covers called Seals. By 2016, the year Nicole would turn ten, Michelle was restless, nearing middle age, with not a lot to show for it. She had married and divorced and had a daughter, but she was, in many ways, alone. She wanted to find someone and start really living her life—that was apparently her frame of mind when she met Fotis Dulos at the Greater Miami Ski Club in Doral, Florida.

Fotis looked like many other members of the leisure class, well-dressed and slim and seemingly wealthy enough to do whatever he wanted any day of the week. She knew he was married with kids, but why should that matter? The marriage was clearly troubled. Why else would Fotis be here without his wife? What's more, Michelle has claimed—on Instagram—that Fotis was accompanied by another woman when they first met and in fact had other girlfriends, mostly Greek women he'd met at ski competitions.

But even if this were true, Fotis's affair with Michelle would've seemed different to Jennifer. It was clearly more than a fling. Fotis was in love.

"Her name is Michelle Troconis and they call her Michi," Jennifer said in 2017. "She is living in Miami and she's Venezuelan. Fotis told me she has a daughter named Nicole, who is ten. Nicole's father lives in Argentina and Nicole spends all of the summer with her father in a ski resort because it's winter there and they want Nicole to be a champion downhill skier."

Fotis encouraged Petros to befriend Nicole. This would have a strange vicarious charge: living a fantasy through your ten-year-old son. And it gave Fotis an excuse to keep in touch with Michelle.

Jennifer regularly checked Petros's phone, where she could see Fotis's Instagram. Seeing photos of Nicole in a post is what first set her suspicions ablaze.

"Petros had a relationship with Nicole as early as 2016," Jennifer said later. Petros said he and Nicole "were boyfriend and girlfriend." Jennifer then added, "I asked him what that meant because he was ten."

Petros said it meant, *He likes her and she likes him.*

"Fotis promoted this relationship, and was proud of him," said Jennifer.

"Nicole is Petros's first girlfriend," Jennifer said in 2017. "This was promoted by Fotis and Michelle as a cover for them and as a way to be closer. They used their own kids. It's distasteful and a touch insane."

Fotis flew to Miami in November 2016 to celebrate a friend's birthday. Michelle spent the weekend with Fotis at a hotel near the beach—seemingly the first time they were really together.

When looking for a way to communicate secretly with Michelle, Fotis went to Petros, who signed his father onto Houseparty, an app Petros used to talk to friends. In this manner, Fotis involved Petros in the betrayal of his own mother.

Had Fotis really been unfaithful before?

"He absolutely had other affairs," D. J. Paul told me. "Jennifer might not know all the names, but she knew what was going on. I'd be shocked if it were limited to two. Fotis was the kind of guy who always had something on the side. He was a player. He gave off the sense that he was European royalty."

"That man took a lot of vacations on his own, whether it was to Greece or California or wherever," a Farmington friend of Jennifer's told me. "Where was he the night his own mother died? Greece! I know Hilly was upset because Fotis was constantly traveling even though he had five children. Was there proof that he was cheating? I don't think so. But was Jennifer suspicious? Yes. It drove her crazy."

"She knew he'd had affairs, but [Michelle Troconis] was different," said D. J. Paul. "It was more emotional, more intense."

Even so, Jennifer did not give up on the marriage. That was not her nature. When there was a problem, she tried to fix it. She tried to become the woman she believed Fotis wanted.

"I remember in Greece, during Clea-Noelle's baptism, Jennifer was taking water-ski lessons," a family friend told me. "Maybe she sensed

Fotis was cheating and thought the answer was to be with him everywhere, even out on the water."

Jennifer insisted on seeing a marriage counselor. The fact that Fotis, who loathed psychologists and psychiatrists, agreed suggests he knew Jennifer was onto him and understood it was not in his financial interest to alienate his wife.

Fotis had one requirement: the counselor could not be Jewish. Perhaps he believed a Jewish doctor would take the side of the Jewish spouse, or the spouse who'd once been Jewish. Or perhaps he did not trust Jews. At times Fotis seemed to think the Jews of the world had joined in a conspiracy against him.

Jennifer and Fotis engaged Mark Lucyk, a clinical psychologist in West Hartford. In court they would argue over just how many sessions they'd attended.

Fotis: "Did we go to marriage counseling with Dr. Lucyk for over ten sessions?"

Jennifer: "No, not . . ."

Fotis: "Okay. Thank you."

Jennifer: "Maybe I did, but you didn't."

Fotis: "Okay, all right."

Jennifer: "You were there for like four. Sorry."

It never would have worked anyway, no matter how many times Fotis attended. He was having an affair with Michelle Troconis, which made everything he said in those sessions a lie. Fotis had an economic interest in maintaining the marriage, but not the desire.

Meanwhile, Hilliard Farber's health took a bad turn. "I was trying to work on our marriage, marriage counseling had failed, and my father was getting very, very sick and getting sicker," Jennifer explained in court. One night, she said, she had a terrible realization: "My father isn't going to live much longer."

Hilliard was eighty-three. He'd been diagnosed years earlier with Sweet's syndrome, a chronic wasting condition. He'd retired in 2008, selling his business to Tradeweb for as much as $40 million.

Hilliard collapsed on vacation in the Caribbean island of St. Barts in 2016 and was never the same. On January 8, 2017, when he died, he went out like a patriarch, massive and stoic, surrounded by friends and family, but preoccupied with a crucial last task: taking care of his daughters. Melissa would be supported by funds that would see to her needs. The challenge was different for Jennifer, who'd saddled herself with an increasingly unpredictable husband.

Hilliard had tried to shield his daughter and grandchildren with restricted trusts, money Fotis could not access as long as Jennifer was alive. But how to protect her without provoking him? This was a problem.

Fotis told the court that Hilliard left Jennifer a $100 million trust fund. It is not clear whether Fotis believed this, or whether it was his way of screaming to the judges and lawyers *She is rich, I am poor, help me!* In fact, Jennifer's inheritance, the details of which are sealed, was probably much smaller than what Fotis claimed it was. Hilliard Farber's estate had been estimated at less than $80 million. After Gloria and Melissa had been provided for, perhaps $10 million would have been left for Jennifer. Separate trust funds, valued at around $2 million each, were set up for each grandchild, a fact that would possibly figure into Fotis's machinations. For Fotis Dulos, the money in those funds was like an apple pie cooling in an open window.

The funeral service was at Temple Emanu-El on Sixty-Fifth Street and Fifth Avenue in Manhattan. Jennifer in black, inconsolable beside her Christian children. Lauren Almeida sat between the husband and the wife. Jennifer pulled herself together enough to eulogize her father. The man in the box had been her lodestar. The world was off-kilter without him. The sun was gone. The planets, loosed from gravity, drifted away.

After the service, Hilliard Farber was buried at Beth Israel Cemetery in Woodbridge, New Jersey.

Nearly everyone I spoke to believes Jennifer would still be alive if Hilliard had not died when he did. "As soon as I heard that Jennifer was missing, I knew Hill Farber was dead," a friend told me. "He never would have let this happen."

"Hilliard knew how to deal with Fotis," said another. "He would have paid him ten million dollars and said, 'Go away.'"

It *was* at least partly about money. Hilliard kept the taps open not because he liked Fotis but because he loved Jennifer and feared Fotis. Gloria neither loved nor liked Fotis, so, when the time came, she looked at the account books and asked, "Why?"

Fotis claimed Hilliard had been like a second father to him and supported him because he believed in him, that their relationship was about more than business. In fact, it was about power. Fotis, who described Hilliard as "a powerful man," was intimidated by his father-in-law.

That's what kept him in check. With Hilliard gone, he felt free to do whatever he wanted, even bring his mistress into the open.

Jennifer shut herself in her office and wept when her father died. She mourned fiercely. Later, asked why the marriage failed, Fotis said, "I could not just sit and watch Jennifer cry all day."

Gloria struggled, too. She had taken on a new role. She was the matriarch, the grandmother, the once beautiful woman who'd gradually moved to the back of the family photo. Hilliard had understood Fotis, the nature of the threat and how to handle it, which was gently, as with tongs. He did not make demands or confront Fotis; instead, he maneuvered him with money and promises. If there were threats, they were made vaguely, in the way of inevitabilities. *If you do that, this might happen.* Hilliard had managed his son-in-law like a storekeeper managing a mafia bagman. Cost/benefit. You pay the protection because it's cheaper than replacing the windows. To Gloria, that must have seemed like appeasement. Maybe she knew only one way to deal with a bully: cut him off. She was like a new agent brought in to settle an old account. The strategy she implemented would be different.

Mother and daughter needed each other after Hilliard's death. Jennifer came up with a plan: She and Fotis would sell 4 Jefferson Crossing and move into Gloria's weekend house in Pound Ridge, New York. Fotis would run the Fore Group from the guest house, refocusing the business on Fairfield County. Jennifer could more easily visit her mother from there—Manhattan is a much shorter drive from Pound Ridge than from Farmington—and Gloria could stay with her daughter and grandkids on weekend visits. The children would attend the New Canaan Country School, across the border in Connecticut.

Fotis approved of this plan, detailing the particulars to his staff at a dinner in February 2017.

Jennifer completed the New Canaan Country School applications, the kids were accepted, and Gloria made the first tuition payments, which together amounted to around $70,000.

The Dulos family flew to Aspen for spring break in March 2017, the best month to ski Colorado. It's blue skies and deep powder in March, and a western sun that tans the lift operators purple. Fotis complained about Jennifer's behavior on that trip. He said she vanished for hours at a time and never went up the mountain. When they skied, she shopped. "I hired a World Cup skier from Argentina to work with the kids," Fotis said in court. As for Jennifer, she'd help get the kids ready, then disappear until dinnertime, which Fotis called a joke, saying, "Jennifer doesn't eat."

If Jennifer did have an eating issue, Fotis was probably as much to blame as anyone. According to Richard Weinstein, Gloria Farber's estate lawyer—who told this story on television not long after Jennifer's disappearance—Fotis insisted on ordering food for Jennifer, telling her, with her weight in mind, what she was and was not allowed to eat.

Three days into the Aspen trip, several of the kids came down with the flu. The parents cut the vacation short and returned home—better to be sick in your own bed. Then they traveled to Miami, where the subtropical heat would burn off the last embers of the illness. Gloria went along.

Jennifer and her mother sat by the pool at the W Hotel in South Beach as Fotis and Lauren Almeida took the kids to the ski club in Doral. Lauren noticed a tall skinny woman with long hair who always seemed to be hanging around. It was the first time Lauren Almeida became aware of Michelle Troconis.

The trip was upended when Gloria hurt her foot at the pool. She decided to go back to New York to see her doctor. Jennifer went along to help. Lauren stayed with Fotis and the kids in Miami.

It was later that night, when she was alone in the house in Farmington, that Jennifer really began to clue in on the affair. An old email had made Jennifer suspicious about an unexplained trip Fotis had taken, supposedly by himself, to Colorado. Then Lauren called and told Jennifer that, for some reason, Fotis had left her and the kids at the W and checked into a different hotel. This was enough to send Jennifer onto the internet, where she fell down a rabbit hole that went from Instagram to Facebook, where she came across pictures of Fotis with Michelle.

Jennifer confronted Fotis by text. She wanted answers. He wrote back, saying he could not talk at the moment but would explain in the morning.

Fotis said news of the affair should not have come as a surprise. He and Jennifer had not had sex in years. The marriage was broken. It was just that he was willing to admit it.

That's not how Jennifer felt. She wanted to save the marriage. Because that's what you're supposed to do. You make the vows. You keep the vows. She was devastated by the affair, by the humiliation of betrayal.

Fotis's behavior seemed needlessly cruel: Hilliard had died on January 8. Fotis confessed adultery on March 25. "Learning about the infidelity was horrible," Carrie Luft told *Vanity Fair*. "That was a deal-breaker for her."

Jennifer probably knew the marriage was over even before Fotis got back from Miami. If he'd once loved Jennifer, that love had faded when she stopped heeding his every command. She did not adore him as she had in the beginning, and Fotis Dulos needed adoration.

Fotis wanted to separate immediately. He even had a plan: Jennifer would move to Pound Ridge; Michelle and her daughter, Nicole, would move into 4 Jefferson Crossing in Farmington. The Dulos kids would split their time between the two houses while finishing the semester at Renbrook, then attend the New Canaan Country school in the fall. Fotis would come and go from Pound Ridge as he pleased—he still had a key to the guest house. Jennifer would do the same at 4 Jefferson Crossing. Fotis promised to leave Jennifer's office untouched. "It's still your room," he said. "We can even put a lock on the door."

To Fotis, this seemed like a sensible modern arrangement. The kids would not lose their mother or father, but gain a parent and a sibling instead. He used the word "blended." He wanted to blend Michelle and Nicole into the family as you might blend crushed walnuts into pancake batter. To Jennifer, this new blended family sounded a lot like the old family minus a single ingredient: Jennifer.

She asked Fotis to wait on the separation at least until the kids finished the school year. He reluctantly agreed.

"What Jennifer asked me, specifically, was not to get a divorce until later," Fotis told the court. "She said, 'Please, don't even mention the word divorce to the kids.' And I said that's fine. I don't need to get married to anybody and I'm sure you don't. So, I don't need to talk about a divorce, but I definitely want to separate."

Jennifer spent a few days with Petros in London that April. Maybe she believed the time away would do them both good. It irritated Fotis that she had picked Greek Easter weekend. "Easter is a big holiday for us— the Greek Christians," he said. "And Jennifer decided that she's going to take Petros and go to London and deprive him of having Easter with us. So, I had Easter with the four kids and Jennifer was in London with Petros." They did the tourist circuit—museums and towers, the big clock, the famous department store.

How great it must have been for Jennifer to get away—away from Fotis, the pond, the paramour, away from the headache life had become. Hotel mornings with the silver coffeepot on the silver room-service tray, the waiter in white, the heavy curtains with London beyond. She had time to think on that trip, time to walk and linger and browse. Window shopping for *another* life. She was a city person at heart. The sounds of the metropolis, the car horns and engines, the crowds, the surf-like break of traffic, a siren fading in the distance—it was ambient noise for Jennifer, a soundtrack of her true home. Best of all was the time spent with Petros. The attention of a mother of five is scattered by necessity. Some to all, all to none. Now and then it's important to get one of them alone.

Meanwhile, back in Connecticut, Lauren Almeida spotted Michelle and Nicole at the Avon ski club. It was Michelle's first official visit to Farmington. She and Nicole stayed in a house owned by a Fore Group employee. "I saw Michelle on the boat and I must have made a look on my face because the boys said, 'Oh, we're going to tell Mommy!'" Lauren said later.

Jennifer didn't have to wait long to find out. There were soon pictures of Michelle and Fotis on Instagram. It was the disrespect that bothered Jennifer most. Fotis did not even have the decency to be discreet. Just the opposite. He was flaunting his infidelity in front of the kids.

Jennifer must've been reeling when she took Petros to Buckingham Palace. She could not focus on the tour, listened but did not hear, stared but did not see. Petros went ahead. There were so many people, so many faces. At some point, she realized she'd lost him. She called out, calmly at first, then in a panic.

Petros wandered in a daze. Everywhere he looked—strangers. His heart thumped, his knees weakened. A cop spotted him in the crowd. He was clearly lost. Petros told the officer he could not find his mother. The officer reported a missing child to HQ, then radioed other police in the area. Many were on horseback and could see over the crowd. Jennifer was spotted and reunited with Petros. The entire episode lasted a few minutes, but Fotis would later cite it as yet another reason Jennifer should be denied full custody.

"Petros told me he was terrified," Fotis said in court. "He told me that Mommy said, 'Don't tell Daddy what happened.' And then, when I kept on asking, he told me that he was lost for a half hour and that he had to approach a police officer. He was completely terrified. He said: 'Everybody looked like a giant around me. I didn't know where Mommy was. I saw somebody wearing the same boots and I tapped her and it wasn't Mommy and that scared me even more.' He said [he] approached a British police officer and they were able to find Mommy. He said he was scared because the officer filed a report so he thought they were going to get arrested."

"He just walked ahead," said Jennifer. "I knew he was right there, and the bobbies are up on horses, and can see and communicate with each other, and we found him. It was ten minutes."

The mood in Farmington worsened when Jennifer and Petros returned. There had been anger and suspicion before, but it had been sublimated. Everything was suddenly out in the open. "It became a very hostile house when they were both there," said Lauren Almeida. "It was an anxious place because we really didn't know what was going to happen or when they were going to have an argument. So, when an argument did occur, I tried to take the kids away. I felt anxious. I would look forward to the days when it was just Jennifer in the house."

The last weeks of the marriage were defined by a handful of fights at 4 Jefferson Crossing. Jennifer and Fotis had always squabbled, but Jennifer tended to retreat, withdraw, give in, and move on. "She was capable of snapping back and had a sharp tongue and could stand up for herself," a friend told me. "But she's always been different when it came to Fotis. With him, she became almost less able to defend herself, probably fearful of the repercussions. She did not want to rock the boat. And she did not want to set him off in front of people, which would be embarrassing."

Patterns and attitudes—it all changed in those last weeks of marriage. For the first time, Jennifer, betrayed and humiliated, began to defend herself. Fotis believed wives should be subservient to their husbands, which Jennifer had always been. When she finally began saying no, it surprised him, then infuriated him.

"Things are different because we are breaking up," Jennifer explained in court. "Now I know about his plan for a new life and so I started saying 'No' to him a little bit more. And he's not used to hearing 'No' from me, and so he's getting more and more volatile, and more and more controlling, and more and more unhinged, and doing things that he's never done before."

The first real fight took place on May 4, 2017. Lauren later gave the following testimony in court:

> The kids had gotten back from school. They had finished their homework. It was probably around 6:30, so they didn't eat din-

ner yet or have baths, and they had school the next day. Fotis asked Constantine and Christiane to go with him to the waterski site to watch him ski. They weren't going to ski, but just watch him. And it was also really cold that day. And as he was leaving with them, Jennifer pulled in at the same time and she saw that they didn't have jackets or anything on, and she said "No." They hadn't even had dinner yet. It was already 6:30. And so [Fotis] came back into the house and into the kitchen, where they were, and Jennifer was saying, "No, they're not going." And they were fighting back-and-forth. I took the kids upstairs to Christiane and Constantine's bedroom and I closed the door and we were just doing puzzles to try and, you know, to avert the attention. And then we heard yelling coming up the stairs and Fotis opened the door and said, "Come on, let's go. We are going to the pond." And Jennifer was saying, "No, they're not going, no, they're not going." And I was trying to pay attention to the kids, making sure they are not paying attention to the fight.

Jennifer went upstairs and the yelling continued. Then I heard Fotis start yelling at Jennifer, saying she's certifiably crazy, just screaming it . . . This was the first time I'd seen Jennifer really stand up to him and say, "No, they are not going." And she kept sticking with that—they are not going. And he said, "If you come at me, I come back one hundred times harder." I remember that, because I was shocked. I didn't understand it.

The second fight happened on May 30. The kids had returned from school. Lauren was going through their backpacks, digging out and handing around homework. Jennifer was in the kitchen when Fotis stormed in. He began to dictate the terms of the coming separation—who would stay with whom, when and where. He'd written it all down. He called this a contract and ordered Jennifer to sign it. She refused. He went into a rage. Lauren peeked in from the mudroom. "[Jennifer] looked terrified," she said. "She was hunched over. Her arms were crossed. She was just saying, 'I'm not going to sign it.' And he was aggressive, saying, 'You need to sign, you need to sign it.' And then I heard him say that he would take the kids to Greece and disappear."

Lauren brought the children upstairs. They went into one of the bedrooms, closed the door, and started to work on a puzzle, but could still hear screaming. Fotis ripped the "contract" to pieces and shouted: "We're just going to live in this house in Farmington for the next ten years in misery and I will never divorce you."

Jennifer wanted to get away from Fotis, but, for the moment, while her kids were still in school, she felt there was nowhere to go. On June 1, 2017, she moved into a separate bedroom. By then, Lauren, who'd been working for Jennifer as a nanny and for the Fore Group in client relations, had quit the Fore Group and cast her lot with Jennifer. Fotis perceived her resignation as a knife in the back and reclassified Lauren from friendly to hostile. He accused her of stealing a watch and filed a police report. He said she couldn't be trusted.

If you come at me, I come back one hundred times harder.

Members of Fotis's extended family paid frequent visits to the house in Farmington. On June 3, 2017, the Duloses were hosting Fotis's thirty-two-year-old niece—Rena's daughter—and her husband when the third big fight took place. Jennifer believed it was only their presence that kept Fotis in check. Perhaps he did not want word of his temper to get back to his sister.

The day started with Petros in his room, getting dressed for a soccer game. He was excited when Lauren went in to see him. Waterskiing usually kept him away from soccer. He was finally getting a chance to play with his team. Fotis had agreed to drive Petros—Jennifer would be with Clea-Noelle at the horseback riding academy—then said he wouldn't. He was taking Theodore to the pond. Driving to the field was a waste of valuable time, Fotis said, and would "ruin the entire weekend." Lauren rearranged her schedule to drive Petros, and the two went to the kitchen.

Fotis became agitated. He began muttering as he stood at the stove making crepes, which he did—with the help of a housekeeper named Kazimiera Kaminski, aka Katia—every weekend he was home. According to Lauren, Fotis said he didn't "understand why [Petros] needed to do these sports [like soccer], that it's very selfish of him to want to be cheered on during these games . . . [Petros] just sat there with his head down."

Lauren dropped Petros off, ran errands, and then went back to the field, where the game was still in progress. Petros seemed exceedingly joyful. When Lauren looked questioningly at one of the parents, the parent smiled. Petros is having a great day, she said. He's already scored twice.

No one from the family had been there to see those two goals, which made Lauren sad, but she was glad to be in perfect position to see the third. Petros came up the wing, say, socks and shins covered in mud, jersey flagging. The center kicked the ball across the field. Petros struck it as it came, sending it over the goalie's right shoulder into the net.

After the game, Lauren took Petros to Dunkin' Donuts to celebrate. He recounted the particulars of each play. He was muddy and wet—it had been drizzling—but exhilarated. "He was really happy," said Lauren. "He had scored three goals, the only three goals either team scored that day."

Then she drove Petros to the pond. Fotis was waiting when they arrived, tense with anger. He motioned for Lauren to roll down the window, leaned into the car, and lectured Petros. Again he said it had been selfish of Petros to insist on playing soccer, and now it had begun to rain, and the weekend had been ruined. He told them to turn around and go home. He said, "I don't feel like skiing anymore."

Jennifer was out with Clea-Noelle when Lauren and Petros got back. Lauren went upstairs to play with Christiane. Fotis came in. He was in the kitchen with his niece and her husband when Jennifer returned. Lauren heard the car door shut, the house door open, then Fotis screaming at Jennifer about Petros.

Jennifer said later in court that she did not want to have this conversation because Fotis was too angry. "But he kept letting me have it about the waterskiing and missing his perfect Saturday," she recalled. "His perfect Saturday was ruined, and it's going to rain tomorrow, but it was really that his girlfriend, Michelle, was coming tomorrow—that's why it had to be today. He was very, very angry at me, and wanted to let me know, and wanted to let me have it."

Fotis moved close. He suddenly seemed menacing. She recoiled as if she'd caught a premonition, turned, and ran. She went up the stairs and into the room where Lauren was playing with Christiane.

"Jennifer looked terrified," said Lauren. "Fotis came in after her and closed the door and barricaded the door. Jennifer was shouting, 'Let me out! Let me out!' Christiane and I were on the rug, and Fotis had this stone face. Jennifer was begging him, saying, 'Please, I don't want to talk about it now.' And he was saying, 'I want to talk about it *now*.' And she kept saying, 'Let me out! Let me out!' And she tried opening the door, but Fotis is stronger, and she couldn't get it open."

Then Jennifer screamed. And that scream is at the center of this story. It was a cry of panic and desperation. Everything that had already happened was in that scream, as were all the terrible days to come. It was a horror-movie scream—long overdue and honestly earned. It expressed Jennifer's fear of Fotis, the years of mistreatment and alienation. The affair was in it, the sense of betrayal. "I started to scream at the top of my lungs," said Jennifer. "That's when Fotis let me out. And the only reason he did is because his niece and her husband were downstairs and he was embarrassed."

"I was scared," Lauren said. "I didn't know what to think. I had a little girl next to me. And she looked at me and said, 'Why is Daddy doing that to Mommy?'"

Fotis went down the stairs and out the door. Christiane followed. A few minutes passed. Quiet minutes. Too quiet. "I walked into the kitchen," said Lauren. "Jennifer came out of the dining room with this face that was, just like, scared and terrified. I asked, 'What's wrong?' And she said, 'He has them driving the car.' And I was like, 'What?' And so, I went to the dining room from where you could see the front of the house. And then I saw Christiane in the front seat and Fotis in the passenger seat and I watched them pull out of the driveway and go around the neighborhood and come back. And then Christiane got out and Petros got in and they went down the street. He didn't stop when they got back to the house but kept going. Petros turned onto Avon Mountain Road, a very windy road that even adults have a hard time driving."

"He took Theodore who's eleven, Petros who's also eleven, and our daughter Christiane who's eight, and put them each in the front seat of a car and they were in full control of the wheel, the brake, and the gas, and had them driving around the neighborhood, which was terrifying," Jennifer said. "Then he took Petros alone. He took Petros out on the main road, which is very swervy and there have been many accidents."

Why did Fotis let his eight-year-old daughter and eleven-year-old sons drive his Porsche around Jefferson Crossing and out onto Avon Mountain?

What did it mean?

Jennifer believed Fotis did it to scare her, to ratchet up the pressure. If the situation became intolerable, maybe she'd give in to his demands. It was not divorce he wanted, which might diminish his status and income, but a separation in which Michelle replaced Jennifer but everything else stayed the same. Fotis was showing her that he was in control, that he could do with their lives what he wanted, even if it meant risking the safety of the children. The term for such behavior, coined in 2006 by the sociologist Evan Stark, is "coercive control." It's like violence, but its effects are not physical. Indeed, the journalist Rachel Louise Snyder titled her 2019 book on domestic violence, which cites Stark's work on coercive control, *No Visible Bruises*. Jennifer's experience demonstrates the way one spouse can terrorize the other before physical violence ever occurs.

The last day of school was Thursday, June 8, 2017. Jennifer and Fotis gathered the kids that afternoon to explain the situation. "We said that mommy and daddy love each other but they're going to separate," Fotis said. "We're always going to love each other, but not in the same way. We're going to move the kids and Jennifer to Pound Ridge. I'm going to stay in Farmington. I'm going to have them every Wednesday and on the weekends in the summer."

Many historians will tell you that the First World War and the Second World War, though usually considered separate events, were a single conflict with a twenty-year intermission.

It was like that with Fotis and Jennifer. There were many fights in the spring and summer of 2017, but, in a historical sense, it was a single fight with just enough time between rounds for the participants to curse and cry, make phone calls, and catch their breath.

The fourth big fight took place on June 14. It started with Fotis reading a schedule of upcoming waterskiing events out loud at breakfast. Petros muttered something. Fotis asked him to repeat what he'd said. Petros told Fotis he no longer wanted to ski competitively. Petros had said this before, but Fotis had always ignored him. He believed it was not that Petros didn't like skiing but that he didn't like being outperformed by his twin brother, Theodore. On this occasion, with the tension in the house, Fotis focused his ire on his son and, according to Jennifer, "let [Petros] have it."

Fotis, who believed Jennifer had put Petros up to this act of rebellion, stormed upstairs looking for his wife. Lauren heard Fotis yelling on the second floor. The quiet between shouts was Jennifer whispering in response.

Fotis called Petros upstairs. "I heard Fotis say to Petros that if he didn't waterski, he would become a loser," said Lauren.

"He told Petros he'd be a loser if he didn't waterski," Jennifer told the court later that summer. "He said to Petros, 'I'm going to take a picture of your body now and I'm going to take a picture of your body a year from now. You're going to sit around. You're going to get fat. You're going to grow up and be a loser. And you're going to smoke pot."

Lauren was in the car with Petros a few minutes later, driving him to a practice. The life of a suburban kid with ambitious parents is a succession of practices, sessions, examinations, games. It's not his life, but the life someone has imagined for him. When the vision of one parent diverges from that of the other, the kid feels like he's being split in half. "I'm not going to be fat," Petros told Lauren. "I'm going to play some sports."

If anything, Petros's resistance accelerated Fotis's plans. Once he'd gotten Jennifer out of the picture, he'd be able to put Petros back on track. To do this, he had to really scare Jennifer. Yelling and threatening and letting the kids drive the car wasn't going to be enough.

Jennifer was probably meant to find the receipt for the "gun box." When she asked about it, Fotis said, "That's right," then took her up to the master bedroom, where he retrieved a hard plastic case from the closet. He got the key and opened the box on the bed. There was a stubby black pistol inside, a 9mm Glock. This information comes from police reports, court filings, and Jennifer's friends, to whom she told the story. She said she stared at the pistol, heart racing. It was like seeing the instrument of her own death. As a playwright, she knew Chekhov's maxim: a gun seen on a wall in the first act must be fired in the second or third act. "We always said we would never have a gun in the house," Jennifer said later. "Children can get ahold of them and kill themselves. And we also have a son who is fascinated with guns, who is depressed, and he talks of suicide."

Fotis said he "bought the gun from his friend Chet, a waterski coach in Florida."

He said he bought it "for protection."

In most cases, Jennifer told him, it's not the intruder who gets killed by the gun, but the gun owner or a member of his family.

"That's just what Michelle said," Fotis said. "She didn't want it in the home either. She didn't want it around Nicole."

Jennifer asked Fotis if he even knew how to use the gun. He said he was learning. "He said that he went to shoot with Michelle and he shot so beautifully and so perfectly on target that she could not believe he'd never shot a gun before," said Jennifer.

When Fotis was gone, Jennifer found the key, opened the box, took a picture of the pistol, and wrote down the serial number. "I did not even know if it was legal for him to have a gun," she explained. "I didn't think he had a permit."

The Glock, ominous in its case—that's when she knew it was time to take the kids and get out. But do it stealthily. If Fotis caught her in the act, who knows what he'd do?

"Fotis had become more controlling, bullying, and volatile since I learned of his affair," Jennifer said. "Then we started to discuss separation and maybe divorce. And so, over the course of these three months, he had threatened to disappear with the children. He'd obtained a gun. He'd bullied us and the kids. When we said 'No,' he wasn't hearing no. It became increasingly volatile at home. He cornered me in a room, chased me out of the house. It's just become very frightening. But the gun and the threats to take the kids away—really are very serious to me."

There was the house in Pound Ridge, but Jennifer did not want to go there because Fotis knew the house and had the key. She rented a house at 153 Chichester Road in New Canaan instead, then hired a moving company to pack her possessions in an unmarked truck on a day she knew Fotis would be away. Movers practiced in the art of the "stealth relocate" are not uncommon in Fairfield County, that kingdom of divorce.

June 18, 2017, was Father's Day. Fotis spent it with the kids at the Avon ski club. Flawlessly blue Connecticut. Eighty-four degrees at noon. Seventy-three at sundown, pond glassy and black. They took turns behind the boat, carving the water into spray, the boat slowing to make the wide turn when one of the skiers bit it and went cartwheeling across the surface. Bliss for Fotis. His kids, his command, his world. If he could have picked one day to live over and over, this might've been it.

Jennifer and Lauren used the occasion to pack. The unmarked truck came for the boxes at 2:00 p.m. the following day. The co-owner of Daley Moving & Storage, Gina Bunch, told Hartford's Fox61 that Jennifer was shaking when they arrived. "She was absolutely scared," said Bunch.

Jennifer had told Fotis she planned to take the kids to Pound Ridge that night. It was a Monday. They would sleep over at her mother's, then drive to New Jersey in the morning to visit her father's grave. The day before had been her first Father's Day without Hilliard. Fotis stood watching them go. He later recalled the last words he said to Jennifer before she left: "I said I was very proud of us. I know this is a tough situation and compared to other couples, we're probably at the top 90 to 95 percent."

Jennifer promised to have the kids back in time for a ski lesson the following afternoon.

They took two cars: Jennifer would drive one group in the Range Rover; Lauren would drive the other in the Suburban. It began to rain. Fotis told Lauren to drive carefully and call when they arrived.

Here's how I described the scene in a piece I wrote about the case for *Air Mail* in 2020:

> *Money can't protect you.* This is what Jennifer Dulos should have been telling herself as she loaded her kids—three boys and two girls, all under 14—into her car and drove away from the husband and marriage and house and life she had lived in Farmington, a trip that would have taken her south on I-84 to Route 7, past the Danbury Fair Mall and adjacent airport, its runway lit like the Vegas Strip in the dead of night, through the Wooster Mountain cut that opens like a gateway to the affluent towns along the Connecticut coast . . .
>
> Fotis had left her long before she had left him. He'd been no more than a ghostlike presence from the earliest days of their marriage. It was no surprise that he'd been cheating; he'd probably been at it for years. And things had only gotten worse. His mood swings, outrages, and flashes of temper had come to seem like a danger. At 50, she knew it was time to start yet another chapter in her life.

Fotis, left alone in Farmington, became suspicious. What Jennifer had said suddenly made no sense to him. *Hilliard's grave is in Wood-bridge, New Jersey. To visit it on Tuesday, they are going to Pound Ridge on Monday?* He walked through the house, opening closets and drawers. What he found, or did not find, stunned him. Clothes, toys, gear—gone, all of it was gone. She'd even taken the toothpaste.

Fotis called Jennifer. No answer. He called Lauren Almeida. Same.

"They wouldn't pick up," Fotis said later. "I tried to call my mother-in-law. She didn't pick up. I tried her cell phone, her landline, no response. I tried to call the Pound Ridge house, no response. I sent them a message and said, 'Guys, I'm really worried. I don't know what's going on. I'm going to have to call 911. Please respond to me.'"

He added, "It made me nervous. I'm their father and I'm nervous and there's things in my culture I consider way more dangerous than letting your kid drive . . . So of course, I was concerned. There was a lot of rain so I kept on texting and saying, 'Are you guys OK?' Nobody responded."

Fotis called the Farmington police. He said his children had been abducted by their mother. He said he was worried about their safety because it was dark and rainy. He also wanted to report stolen property. Jennifer had taken several items that did not belong to her.

The police asked for Jennifer's and Lauren's cell numbers and promised to investigate. A few minutes later, they called Fotis to say all five kids were safe and accounted for. The issue, as far as they were concerned, was resolved.

Fotis received the following text from Lauren Almeida at 9:00 p.m.: "We made it."

"I felt horrible," said Fotis. "I think that this was the worst thing anybody had ever done to me."

Part
FOUR

JENNIFER MET WITH a lawyer named Eric Broder the next morning in Westport, Connecticut, and filed for divorce.

When I asked Broder, a leading Fairfield County attorney, about his involvement in the case, he spoke of it sadly. He said Jennifer's disappearance has been the worst event of his professional life. "I couldn't believe it, when I heard," he told me. "I'd seen her a few days before. She had switched attorneys, which is not uncommon in cases like this, but we stayed in touch. I checked in on her. It was just before the holidays, lunchtime. She was eating alone in a diner near the Stamford courthouse. I was shocked the case was still going on. It seemed like it had already gone on forever. I sat with her for a few minutes, then said, 'I'm so glad to see you. I just wish it wasn't here.'"

Broder continued: "The newspapers were filled with pictures of her when she vanished, but she did not look like that in 2017. When I meet a client, it's often at the worst moment in their life. And that's how Jennifer looked—like it was the worst moment of her life, skinny, frail, and scared. She seemed like she was in a dangerous situation and needed to get out of it as quickly as possible."

That first morning, Broder filed an ex parte motion for a restraining order against Fotis—if granted, such an order cannot be contested by the defendant. Fotis would not be allowed to contact Jennifer or the kids or get within five hundred feet of them until a judge had heard from the lawyers and studied the facts, at which point the motion would be either removed or elevated into an order. Such motions are rarely upheld in cases that do not involve domestic violence. Fotis never hit Jennifer—but Broder believed the extenuating circumstances, particularly Fotis's acquisition of a gun, might convince the judge.

The ex parte motion was Jennifer's document, with Broder facilitating as a kind of ghostwriter. There was an introduction, followed by a bulleted list:

> Over the past three months, my husband, Fotis Dulos, has exhibited irrational, unsafe, bullying, threatening and controlling behavior. This behavior has significantly intensified in the last three weeks and I'm afraid for my safety and the physical safety and emotional well-being of our minor children:
>
> - My husband has threatened to kidnap our children.
> - Our children's mental and physical health is suffering as a result of my husband's compulsive and abusive behavior with regard to the children's participation in his obsession: water skiing.
> - I am afraid that my husband will harm our children to punish me.
> - My husband exhibits complete disregard for the physical safety and emotional health of our children.
> - My husband has recently acquired a gun.

The motion was granted, and the restraining order went into effect on Tuesday, June 20, 2017, the day after Jennifer fled Farmington. A marshal attempted to serve papers on both the order and the divorce—Fotis would know nothing of either until the documents were delivered—at 4 Jefferson Crossing at 12:30 p.m.

Fotis was there, but, speaking through the closed door, he said he would not accept the papers. What he'd apparently seen on cop shows led him to believe they were not binding if they could not be served. The marshal told Fotis this was not true, that the restraining order would be in effect whether or not he opened the door. Fotis said he wanted to call his lawyer. The marshal left the envelope on the porch and went away.

The police confiscated Fotis's Glock the same day. Fotis came and went from the house, but he claimed he did not pick up or look at the court papers until the next afternoon. Meanwhile, by calling Jennifer, Lauren, and the kids, by screaming, cajoling, and threatening, he had already violated the restraining order several times.

Fotis later told a judge that he believed that he had not violated the order because he had not examined the papers. When Eric Broder read the marshal's affidavit—"I told him I would be leaving [the documents at] his front door and for him to read them before he did anything else"—Fotis said the marshal was lying.

"I don't believe he didn't read the papers when they were served on Tuesday," Broder told the court. "There is no way. I don't buy it. He's way too smart. Then he communicated in violation of those orders, which I know he understood because he had to understand those documents. So, he violated those orders. Control. Lack of control. That is one of the issues here."

In the vast majority of cases involving ex parte orders—which are rare—the opposing lawyers work out a deal before the first hearing. That's what Broder expected to happen with Dulos. Broder is known for negotiating, for reaching amicable agreements. "My goal is always to settle quickly," he told me. "The whole time this process is going on, you have stress. And stress can lead to bad things." But Fotis felt he had been wronged, and refused to settle.

Jennifer had signed a twelve-month, $300,000 lease for the six-bedroom, eight-bathroom, fifteen-thousand-square-foot mansion at 153 Chichester Road. Zillow, which currently values the property at $6.2 million, describes it as a "stone and shingle English Manor House [that] sits high on 4.6 private gated acres." Gloria paid for the rental, which, with its fence and wall, seemed to offer protection.

New Canaan is more than a step up the social ladder from Farmington. It's another world. The town bills itself as "the next station to heaven." It was much closer to the milieu Jennifer had left when she married Fotis. It might look like the Virginia horse latitudes but is in fact faux country, wired with every service and convenience available in Manhattan. It's all winding lanes in New Canaan, intentionally dilapidated barns, manicured groves and orchards, private schools, dance academies, Botox day spas, and five-star restaurants. Farmington is rich. New Canaan is wealthy.

Jennifer had good reasons to choose New Canaan. It's the home of the New Canaan Country School, to which her children had been admitted before she even left Farmington. And it's within the jurisdiction of the Connecticut Superior Court in Stamford, where she could file for divorce. It also had the perhaps unintentional benefit of seeming like a mocking rebuke to Fotis, who dreamed of moving his business to Fairfield County but never quite managed it.

Later, when Jennifer vanished, reporters dug an exchange out of the court transcripts that reads like the conflict in a nutshell: Fotis claimed Jennifer had told the kids he was not successful because "successful people don't live in Farmington, they live in New Canaan." Every friend of Jennifer's I have spoken to dismissed this quote as invention or fantasy. Jennifer did not think that way. After all, she had raised her kids and spent some of her best years in Farmington. But the point was not what Jennifer had said, but what Fotis had *imagined* her saying.

The issue of money and status, who was up and who was down, who had made it and who had failed, played on his insecurities and demonstrated a class consciousness that is less American than Greek.

Jennifer was terrifically nervous in the early days of the separation, too jumpy to be in any room but a room filled with people. So, after she filed the ex parte motion, the entire crew—Jennifer, Lauren, the kids—spent a week at the Mandarin Oriental, a five-hundred-dollar-a-night hotel at Columbus Circle in Manhattan. "I know that filing for divorce and filing this motion will enrage [Fotis]," Jennifer explained. "I know he will retaliate by trying to harm me in some way."

Here's a fact: when you have money and have a problem, people will appear with a solution. The problem for Jennifer was her fear of what Fotis might do. The solution, at several thousand dollars a week, was bodyguards: beefy, pistol-carrying men hired by Gloria. The presence of these torpedoes angered Fotis. He suspected that Jennifer was having an affair with one of the bodyguards and hated the fact that his children were spending many hours a week in their presence. Asked in court why she felt she needed this professional protection, Jennifer said, "I was terrified that [Fotis] would come and take the children, and retaliate."

As Las Vegas is the capital of gambling, and New York is the capital of banking, and Los Angeles is the capital of entertainment, Stamford, Connecticut, is the capital of contentious divorce.

Over half a million Americans split every year, which amounts to over 250,000 lawsuits. Though these cases and their accompanying miseries are uniformly distributed across the United States, many of the ugliest, most mean-spirited, and most expensive end up in the

Connecticut Superior Court in Stamford—which serves Greenwich, Darien, and New Canaan, the habitat of some of the richest people in America: hedge fund managers, venture capitalists, oligarchs, celebrities, and star athletes who have drifted north from New York City.

The lawns in Lower Fairfield County are arsenic green, the oaks cast cool shadows, and the marriages fall apart, with the first wife replaced by the second, or the second by the third when the second is caught in flagrante delicto with the tennis pro from the club. Such a situation, if it leads to divorce, means a growth opportunity for local attorneys, who file motions and orders, delays, and charges of contempt in the aforementioned courthouse, or get into fiery exchanges in front of a jury, or nail the witness on direct, cross-, or recross-examination, each minute of which, not to mention the phone calls and the meetings and the working breakfasts and lunches, is billable at $1,000-plus per hour.

According to Lisa Nkonoki, the wife often discovers that her husband has filed for divorce when her credit card is rejected. "The husband cuts off the American Express, which the spouse only learns about at the end of a long expensive lunch," Lisa told me. Or "they roll up to the gates and they are told they are no longer a member of the Greenwich Yacht Club. 'Call your husband. You can't come in.'"

Famous Connecticut Superior Court divorce cases include that of television industry mogul John Kluge, founder of Metromedia, whose third wife, Patricia—he was cheating on her, she on him—aimed to come away with half of their $6 billion estate; that of New York Mets disappointment Bobby Bonilla, who battled for assets with his estranged high school sweetheart, Millie; that of the talk-show host Montel Williams, whose wife, a retired exotic dancer he met on his TV show—she'd seen pictures of Williams cavorting with a lanky Swedish model—tossed his clothes out the door of the couple's mansion in Greenwich.

In the end, the Dulos divorce would outdo them all. The case would drag on for twenty-three months and never reach the starting line— the parties were still involved in preliminary discovery when Jennifer disappeared. By then there'd already been more than four hundred filings.

It's said that many second wives move to Fairfield County specifically so that, when the time comes, as it usually does, they can file in Stamford, the most punishing, money-friendly divorce court in America. If the process takes longer there, is nastier, and is more costly, that's seemingly by design. Divorce is Fairfield County's great industry. By filing many often-nonsensical motions, by requesting many often-unnecessary hearings, a lawyer can survive for years on a single instance of marital heartache.

Fotis believed that Jennifer moved to New Canaan instead of Pound Ridge so she could file for divorce in Stamford. If Jennifer wanted to make Fotis suffer for his betrayal, there was no better way.

When asked to name a culprit in the Dulos disaster, many veterans of the process point to the system itself. "When I go to meetings with the powers that be in Hartford or Wethersfield they just shake their heads at this judicial district," Judge Michael Shay, who presided over the Dulos case for a time, said in court. "It's like we're a different animal. There is no other judicial district in the state of Connecticut that handles the volume of high conflict cases with this much assets in them but that just does not seem to be able to get these cases closed within a reasonable time."

"There are an incredible number of wealthy people in Fairfield County who have been legitimized in their own psychopathology," the divorce attorney Alan Rubenstein told me. "They find lawyers who find judges who allow them to get away with behavior in Stamford they'd never be allowed to get away with anywhere else. An especially litigious lawyer once gave me his description of the ideal client: 'Very rich, very angry, and very wrong.'"

Rubenstein added, "Fotis was clearly a sociopath. But there is always corresponding pathology. I'm not a psychiatrist, but I can tell there was a lot that led up to what eventually happened in that divorce. I promise you that Fotis Dulos did not become the person he ended up being without the help of the Stamford divorce court."

"The divorce lawyers involved in this case share a good portion of the culpability for what happened," said the attorney Lindy Urso, who represented a witness in the criminal investigation. "You're playing with lives when you mess around with a person's ability to see their children to gain advantage in a divorce. If you do that enough times, you're going to come across somebody who is going to snap."

Fotis would be represented by three different attorneys during the divorce, starting with Alan Rome, a West Hartford lawyer who was friend as much as counsel.

Alan Rome was born and raised in the state—a pure product of Connecticut. It's a distinction you start to notice. Whereas Jennifer's lawyers and doctors tended to arrive from Manhattan with degrees from Harvard or Yale, members of Fotis's team got their diplomas from the University of Connecticut or other regional institutions. Rome, who graduated from UConn in 1985, studied law at Western New England College's school of law in Springfield, Massachusetts. He had done legal work for Fotis for years. His selling point for the divorce was possibly his relationship with Eric Broder. The attorneys respected each other and had worked out agreements in the past. In a divorce case, it's to the advantage of both parties to settle. If the case does not settle but goes on and on, it usually means that something other than money or property is at stake.

Broder was surprised when Fotis, rather than getting on the phone, filed a legal response:

> On Monday, June 19, 2017, the plaintive/mother [*sic*] left a marital home with five children. Telling defendant/husband that they were going to visit her father's grave. Defendant/husband made numerous attempts to contact plaintiff/wife, the babysitter, Lauren Almeida, and the minor children throughout the day to ensure they arrived safely, with no response. Due to lack of response defendant/father became frantic that something happened to plaintive/wife and the children and he called 911, as well as the Farmington police dispatcher to inquire about their safety. Per information and beliefs, plaintive/mother took the children's cell phones away from them, leaving them unable to contact defendant/father. It wasn't until defendant/father received a text from the babysitter, Lauren Almeida, later that evening, did defendant/father learn they were all safe.
>
> On Tuesday, June 20, 2017, defendant/father was serviced application for emergency ex parte order of custody, application for relief from abuse in order of protection, and dissolution of marriage summons and complaint. Said pleadings were all filed in the judicial district of Stamford and listed plaintive/wife's address as 153 Chichester Rd., New Canaan, Connecticut. Plaintiff/mother had given defendant/father no warning

that she was moving out of the Farmington residence the prior day and taking the children with her, nor did he have any advance notice that these court proceedings would be filed.

Jennifer responded with a filing of her own:

My husband is obsessed with water skiing and insisted that the children must train to be world class water skiers, despite the children's wishes to participate in other extracurricular activities, sports and social events. For years, my husband has insisted that the children follow a rigorous training schedule that is both dangerous and excessive. He expects the children to travel all over the United States and overseas to compete, and regularly scheduled grueling trips to competitions. Each day since school ended, the eldest children have been forced to train at a nearby waterski pond from 8 AM until as late as seven at night, regardless of temperature or weather. The children are skiing at high speeds and forced to perform dangerous jumps. The children have told me that they do not want to water ski at this level. They are physically and emotionally exhausted and have begged me to do something about it. We are all terrified to disobey my husband.

If the children try to quit water skiing, my husband threatens and bullies them. For example, on one occasion when my son felt too tired to ski, my husband threw one of his skis against a rock and broke it in a fit of rage.

I am afraid of my husband. I know that filing for divorce, and filing this motion will enrage him. I know he will retaliate by trying to harm me in some way. He has the attitude that he must always win at all costs. He is dangerous and ruthless when he believes that he has been wronged. During the course of our marriage, he told me about sickening revenge fantasies and plans to cause physical harm to others who have wronged him. For example, flying a plane over an ex client's home and dropping a brick on his house. I fear for my family's safety and I believe him highly capable and vengeful enough to take the children and disappear. Furthermore, I believe that the children's suffering will continue, and worsen if they continue to be exposed to the defendant without supervision.

The Connecticut Superior Court is housed in a modern building at 123 Hoyt Street in Stamford. It's been the setting for many notorious cases, criminal and civil. It's where Michael Skakel, the Kennedy cousin convicted of killing fifteen-year-old Martha Moxley in Greenwich in 1975, appeared when fighting for a new trial, which he was granted in 2013. It's where Alex Kelly, who committed two rapes in four days in Darien in 1986 before fleeing to Europe, finally faced justice. Reporters gather outside the big glass entrance on red-letter days. They shout questions at the victim and the accused, interview the lawyers, photograph the judge, and then go down the street to talk shop over coffee or drinks.

Jennifer and Fotis made their first appearance on June 26, 2017. Broder and Rome argued the merits of the ex parte motion before Judge Thomas Colin, who'd been a prominent divorce attorney (he represented supermodel Stephanie Seymour) before being appointed to the bench.

Jennifer was terrified. She had not seen Fotis since the night she left Farmington in the rain. That initial hearing occupied three courtroom days.

Broder called his client to the stand.

"Are you afraid of your husband?" he asked Jennifer.

"Yes, I am."

"Why?"

"Because he's very volatile. He doesn't take no for an answer. He hates—he doesn't accept—losing. He said to me, 'If you hit me once, I'll hit you a hundred times more.'"

To Alan Rome, the case against the ex parte motion was simple: no history of violence. "Yes, there's a bad divorce," he told Judge Colin, "but you've seen thousands of cases where people get together and fight. I mean, anybody who has come to this courthouse, I guarantee you they have gone behind closed doors and raised their voices. When it escalates to a punch, a touch, a push, I agree: restraining orders come into place. But when there's no touching? No police intervention, nothing else? This is a case that should go through the regular custody battle and process, not with these ex parte orders. One party doesn't get to unilaterally decide to take the children out of the state and move to a different jurisdiction."

Eric Broder believes he and Alan Rome came close to settling. They were in a conference room in the courthouse, talking terms before the judge arrived. They were making real progress; then something happened. Broder is not exactly sure what triggered it. Maybe it was that he told Fotis he could imagine how he felt. For some reason, putting himself in Fotis's place—showing empathy—set him off. Fotis was suddenly on his feet, screaming. For a moment, Broder thought Fotis was going to hit him. That's when Broder knew Jennifer had not been exaggerating about her husband's temper.

Judge Colin addressed Jennifer and Fotis at the end of the second day. As if turning to the camera, he broke the fourth wall to warn them from the depth of his experience. He was trying to snap them out of their bad dream and make them see where they were and what they were about to do.

"I've known you now for no more than twenty-four hours and you seem like nice people with wonderful children," said the judge. "[You have] all the opportunities in the world that many families don't have—with healthy children, wealth, and all that provides. But the one thing it doesn't provide is happiness. I hope that you can put this all aside and maybe, in the next week or ten days, as things cool down, figure out a way to solve the problem yourselves instead of having three or four lawyers, a judge, a court monitor, a clerk, all involved in your life because, obviously, it's not ideal to have the government involved in your life like this. If you can't do it, then the court's here to do it. But I encourage you to think about all the fortunate things that you have in your lives that many people don't, and think about how the kids would feel if they sat in back of this courtroom and watched this hearing."

This speech was like the sign you see before you enter Manhattan on Route 9A: LAST EXIT BEFORE TOLL. But they blew right past it—because they did not understand its importance, or because they did understand but did not care.

Judge Colin struck down the restraining order—Fotis would be allowed to see his kids—but upheld Jennifer's order of protection, as well as an additional instruction that became an issue of brutal contention: "The Dulos children are to have NO contact with Michelle Troconis." This addressed Jennifer's fear of being replaced, blended out, but seemed especially harsh to Fotis, who loved Michelle and wanted to get on with his life.

Though the ruling was temporary—it would stand only until the divorce was resolved—Fotis spent the next several months, which could have been spent settling the case, looking for loopholes or simply violating the injunction. It was this dynamic—Fotis's refusal to follow the order and his talent for getting caught breaking it—that set off the chain of events that would end in tragedy. Everything that followed, followed from here, starting with the machinery that kicks in to gear when a bad divorce becomes contentious. This meant all sorts of strangers, including court officers and specialists, entering what had once been a sacred space—the private life of the family.

The court appointed a guardian ad litem: a GAL is a neutral party meant to represent the interests of minor children during a divorce litigation. Over time, this system, created to protect the defenseless, has itself become a weapon in the battle, with the warring parents competing for the approval, attention, and aid of the GAL, who is usually an attorney working for supplemental income. The task is remunerative but thankless. No matter what a GAL decides, someone hates him. "The GAL serves as a kind of investigative reporter," the lawyer Alan Rubenstein, who has often served as a GAL, told me. "You start by gathering all the data and information you can on the mom and dad and children. You meet with everyone. First the parents, then the kids, then, if possible, the grandparents, teachers, psychologists. Then you meet with the lawyers. If all goes as it should, you work with the lawyers to come up with a parenting plan—who lives with who, where, when—that's in the best interest of the children. Your job is to do this just long enough to get them through the rough patch. When the divorce is finalized, you are done."

Michael Meehan, a bald, middle-aged graduate of the University of Hartford and the Quinnipiac University School of Law, was appointed GAL in the Dulos case. He required a $20,000 retainer up front, then billed $500 an hour, a fee the couple had been ordered to split. Fotis skipped his payments, forcing Jennifer to cover the balance, which led Fotis to dismiss Meehan, saying, in essence, *How can you call him neutral when all his bills are paid by Jennifer?*

Meehan met with Jennifer and the kids at the New Canaan house on July 21, 2017, for an introductory meeting. The Dulos divorce was a rare occasion of the superrich falling into the guts of the bureaucracy, into the circuitry and among people their wealth normally insulates them from.

Meehan became the hub of the relationship. When Jennifer had a request, a beef, or a change of plans, it was not Fotis she contacted but the GAL, whose inbox filled with the minutiae of marital intrigue.

Jennifer was still looking for a psychiatrist for Petros in 2017, though the signs of depression went disregarded by Fotis. If you bring him to a psychiatrist, said Fotis, the psychiatrist will of course find something. That's the business. To a psychiatrist, a kid like Petros is an "annuity."

The court sided with Jennifer, forcing Fotis to give in. It was simply a matter of agreeing on a doctor. Names were suggested and rejected. Fotis whispered his usual caveat: No Jews. They settled on David Lopez, a psychiatrist with offices in Greenwich.

Fotis had problems with Dr. Lopez, who, he claimed without evidence, had been handpicked by his wife and her family. Fortis resented the fact that the doctor was in Greenwich, which is much closer to New Canaan than Farmington. For Fotis, driving to Greenwich meant losing an entire day. He talked about being self-employed and needing to take a second job—as a coach—to sustain himself. Once again, he made reference to Jennifer and her "$100 million trust fund," a clear exaggeration. (As noted earlier, Hilliard Farber was rich, but not *that* rich.)

Dr. Lopez had numerous sessions with Petros between 2017 and 2018. He felt the presence of Fotis in these sessions, even when he was alone with his patient. Petros told Dr. Lopez that he wanted his father to have full custody. The way he said it convinced the doctor that Petros had been coached. The eleven-year-old was under tremendous pressure, caught between parental pincers. By telling him to lie to Jennifer and Dr. Lopez, Fotis put Petros in a no-win situation: either he lies *for* his father and betrays his mother, or he tells the truth and betrays his father.

In the fall of 2017, the court warned both parents that, as parties in a high-conflict divorce, their main responsibility was to shelter the children. And yet, in the sessions that followed, Dr. Lopez came to believe Fotis continued to coach his children to obfuscate. "Based on what Dr. Lopez told me, Petros was at risk and is worsening because he was afraid to lie on his father's behalf and is very conflicted," Jennifer testified. "He's at risk of a mental breakdown and that's concerning to me."

Whenever Jennifer confronted Fotis—by email, by phone, or on an app made for divorcing parents called OurFamilyWizard—he denied the fact that Michelle and Nicole had been socializing with the Dulos kids. But Jennifer could see the evidence for herself on social media, in posts and updates Fotis did not try to hide. Jennifer learned that pictures of Michelle and Nicole had been put on the mantel at 4 Jefferson

Crossing beside Dulos family photos, and that Nicole had begun to refer to Fotis as her stepdad.

Jennifer was driven to distraction by a particular Instagram post, which showed Petros in a ski helmet and goggles with a long blond braid. It confused her at first. Petros had short hair and would never wear a braid even if he could. Then she got it. Nicole Troconis had a long braid. Jennifer was looking at an image with Nicole's braid photoshopped onto Petros, as if her son had been digitally mated with Michelle's daughter. The comments below the post—"hilarious," "a bomb," an emoji of eyes laughing so hard they were crying—were nauseating to her.

Exasperated by the obfuscation, Eric Broder hired a private detective to prove that Fotis Dulos had in fact been blending the families. Rob Artus was a middle-aged investigator, handsome though not distractingly so. He'd grown up in the United Kingdom but had resided in Connecticut since 1989 and become an American citizen in 2004. Covert surveillance is his specialty. Artus tailed Dulos around Hartford County for three days in November 2017, when Fotis was under legal order to keep his kids away from Michelle.

Jennifer and Fotis were in court, still embroiled in the battle over pretrial custody, when the detective reported his findings. Eric Broder orchestrated the testimony to unfold like an episode of *Perry Mason*. In the morning, he asked Fotis if he had mixed his kids with Michelle and Nicole at various Connecticut locations—a go-kart place in Wallingford, a movie theater in Simsbury, a ski resort in New Hartford. Fotis, probably believing Jennifer got her information from Petros, said no. Then Broder called the detective to the stand. "Mr. Dulos, Ms. Troconis, and four children arrived at the Ski Sundown skiing facility in New Hartford, Connecticut approximately at 10:00 a.m. and departed the area together just before 12:00 o'clock," Artus told the court. He then testified to Fotis's presence, with Michelle and Nicole and several of the Dulos kids, at the go-kart place and the movie theater.

Fotis stuck to his story when called back to the stand. He said the detective must have mistaken some other man for him. Or maybe, said Fotis, this new evidence had been fabricated. He made much of the fact that Artus did not seem to know there was a back entrance into Ski Sundown.

Fotis persisted in denial right up until he learned the detective had video of Fotis and Michelle and the kids at each location. When arrangements were made to show the footage in court, Fotis asked permission to change his testimony. He said he had confused the dates. His answer should have been, yes, he had in fact gone to all of those places with Michelle and the kids. The judge found Fotis in contempt. Jennifer's attorneys filed a perjury charge.

One afternoon, Lauren Almeida drove to Farmington to collect some items Jennifer had left at 4 Jefferson Crossing. Fotis was supposed to leave them in a box on the porch and keep his distance—an instruction he promptly violated. Lauren memorialized the encounter in an email. She said she had the box in her hands and was heading back to the car when Fotis rushed from the house calling her a liar. He said Jennifer had paid her $80,000 in return for testimony she gave in the divorce court. He threatened to sue Lauren, access her bank statements, and prove she'd been bribed. Lauren said she had been given nothing and had only told the truth. Then Fotis's tone changed. He said he wanted Lauren to play the role of peacemaker. "In a few seconds he went from threatening me to asking me to be the voice of reason," Lauren wrote. He said he was concerned about Jennifer's health.

He said he was not worried that "he would pass [the psych evaluations] because he had all his marbles but worried about Jennifer." Then, as Lauren headed to the driver's door, his tone changed again. He accused her of lying on the stand, saying he'd never barricaded Jennifer in a room at 4 Jefferson Crossing. Lauren reminded him that she'd been there and seen it with her own eyes. He said he had only "closed the door because his niece and husband were at the house." She said, "No, I saw what I saw."

"He tried telling me what I saw didn't happen," wrote Lauren. "He told me again to be the voice of reason. If I cared for the kids at all, I would be the voice of reason for Jennifer."

Jennifer was building a new life in New Canaan. Her kids were thriving at the New Canaan Country School, and she was looking for a house closer to the campus. She'd made new friends and reconnected with old friends, including several members of the Playwrights Collective. Veterans of the company met in the city to see a show of Carrie Luft's, then went for drinks.

Jennifer had not seen most of these people in more than ten years. She'd made her exit as an artist and heiress, beautiful and young. She returned as a suburban mom embroiled in a contentious divorce. She'd been through hell. Her friends quickly registered the change. It was not that she looked older; it was that she looked distressed, gutted, gaunt to the point of being sickly. The bones could be seen beneath the skin. Her eyes, which had been lush and dark, were haunted orbs peering out from the hollows of her face. The hundred-watt smile was still there, but different: what had once been natural and spontaneous seemed forced and intentional.

"Jen had written me about what was going on since her marriage started falling apart, but that night was the first time I'd actually been with her in years," Dan Rybicky told me. "It was a special night for Jen. Maybe there were ten of us. She was so happy to be with us again. She cried. It definitely seemed like something had been taken out of her. She was still beautiful, but she was a shell. She spent the whole night telling me what had been happening in her marriage. She did not mince words. It was scary. It felt like something bad was going to happen. It wasn't like I said to myself, 'Oh no, she's going to be killed,' but I was truly disturbed by everything she told me about Fotis—his behavior, his anger, his gun."

Even so, Jennifer's life showed signs of improvement. She still used bodyguards, though not as often, or as many. There were hours when she felt she needed no extra protection at all. Fotis was fifty miles north, and occupied with his own problems. Parental interactions, though hostile, were conducted via third parties: the lawyers, the psychiatrists, the guardian ad litem. When Jennifer and Fotis did communicate directly—through email, app, or text—the exchanges would usually deteriorate into a chain you can spend hours trying to parse.

Oct 24, 2017, at 10:09 a.m.

Jennifer,

I noticed Christiane had a wound under her chin and when I inquired she told me she had an accident while horseback riding. I am not in any way trying to put you on the spot (and have not copied Michael Meehan), and I understand that injuries are part of sports. However, being thrown off a horse is not to be taken lightly and I would like to be informed directly by you when these things happen. I also understand that you leased two horses for the girls. Did the accident occur with the new horse? Are these horses trained adequately? You can appreciate that I am concerned. Not trying to make waves.

Best regards—Fotis

~

Oct 24, 2017, at 10:30 a.m.

Dear Fotis,

She did fall and she was fine, just the chin nick. I was there. I spoke with the people in charge and Christiane is no longer riding that pony. We leased one pony—Lorenzo—who is beyond excellent and safe for Noelle to ride. Christiane gets to ride another pony. We were trying this one out, Little Jack, and now she is riding Sham, who is slower and very safe. I was on it immediately. I appreciate your wanting to be in the loop. I found this barn in particular as Jill Shulman puts her rider's safety first and foremost and the girls ride beneath their ability to make sure they are safe. Jill is a mother of 4 herself and treats the girls as her own.

Regards,

Jennifer

~

Oct 24, 2017, at 12:30 PM

Jennifer,

Thanks for getting back to me. How did she hurt herself under the chin? I am assuming she had a helmet on.

Did it come off? Did she get dragged? Did you check for a concussion?

Fotis

~

On Oct 24, 2017, 12:38 PM

This is absurd. Of course she had a helmet on. Nothing you mention below occurred. If you'd like to harass me about it I suggest you use OFW and cc Mike [Meehan] or have Alan [Rome] send a letter. Back off please.

~

On Oct 24, 2017, 12:42 PM

Jennifer,

I am not harassing you. I was not informed by you or anyone else about the accident, and I am just asking the questions any parent would ask. You are being aggressive. I had not even copied Michael in my communication because I did not want to escalate this. Head injuries are serious and everyone knows that. I have the right to know what happened and what steps you took afterwards. This is the second time that Christiane comes to me with a head injury. The first time back in June, she was diving in a 4' pool and hit the bottom. Lauren took a video of Petros performing front flips on the same spot and barely clearing the bottom. Our children are coordinated and cautious, but they are still children. Good parenting in sports is more than being a bystander or hiring baby-sitters to do our job. Accidents will always occur, it is what you do before and after that makes the difference. And unfortunately, I think you are weak on this department.

Best regards—Fotis

~

Nov. 3, 2017

Jennifer,

I think we fall very short of demonstrating anything to Mike and the court system, other than that we are two spoiled people arguing about waterskiing, polo and ice-hockey. Jennifer, you have not worked with me to co-parent our children. I have proposed a holiday schedule since September, sent follow up emails, and we are now in November and there is still no response from you or your attorneys who instead brag about your neediness and hourly rates behind your back. I have proposed activities and there is still no response from you. The holiday schedule was the simplest of matters to agree on. You only push your agenda thru, which is simple "make Fotis' life miserable, drain him of funds, catch Fotis breaking the court orders and obtain sole custody or at least sole decision making ability for the children." We all see this, it is not rocket science. Including the children. They do not like what you are doing and they will resent you for it. I keep on speaking nicely about you, but they wonder why you say terrible things about me, such as "your father did not work enough to make more money," "your dad is a psychopath," "you are your father's slave," "asshole," "your dad does not care about you, he only cares about Michelle and Nicole," "your father is a cheater," "your father likes Farmington because he is not that smart, successful people live in New Canaan," etc. etc. I have asked you multiple times in the past to stop speaking badly about me, especially to our children. Additionally you censor their conversations—just yesterday you hung up the phone because Noelle was describing how she fell from the pony you bought. This is all very damaging and no matter what happens in court, you are scarring our children. The children have a blast when we are together. They adore me and I adore them. We will always have a bond. And I sincerely wish the same for you. I actually work towards it, time and again. I want our children to have a sane mother, and I think you have a lot to offer. But, focus on them and not on Michelle and ruining me. I texted you on Thursday and asked to speak to you. But you ignored me, as always, because this is what your attorneys advise and want—they want the conflict. At this point I am a bit disgusted to be honest with you. So, please have the children to me by 10 am on Saturday. Anything else, I will consider a violation of the court orders.

Fotis

~

November 3, 2017

Fotis,

Again, from Wednesday, November 1st, 2017, when the children were dropped off with you until the morning of Thursday, November 2, 2017, the children and you shared the marital home with your romantic partner and her daughter who reside there. This is in contempt of the court orders. Again. Worse still is you continue to ask the children, all 5, to LIE on your behalf to their mother. It causes them confusion and distress. Stop it.

Jennifer

If Jennifer did see Fotis in person, it was only for a few minutes during pickup or drop-off as the children moved from one house, from one suburb, from one suzerainty to another. In this, they lived like nomads. Their life was a matter of crossing borders, changing residences, moving from parent to parent, with different bedtimes and rules. It meant always being in a house where one parent was at war with the other. It meant being asked to take sides in that war, even if the request was not explicit.

Fotis and Jennifer were born in the 1960s. This means they grew up in the 1970s, the height of the divorce boom. They knew what divorce was like from a kid's point of view, even if it was from secondhand experience. The nightmare of court dates and joint custody, the hellish life of a child whose parents never stop bickering and repeatedly fail in their promise "to do better," parents who act how they want and justify it with the phrase "for the good of the children." They were part of a generation that learned to fear certain sentences: *Your father and I need to talk to you kids*; *Your father and I still love you*; *It's not your fault*; *Sometimes people fall out of love.*

Many members of that generation dreaded the appearance of a person like Michelle Troconis and imagined screaming, *You're not my mom! You can't tell me what to do!* They feared the late-night ride from house to house, the sad car trips in the rain, the clack of wipers that wake you to a domestic nightmare, weekends in an unfurnished apartment in a strange city or town. Psychiatrists, counselors, court officers—they loathed the prospect. Or the understanding way the teacher looks at you and makes special allowances. They promised themselves that, no matter what else they did in their lives, they would not do to their kids what was done to them.

The author Rick Moody, who grew up in New Canaan and attended Brown, wrote about a marriage gone wrong in his 1994 novel, *The Ice Storm*, set in Fairfield County. When I asked him about it, he described the work as a "depiction of the kids who lived through the social revolution of the 1970s" and "a response to John Updike's Rabbit books from the perspective of the children who bore the consequences of all that libertine behavior."

And yet here they were—Jennifer and Fotis, people who had lived through that era and should have known better, doing to their kids exactly what had been done to their own friends.

Why did they fall into the same trap?

Maybe it was because, having been raised by parents who stayed together, they had no personal experience of divorce. In that case, theirs was a failure of imagination. Or maybe, when you get that deeply embedded in a conflict, when you lose yourself in animosity, you forget everything else. You need someone to slap you in the face and scream, *Wake up! Look what you are doing to your children!*

That someone might have been Hilliard, but Hilliard was gone. It also might have been the judges in Stamford—Judge Colin tried—but most of the judges were too ensconced in the system, or too weak, to stand up to the lawyers who fanned the flames because there is more money in a fire than a rescue.

As the number of filings and court hearings increased, so did Fotis's anger and frustration. Now and then, the depth of his rage could be glimpsed. One afternoon, as he was driving down Chichester Road in New Canaan for a pickup, he spotted Jennifer in the street, walking home from the house of a neighbor. He looked at her; she looked back. Rather than slowing the car, he accelerated. He drove directly at Jennifer. His eyes were empty, exhausted, and black. Then, at the last minute, as if he could suddenly see his own future behind bars, he swerved away. Jennifer ran to the house and fell into Lauren Almeida's arms, crying.

One afternoon in the Stamford courthouse, Jennifer bumped into Lisa Nkonoki, whom she remembered from Renbrook—Jennifer had been the class mother to one of Lisa's grandkids. Jennifer knew Lisa was a life coach who'd helped grease the skids in several high-profile divorce cases. When Jennifer asked for advice, Lisa handed over a business card. They met, talked, and texted several times in the weeks that followed.

Lisa told me Jennifer did not seem well. She seemed stressed. She'd been through a lot and still had a lot to go through. She told Lisa she expected to pay $1.8 million before it was all over. These lawyers and these courts hire doctors and psychologists, said Lisa, but does any of it help?

"Jennifer's lawyers let her believe she was going to get sole custody, but that was never going to happen," Lisa recalled. "You are letting people ratchet this up. You are still going to have to co-parent. Those kids deserve to have both parents. The court can't solve this fiasco."

She then described the dangers of a situation like Jennifer's: "People are always scared in criminal court, but those criminals have already done their crime. It's civil court you need to be concerned with. You

don't know anybody's mental state. And when you leave the courtroom and they say, 'You're divorced or lose custody,' you don't know
how people are going to respond."

Fotis met Lisa in the courthouse a week or so later. He knew that
she'd been talking to Jennifer and wanted to tell his side. "He said, 'I'm
a father trying to fight to get my kids,' blah, blah, blah, blah," Lisa said.
"He was well put together, very handsome, but, to be honest, he cried
broke constantly. I'll never forget. He was wearing a rust velvet jacket
and a really nice watch. I listened to him for a little while, then said,
'Well, I'll see.' I didn't really know the story, but it sounded like he was
being treated unfairly. He wasn't able to see his kids."

Lisa arranged to meet Fotis at her house but changed her mind after she'd made some calls. One of those was to Richard Gordon, a developer whose son David had built her house. David's son Mason had
been at Renbrook with the Dulos children. Richard told her about a
party at the Dulos house to which everyone in the class was invited but
Mason. That bothered Lisa. She later learned that Fotis had crossed the
kid's name off the guest list because he didn't want the son of his com-
petitor in his home. Lisa thought that was crazy. She then called one
of the Duloses' neighbors, another Renbrook family. They had moved
from New Canaan into a Fore Group house. They told Lisa there had
been problems with the property. When asked for redress, Fotis became incensed. He could not stand being criticized. From then on, he
would not even acknowledge their existence. It was icy. "Not a good
person"—that's what Lisa was told. "Don't get in his way. Don't cross
him. He's very vindictive."

Lisa asked herself, *Do I really want to be alone with this person?*
The answer being no, she moved the meeting down the street to Rebel
Dog Coffee, where she and Fotis talked for about an hour. Fotis did a
lot of complaining. He felt sorry for himself. "He wanted everything,"

said Lisa. "He wanted the money, he wanted the kids, he wanted the girlfriend, he wanted his soon-to-be ex-mother-in-law to pay for all this shit." She added, "What the court did to him—kept him from his kids—wasn't right, but what he wanted wasn't right, either."

She went on: "Then he started talking about Troconis. He said, 'My kids like my girlfriend better than they like their mother.' I snapped. I said, 'Why would you tell me anything like this? That's not helpful. I'm not the lawyer. I'm trying to help you with your kids. Being negative about their mom does not help. You shouldn't ever say those things.'"

"In the end, I think it really became a question of money," Lisa told me. "Jennifer, her mother, and the lawyers were going after Fotis's business and house, and I think that's when he started to panic. He suddenly realized he could lose everything."

The Fore Group, which had built or renovated forty-five homes since 2004, had just a handful of projects in the works by 2018. Meanwhile, the company's outflow of cash swelled to a torrent. There were the usual business fees—land taxes, salaries, permits, equipment, supplies—plus the cost of living. Food, mortgage, travel. A mistress is more expensive than a wife. There was the astonishing price of the divorce itself: the lawyers, the shrinks, the guardian ad litem. Jennifer covered the vast majority of these fees, but Fotis still owed more than he could pay. He was $4.5 million in debt. Some of this was owed to banks, but a large part was owed to the Farbers. In the interests of the grandchildren, Hilliard might have let the debt slide, but Gloria was less forgiving. She demanded repayment. When Fotis balked, Gloria sued.

"Hilliard Farber had fronted Fotis Dulos millions of dollars over the years for mortgages and land acquisitions," *The Providence Journal* reported in 2019. "After Farber's death in January 2017, the flow of funds ceased, and Dulos, according to a lawsuit by Hilliard Farber's estate, stopped re-paying the loans. Dulos now owes $2.5 million, the lawsuit states."

Fotis carried on as if nothing were amiss, as if he had money to burn. In August 2017, Michelle and Nicole, who'd been spending every free weekend at 4 Jefferson Crossing, finally made the move from Miami to Farmington. Nicole would attend Renbrook in the fall. Fotis said he tried to hide this, but Jennifer found out when he "accidentally" sent a picture of himself behind the wheel of a rented moving truck flashing what looks like a gang sign. Jennifer suspected the picture was "accidentally" sent because Fotis wanted to rub her face in it. He's sticking out his tongue in the picture.

"This is the lovely photo Fotis sent to me (and Lauren!) as a 'mistake,'" Jennifer wrote in a note she sent with a JPEG. "Him driving Michelle's stuff to Farmington from Miami. Thanks, Fotis, for the gesture."

"That's one thing I never could understand," Lisa Nkonoki told me, referring to the way Michelle took up residence in Jennifer's house, room, life. "As a woman, I'm thinking, 'How crazy is this dumb girl? I don't care what you call her . . . How dare you think you're going to move in? To me, it's just crazy.'"

Michelle's daughter, Nicole, bunked in Clea-Noelle's bedroom. Clea-Noelle had to share it with Nicole when she visited Farmington. Referring to her children's visits, Jennifer said, "I just think being in the house, which isn't quite their house anymore, there are pictures on the wall of Petros as a baby next to Nicole as a baby, and it's strange. Noelle's room, she walked in there with an N on the chair, and she said, 'Oh, Daddy, did you redecorate?' That's now Nicole's room."

Jennifer continued: "While I don't doubt Fotis may love the children,

I don't think he takes into consideration that they also need to have a process, and go through things. I think he's just rushing what's good for him without thinking that these are children in a divorce and there are stages and we have to go slow and be careful and not just say this is the new reality because it works for me."

Nicole's enrollment in Renbrook caused a stir among the eleven-year-olds and their parents. "I remember being at a playdate with my grandson in Rocky Hill when the moms were all talking," said Lisa Nkonoki. "Because I was older, they regarded me as a bit of an elder statesperson. They called me over to ask my opinion. 'Hey, G.G., there's a girl who was just put in with the fifth grade and we're going to have a sleepover, but we don't want her to come. The mother's having an affair with the father. What do you think?' And I'm like, 'Why would you hold something like that against a fifth grader? She's a kid! She's in the middle of it!' I hated the fact that Fotis and Michelle put all those kids into this ugly situation. Why did Nicole have to go to the same school?"

Jennifer filed a complaint. She believed Fotis had violated the court order by moving Michelle and Nicole into 4 Jefferson Crossing. Fotis swore that he kept Michelle away whenever the Dulos children visited. When Jennifer called this a lie, Fotis characterized her incredulity as paranoia typical of the Farber family.

Fed up with Fotis and his obfuscations, Jennifer switched attorneys, replacing Eric Broder, who is known for settling, with Reuben Midler, who is known for waging zero-sum divorce campaigns. It's not uncommon for the parties in a contested divorce to change lawyers in the middle. It tells you the proceedings have entered a new phase. Act 1 is over. Act 2 begins. The moment Jennifer replaced Eric Broder with Reuben Midler is akin to the moment Michael Corleone fired Tom Hayden because Tom Hayden was not a wartime consigliere.

Jennifer's friends were concerned about this change in personnel. They knew it meant the war would escalate. "She told me about it in New York," said Dan Rybicky. "She told me she'd brought in this really tough divorce lawyer. I heard about the fight that was going to ensue. I think the term was 'scorched-earth lawyer.'"

Why did Jennifer do it? Why did she hire a wartime consigliere?

Maybe it was Gloria. Hilliard had looked into Fotis's eyes and saw madness and instability—what Philip Roth called "the indigenous American berserk." He treated his son-in-law accordingly, carefully. Not because he was scared of Fotis. Because he was scared *for* Jennifer. Gloria saw Fotis just as clearly as Hilliard had, but, unlike Hilliard, did not fathom the rage of the thwarted narcissist. Hilliard would have paid Fotis to exit: *Here's money, good luck, goodbye.* Gloria refused to bend. Rather than pay, she demanded the return of what had already been loaned—hence the lawsuit. Not because she needed it. Maybe because she wanted him to suffer. Gloria squeezed Fotis because Fotis deserved squeezing.

Or maybe it was Jennifer. She did not expect to win money in the divorce. It was not money she was after. It was recognition.

Bringing in the new lawyer was the beginning of the end. "That's what tipped Fotis into the red," said D. J. Paul. "Jen was poking a bear. She had every right to do that, and I understand why she wanted to. But I'm not sure it was the wisest move. When she told me how crazy the divorce had gotten, and how crazy Fotis had become, I was like, 'Jen, if you really think he's that crazy, why are you antagonizing him?'"

Every psychiatrist and lawyer I've spoken to described Jennifer's behavior as typical. She'd invested her entire life—her love, her money, the money of her parents, her past, her future, her identity—in a man who treated it all with disregard, then, when she protested, accused her of being "certifiably crazy." For her, the divorce court was the place to seek justice. Of course, a person with more worldly experience, a person like her father, would have known the ugly truth: there is no justice, not in this world.

"It's the oldest story," D. J. Paul said. "How many breakups have you witnessed where one side tries to exact a price from the other? And people usually have the same reaction: 'Why don't you just settle and move on?' Why? Because they want the fight, because the person on the other side should be punished. And yes, it sounds to me like Fotis really did deserve to be punished. But my question to Jen was, 'Is it worth it?' To me, he sounded like someone you wanted to get as far away from as quickly as possible."

When Jennifer replaced Eric Broder, Fotis, never one to back down, replaced Alan Rome. Like Broder, Rome was the sort of lawyer who settles. Jennifer had hired a wartime consigliere, which meant Fotis needed a wartime consigliere, too. But unlike Jennifer, Fotis could not afford a top-tier attorney, and, unlike Jennifer, Fotis did not believe there was anyone in the game smarter or tougher than he was himself. So began the chaotic period in the marital unwinding when Fotis Dulos was represented by Fotis Dulos. In court he cast himself as the little guy, the penniless underdog who could not afford a fancy attorney and so was standing up to the legal system alone.

It was not just about fees, of course. It was also about performance. Fotis had been forced to sit on his hands as Alan Rome questioned Jennifer and Lauren in those first hearings, all the while surely thinking,

I could do this better. Fotis wanted to cross-examine his wife personally. He seemed to believe that, once he got her on the stand, he could break her the way he broke her in Farmington.

He made his first appearance as counsel on January 17, 2018, shortly before Thomas Colin retired from the bench and turned the case over to Judge Donna Heller. She'd been a partner at Finn Dixon & Herling when she was appointed to the Connecticut Superior Court by Governor Dan Malloy in 2012. Judge Heller's husband, Norman, is a respected New York divorce attorney. The Hellers live in Riverside, an affluent section of Greenwich. Judge Heller is smiling in her official portrait. She has high cheekbones, blue eyes, and blond hair.

Dulos v. Dulos was a mess when she took over. There'd already been over a hundred filings. There'd already been emergency orders, motions of contempt, charges of perjury, and courtroom outbursts. Judge Heller set ground rules at the start, but you sense, reading the court transcripts, that she was trying to control a situation that was inherently uncontrollable. It was the mercury of human emotion running across a flat table.

In explaining why he'd decided to appear as his own counsel, Fotis pled poverty. Not being rich like Jennifer, he said he simply could not afford to pay a high-powered attorney. Some were dubious, given the fact that Fotis was living in a mansion, traveling the world, and sporting a paramour.

Judge Colin had imposed a temporary co-parenting order that gave Jennifer ultimate decision-making authority. Reuben Midler, Jennifer's new lawyer, wanted it made even more restrictive. Fotis had perjured himself and had routinely violated the court's orders. Midler called witnesses, including Jennifer and the psychologist David Lopez, to the stand to make the case. He was a relentless questioner with a special talent for irritating Fotis Dulos, who snapped at Midler, insulted him, and called him names, drawing nearly constant rebuke from the judge.

Reuben Midler often referred to the defendant as "Mr. Fotis," which Fotis corrected sharply, saying: "Mr. *Dulos.*" At one point, Fotis began addressing Midler as "Mr. Reuben."

Fotis's legal maneuvers played like high drama. This was the moment he'd been waiting for—the chance to get Jennifer and her cohorts under oath and barrage them into confession. He seemingly wanted them to admit that he, Fotis, was the better parent and that the kids loved him more. But whenever he attacked, Midler objected and Judge Heller sustained the objection. Because it was not Fotis's turn to ask questions. Because his questions were leading. Because he had referred to an item not in evidence or a topic not at issue. Judge Heller would not let Fotis browbeat or argue with a witness, or share gossip— *everyone knows Jennifer is crazy*—which she deemed hearsay.

The question at issue on most days was simple: Had Fotis Dulos violated the court order? Had he allowed his children to socialize with Michelle Troconis? But Fotis seemed to think parenting quality was the only topic that really mattered. Which one uses antidepressants and which one stays clean? Which one sees a psychiatrist and which one takes the kids skiing? Which one lost track of a child in London and which one has never lost a single kid? "Judge Heller has ruled against me over and over," Fotis complained. "I am not an alcoholic! I am not a drug addict! I am not an abuser! I am a good father and my children adore me."

Then the big moment arrived: On January 31, 2018, Fotis got Jennifer on the witness stand. He paced before her, hectoring and bullying. For a moment, it seemed as if they were back in Farmington, with Fotis waving a "contract" in her face.

The judge interrupted. "If it gets contentious," she told Fotis, "I will step in and ask you to tell me what you want to know and I will ask Ms. Dulos questions." But mostly she let him go. What did Fotis get out of the encounter other than the satisfaction of the whip hand? It did not help his case, nor did it seem intended to. He seems manic in the court transcript, wildly off topic.

Fotis asked Jennifer, "Have you confided in me that you have genital herpes?"

Midler objected. Irrelevant.

"That's sustained, we will strike that," said Judge Heller.

"It's very relevant," said Fotis, "because of their stating that my affair is—is—and belittling her in the eyes of the children, and I need to explain the affair."

"No," said Judge Heller. "You don't need to explain the affair, Mr. Dulos."

"Is it the truth," Fotis asked Jennifer, "that, for the last six years, our sexual relationship has been virtually non-existent?"

When Fotis did not get the answer he wanted, he'd shout, "Yes or no?! Yes or no?!"

If Jennifer said no when he wanted yes, he'd shout, "Yes!"

Fotis asked Jennifer if she could honestly say that he had mistreated the children.

"You ask the children to lie and say that Michelle was not there when you would have been in contempt of court," Jennifer answered. "It's not in our children's best interest to learn how to lie for your case."

She continued: "And there were weekends where you were all together. I got to hear all about Gaston . . . the father of Nicole . . . He was staying there for five days apparently. This just kept on happening. Every time they were with you, Michelle was there."

Fotis pressed on:

> FD: Do you speak in a derogatory way about me to Petros?
> JD: No.

FD: No? You have never made any comments such as your father did not work enough to make more money?

JD: No.

FD: Your dad is a psychopath?

JD: No.

FD: Your father is an asshole?

JD: No.

FD: Your father is a cheater?

JD: We talked about cheating with Uncle Mark [Masiello, one of Fotis's oldest friends].

FD: Your dad does not care about you?

JD: No.

FD: Your dad will drop you in a heartbeat?

JD: No.

FD: Okay. Your dad only cares about Michelle and Nicole?

JD: No.

FD: Okay. Your father likes Farmington because he's not that smart. Successful people live in New Canaan?

JD: No.

FD: I will make sure this divorce takes two and a half years?

JD: No.

Fotis then called himself as a witness. Because self-questioning would be ludicrous, Judge Heller told him to take the stand and just say what he wanted to say. She called it a narrative. It's really Fotis's side of the story:

Our marriage has been broken down since 2011, but we have continued for the sake of the children. In November 2016, we attended therapy in an effort to salvage the marriage. With regards to the stressors, your honor, I've never put the physical or mental health of my children in any danger. I never speak about the proceedings. I do not disparage their mother to them. Ms. Dulos, on the contrary, contracted body guards and exposed the minor children to their presence . . . At the end of December, the plaintiff took the minor children to visit one of the body guards and hang out and hear stories . . . The children get along famously with Michelle. They get along famously with Nicole. They get along famously with me. The GAL came and visited the house and told me at the end, "I am impressed." Those were his exact words . . . The children are stressed by the plaintiff. She lied to them in June when she took them out of the house and told them they are going to the grave of their grandfather. I have never escalated this conflict. Starting from the very beginning, I was the one that said, "Let's be friends and work this out and let's keep our kids sacred." These were my exact words. "The kids are sacred." I was not the one that filed the emergency ex parte and restraining order. I am the one always making gestures . . . I'm exasperated, your honor. From day one, when these children were born, I've been so active in their lives. I'm the one that has been with them every weekend. I'm the one that sees them every day when they come home from school. My office is attached to the house. They open the door and come in. People think that the babysitter was my wife because they never see my wife with us at any event. The children have traditionally engaged in activities with me and continue to do so. Constantly water skiing. They have done great, all of them. I coach them. I was a parent that was very involved with snow skiing.

I would go there on a Saturday and Sunday and sit and watch them and be there for them. So, when they were cold, they could come in and I would take care of them. I would change their gloves, and make sure their boots are right. I've done horseback riding with them. I've done polo. I have done biking. I have gone on trampolines with them. I have taught them to do flips. I play soccer with them whenever they are with me. Have injuries ever happened? No, the children have never been injured on my watch. And we've been up mountains. We have skied mountains like Ajax [in Aspen]. The seven-year-old went down Ajax. Nobody ever got hurt with me. I was accused of having controlling, volatile and delusional behavior. What allegations have been made to support—there is nothing—to support this claim? There has been no support. I was never treated for mental illness. I am not taking medication. I don't do drugs. I don't smoke. I don't drink. I am an athlete. I don't use babysitters or caretakers. I take care of the children. I have never lost a child, unlike the plaintiff.

Judge Heller issued a decision on March 1, 2018: Fotis's visitation rights were suspended and sole physical custody was temporarily awarded to Jennifer. This did not mean Fotis could not see or talk to his children, only that the visits had to be supervised and would be at Jennifer's discretion.

For Fotis—who believed not only that he was the better parent but also that, as the father, the man, he should be in control—it was a brutally emasculating moment. The fact that the ruling had been made by a Jewish woman must have made it even harder for him to accept. For Fotis, this was another turn of the screw.

Judge Heller cited Fotis's behavior in making her ruling. She castigated Fotis, saying that he "does not seem to appreciate in any respect the consequences of lying under oath and willfully violating a court order. His facility in testifying falsely to the court suggests that he is equally comfortable in encouraging the children to lie to achieve his desired outcome."

She said the limits she had placed on visitation were not meant to be punitive but protective: "There is an immediate and present risk of psychological harm to the children if they have unrestricted and unsupervised contact with the defendant, as well as a risk of physical danger."

The decision worried the guardian ad litem. Michael Meehan has been demonized, but he was probably the case's only honest broker. He was dealing with constant incoming from Jennifer and Fotis, the lawyers and doctors, while trying to keep the interests of the children in mind. The fact that, at one time or another, everyone involved was angry at Meehan suggests he was actually doing his job.

"I am concerned that we are now inadvertently alienating the children from their father," Meehan said of the new orders. "These children desperately are seeking some level of consistency in interaction with both parents on a regular and consistent basis. [The current situation] is not helpful for the children, nor has it been helpful for these children in their individual relationships to each parent. The children are very vocal. All of them want more time with their dad. They want to see their father.

"The process is starting to wear Mr. Dulos down," Meehan continued. "I am concerned about this because [Fotis] needs to continue to put forth his best effort on behalf of his children. I say that with respect, because what he needs to do is trust the fact that no one is trying to punish him here in this process. We are actually trying to help the children and in turn help him."

Meehan's testimony was an alarm that caused Judge Heller to order a psychological evaluation of the parents. This evaluation, which was ordered in the spring of 2018 and was finally filed a few weeks before Jennifer's disappearance, hung over the case until the end. Never released to the public, it's the black box amid the wreckage.

Fotis Dulos could have taken Judge Heller's ruling as an occasion to back off and calm down. It was in his interest to lower the temperature, make nice with the judge, and act like a reasonable person. If he did not like the new orders, the best solution was to move as quickly as possible to settlement or trial. In a contentious divorce, such temporary orders, though seemingly harsh, are usually meant to separate the parties only until they've cooled off.

But Fotis was too angry to let the process go forward. Instead of accepting the ruling, he tried to have Judge Heller removed. And he did it in a particularly dishonest way. Perhaps he'd seen a courtroom drama in which a judge, noting a personal interest in a lawsuit—maybe it involves the Exxon *Valdez* and the judge's husband, who owns shares in the company—is forced to recuse herself. Perhaps he'd read a story in *People* about a Hollywood producer who, in preparation for a divorce, consulted every powerful lawyer in Los Angeles, who then, because they'd talked to the husband, could not represent the wife. Whatever the motivation, not long after Judge Heller had taken over the case, Fotis scheduled a telephone appointment with the lawyer Norman Heller. Fotis told Mr. Heller that he was in the middle of a contentious divorce; explained the details (Jennifer lied, kidnapped the kids, and so on); told Heller he wanted to hire him; and then balked, supposedly, at Heller's $25,000 retainer.

A few days later, Fotis claimed that he had consulted Norman Heller about the divorce without realizing Norman Heller was married to Judge Donna Heller. The fact that Mr. Heller took the meeting, Fotis argued, suggests "a reasonable appearance of impropriety." Fotis requested that Judge Heller be replaced. His request was denied.

Fotis then filed a complaint against Judge Heller with the Connecticut Judicial Selection Commission. He said the judge should be removed because she was biased against him as a Greek. This second request was also denied.

Fotis continued to breach court orders. He violated both the letter of the law and the spirit. Since he was not allowed to talk to his children unsupervised, he had friends reach out with messages and information. When caught and scolded by Judge Heller, Fotis, referring to one of his sons, said something like, "Are you telling me that the boy cannot talk to or share messages with his own godfather?"

The most egregiously maddening violation took place in April 2018, when Fotis and Michelle toured the New Canaan Country School, where all five Dulos children were in attendance. Fotis said they did it with the possible intention of enrolling Nicole the following semester, a ludicrous proposition, considering it would mean an hour-plus commute each way. Michelle's presence at the school unsettled Jennifer, who seemed to consider it stalking. She reported the incident to Michael Meehan, who then talked to Fotis.

"When confronted with the issue, he recognized that it was poor judgment on his part," said Meehan. "He did not think he would interact with the children given the fact that they were in school that day when, lo and behold, he in fact did encounter the children while traveling through the campus of the school."

"Michelle wanted to have an interview at the school," said Fotis. "I knew the children's break is from 10:20 to 10:35. So I asked her to make the appointment sometime not during the break. She made the appointment for 10:00 a.m. We arrived shortly after 10:00. I got out of the car and walked her about two hundred feet to the admissions office. I opened the door and she went in. I returned to my car and left. I didn't spend any time in the school. I know the counselor alleges that I was taking a tour, that I was there all day. That's a false statement. I was there probably for less than three minutes. On the way to the admissions office, Theodore's class came out from the building across the street. They were supposed to be in class. I saw Theodore. Theodore saw us and came towards us. I said hello to Theodore, and I said, 'Go on with your class.' I thought that was the appropriate action. I didn't want to ignore my son. I didn't want to engage and I didn't interact with him. I just said, 'Hello.' And I said, 'Theodore, go on.' I never took a tour or entered any building in the school."

For every breach, Fotis offers the same explanation: the other person is lying. *Jennifer is lying about the marriage. The marshal is lying about the ex parte papers. Dr. Lopez is lying about my coaching the kids to lie. The New Canaan Country guidance counselor is lying about the tour.*

Before Michael Jordan shaved his head in 1988, men clung to their hair, no matter how little of it they happened to have. If three wisps remained, they prized those wisps, which they gelled and combed back to front. Such men were in search of "coverage." In some cases, that meant long in back, sparse on top. In others, it meant miracle treatments, Rogaine, implants, or hair plugs. But after Michael Jordan shaved his head and appeared on TV as a chrome-domed futuristic warrior, a certain sort of man, seeking to join the ranks of the powerfully neat, shaved the wisps and faced the world pure and bald—on the field, in front of students, and in the courtroom. For the most part, these bald professionals tended to be of a certain class—aspirational graduates of schools not one but two tiers below Ivy. They were strivers, the last believers in the dream. They drove BMWs and Audi 2000s and played adult softball on the weekend. While others downed Gatorade or talked about stocks on the sideline, they wiped the sweat from their bald heads with a single confident towel stroke.

When Fotis and Jennifer decided to divorce, they went through a portal into a strange world—an invisible world that had always been just a stumble away, a world of not only shyster lawyers, over-billers, and bullshitters, but also strivers, men (all the lawyers involved in this case were men) working for what Jennifer and Fotis already had but were pissing away in a great judicial stream: mansions with three-car garages and outdoor ovens, vacations in Aspen, country clubs, private tutors and private coaches and private schools. For whatever reason, the lawyers who populated this legal netherworld tended to be Michael Jordan bald. Michael Meehan was bald. Fotis's lawyer Rich Rochlin was bald. And Jacob Pyetranker, whom Fotis, perhaps realizing his turn at self-representation had been a disaster, hired to represent him in the spring of 2018, was bald as well.

Pyetranker, who attended Fordham and St. John's, was forty years old when Fotis retained him. He is crossing his arms in the photo on his website. He wears an expensive-looking blue suit, a lavender shirt, and a matching checkered tie. His sandpaper stubble and arched eyebrows bring out his magnificent baldness. His smile radiates confidence. It says, "I've got this." And yet, for Jacob Pyetranker, getting involved in the Dulos divorce so late in the day must have been like stepping onto a train that was already moving a hundred miles an hour.

"I came into the case after Mr. Dulos decided to represent himself, and that didn't go very well," Pyetranker explained.

Pyetranker spent much of 2018 counseling Fotis, highlighting the absurdity of the legal proceedings—hundreds of hours spent trying to determine who would get to spend more time with the kids—and arguing with Reuben Midler. If Pyetranker, who had once worked at Midler's law firm, did not actually dislike Midler—courtroom fury can seem about as real as that of the WWE—he did a good job pretending, as the following exchange shows:

From: Reuben Midler
To: Jacob Pyetranker
Sent: Friday, April 20, 2018, 10:23 a.m.
Subject: RE: Defendant's request for Birthday call to Petros and Theodore today at 5:30 PM pursuant to terms and conditions
Importance: High

Dear Jacob:
I will not attempt to point out how your statements are mere polemics devoid of substance and demonstrative of a lack of an understanding of the outstanding orders of the Court in this case. I suggest that you read the last page of Judge Heller's orders of March 1, 2018 with respect to her granting of the Plaintiff's Motion for Emergency Custody, and then reference the orders of July 25, 2017 by the Hon. Thomas Collin [*sic*],

J. (Ret.) set forth on pages 2 and 3 of the Court's decision. A copy of that decision is attached for your convenience. In particular see orders #s 11, 12, 15, thereof.

I hope the foregoing clarifies what the orders are which are requirements for the call. Your client should also be aware and recall the comments of the Hon. Donna Nelson Heller, J., as the negative effect that any crying would have on the children.

Please confirm that Mr. Dulos will adhere to the outstanding court orders.

I await your advice.

Sincerely yours,

Reuben S. Midler, Esq.

~

From: Jacob Pyetranker
Sent: Friday April 20, 2018, 10:42 a.m.
To: Reuben Midler

Reuben: You're being a complete ass.

Jacob Pyetranker arrived as a voice of reason. That's how he sounded when he stood before Judge Heller, arguing for his client: this case has gone on too long, become too punitive, expensive, and mean. That's how he sounded when he questioned witnesses and made statements. But you also get the sense that he arrived too late. The parties were locked into their narratives. No matter who entered the collective dream and no matter how much they pleaded, the dreamers would not wake up.

Pyetranker started by addressing a situation that began before he was retained. The episode became a focus of much press interest later, when the Dulos divorce became a crime story. Because it had the elements of film noir: a beautiful heiress, a handsome husband, and the hint of underworld violence. It was the first time physical harm was threatened. The fact that it seemed backward—Fotis claimed that he had not threatened Jennifer but that Jennifer had threatened him—is telling. The man who brings violence into the conversation is the man with violence on his mind.

According to Fotis, Petros told him that Jennifer said she had paid someone in the mafia to break his legs. When Judge Heller shot down the credibility of the claim—"To the contrary," the judge wrote, "the evidence supports the conclusion that the defendant fabricated the charge and then pressured at least some of the children to repeat it"—Fotis amended his claim slightly, saying, in essence, "The mafia *could have* broken my legs."

Jennifer accused Fotis of inventing the entire story. Fotis responded by email:

> From: Fotis Dulos
> To: Jennifer Dulos
>
> Jennifer,
> It is easy enough for Mike to confirm the allegations—he can just speak to the children. There are a lot of derogatory and false things you say about me on a continuous basis and despite my repeated requests to you to cease to do so. There is

even a motion about this. However, recently you reached new heights by saying to Petros and Theodore: "I can have the Mafia break your father's legs with a baseball bat." Obviously, this is a highly disturbing comment not just to me, but especially for our children. Needless to say they said "Mommy has changed recently." This is a mild way to put it.

Best regards—Fotis

~

From: Jennifer Dulos
To: Fotis Dulos

Dear Fotis,
What you wrote never happened. There is no truth here.

Regards—Jennifer

Fotis became angry when Dr. Lopez tried to get to the bottom of the story. The psychiatrist believed he was being threatened by Fotis, who said, "Things need to change or you will regret it."

Later, when asked what that meant, Fotis said the process was hurting the children and that everyone involved—the judge, the guardian ad litem, the attorneys, the psychiatrist—would "regret it."

Dr. Lopez quit the case. It was his job to treat a patient to the best of his ability, which did not include risking his personal safety.

Fotis's response was a cosmic shrug: "Because Dr. Lopez is faint of heart, I'm supposed to not express my views to him? And what is he doing evaluating me anyway? His job is to treat Petros."

From this point on, the conflict focused almost entirely on the issue of visitations. Every email and argument was about where and when a drop-off would take place, what could or could not be said or done on a playdate, what would or wouldn't be eaten for dinner, who could be present and who was verboten. Notes taken during these sad afternoons and evenings read like an omnium-gatherum of the playlands, go-kart parks, waterski ponds, diners, and main streets of suburban Connecticut.

Divorce can have an adverse effect on children, especially when it's as contentious as the Duloses'. Symptoms can worsen in children with anxiety, and new conditions can appear. Young children often feel they have to choose one parent over the other—an impossible situation. They often turn on the more tolerant parent, believing that parent will react less harshly to a perceived betrayal. Some kids act out. Others withdraw. Some become compulsive. Others lose faith in the very notion of marriage and the institutions that represent adult authority. Church. School. Town.

The Dulos children continued their regular activities, most of which involved sports, but, for the first time, began to resist. Fotis noted his older sons' reluctance to wake up early and spend all day at the pond, or to travel overseas for competitions. Jennifer saw a new neediness in Petros, who often came into her room late at night. Children are told not to blame themselves for a divorce, but of course they do. The Dulos kids were lucky in that the family had resources that allowed them to see doctors who helped externalize issues that might otherwise have eaten them up from inside. They were even luckier to have one another. They clung together in the way of those in the midst of a disaster. But as bad as the situation was in the spring of 2018, when the divorce was raging and the kids were being passed like a baton from parent to parent, it would soon get worse.

Visitations had to be held in contained areas so that the court-assigned monitor could keep an eye on everything at once, record each notable comment, and intervene if the chatter veered into a forbidden area. You would see the monitor, usually a young woman assigned by Dennis Puebla, the owner of the monitoring company, typing notes into her phone at the perimeter of the primal scene. According to one source, Fotis got angry when the kids said that Jennifer had called him a Turk. He spent the rest of the visit giving the kids lessons in Greek. Jennifer wondered if these lessons might in fact be a way to pass secret messages. Another source claimed Fotis went flying into a rage when one of the kids said that Jennifer had called Fotis a cheater. *Does she mean I am a cheater because of Michelle, or King of the Pond?*

According to that source, Clea-Noelle questioned her father about his first marriage. He asked how she knew about it. She said her mother had told her. It was wrong for the children to know about that, said Fotis, who then changed the subject.

The kids "all say their mom uses bad language, especially when she receives communications regarding the divorce," Fotis complained. "She drops F bombs and treats the children badly. Christiane said that Jennifer said to her 'get the fuck out of here.' The two older boys said she constantly calls [me] an asshole. They said she breaks down and cries and then hugs him and comforts him by saying 'We'll get through this together.'"

With the parties still hung up on the preliminaries, Judge Donna Heller asked a colleague, Judge Michael Shay, to preside over the case for a few days in December to see if he could get these people to move ahead with the divorce.

Judge Shay tried to impose order. When Fotis called Reuben Midler "a liar," Judge Shay scolded him, saying, "We don't talk like that here in court. Mr. Midler is a well-respected member of the bar. This is a legal process. Take it outside guys if you want to do name-calling or want to duke it out. Do it on the courthouse steps, but please don't do it here."

When Midler slammed a book on a table, glared at Fotis, and said, "I can't work with this man," Judge Shay said, "Mr. Midler, I don't need histrionics. I don't need slamming books. I don't need any of that. Nobody needs that. All right? You guys, as I said, take the bad blood outside. You guys leave it at this door. I don't want to hear this. All right? We all know how to conduct ourselves like gentlemen and ladies. We're going to do that. In courtroom 6F, you put the mask on. I don't care what you guys do on the courthouse steps."

Finally, in the way of an exasperated prophet, Judge Shay said, "I'm assuming this case is going to Middletown."

In Middletown, the judicial branch of Connecticut has turned a regional family docket into a "special" court, which, according to the law office of Brian D. Kaschel, "hears lengthy, contested cases involving children." Middletown is akin to a court of last resort. When a proceeding becomes debilitatingly contentious, the lawyers and clients are sent to Middletown, where the case is heard on consecutive eight-hour days until it's done. No one likes the prospect of Middletown, especially the attorneys, most of whom stay at the Wesley Inn, the sort of nondescript dump you remember only if you've been in a fight there. It's like going to the mattresses. Testify all day, sit at the hotel bar all night. When a judge starts talking about Middletown, it means the system itself has lost patience. "There are certain cases," said Judge Shay, "that from day one are basically Middletown-bound."

~

Judge Thomas Colin, who oversaw the first few court sessions, had warned Fotis and Jennifer at the outset. He had told them to settle their own affairs. If they could not, it would be up to the government. That's why we have a divorce court. It's the machinery of resolution, but it's clumsy and dehumanizing.

Fotis and Jennifer soon understood what that machinery looked like. It looked like Michael Meehan and David Lopez and Dennis Puebla and Donna Heller and Michael Shay—the guardian ad litem, the psychiatrist, the monitor, the second judge, and the third. It also looked like Dr. Stephen Herman, the psychiatrist hired to interview the parents and write the evaluation that, in those last months of 2018, was anticipated in the way of test results. In judging the fitness of each litigant, the report would seemingly determine the fate of parental visitation.

Because Dr. Herman, a white-haired man in his sixties, could give me no specifics about the case—he's bound by the rules of confidentiality—I asked about his career and his process in general instead.

"I was a pediatrician first," he told me. "I trained at the Mayo Clinic in Rochester, Minnesota, then practiced in Pennsylvania. I was frustrated by the fact that I had a waiting room full of kids and parents but never enough time to really talk to them, so I left for a year to think, went to work for Pfizer, then realized what I actually wanted was to become a child psychiatrist, but to do that, you first have to become an adult psychiatrist, which is my way of saying I spent a lot of time in school.

"I'm called into a divorce case only when things have gone very badly and can be settled in no other way," Dr. Herman continued. "I interview each parent alone. I ask about their background, biography, education, social history. I ask about their use of drugs and alcohol. I ask each parent what their parents' marriages were like. And how would they describe the house where they grew up? Were they abused physically, sexually, or emotionally? I ask each parent to tell me the story of the marriage, how they met their spouse, the dating, the proposal, and so on. It's not the story I'm interested in, but the differences in how each partner tells it. Certain events or disagreements that might seem small to one loom large to the other—that's interesting.

"Then I talk to each child alone. I talk to their doctors, teachers, speech therapists. I watch the kids together, with each other or with a parent, doing an activity. If they ask me what to do, I say, 'Just hang out.' This makes the parents nervous. They think I'm grading them. I really just want to see how the parent and kids get along. Then I visit each house. I want to see how the kids and the parent interact at home.

"Here's something I never do: I never ask a kid what parent they want to live with. A kid might say, 'I want to live with my father.' In such cases, I will ask them, 'Why?' They might say they love their father more, or that their father is a better cook. The most common answer is, 'Because, if I live with my father, I'll get a puppy.' I could write a book about all the parents who've gotten their kids animals during a divorce."

Dr. Herman spent months working on the Dulos report. He met with each parent around twenty times. Jennifer's side anticipated a document that would strengthen her case. Fotis had been difficult throughout the process. He'd made preparations to contest the report even before it was filed. It therefore came as a surprise when the report, which was finally issued in April 2019—given to the court, sealed by the judge—seemed, from all indications, to conclude that Fotis Dulos was the fitter parent.

On the surface, with the little we know, Dr. Herman's report looks like a "win" for Fotis. How did that happen? Fotis clearly seemed the aggressor—the cheater, the liar, the crazed sports parent who suddenly, after years of marriage, felt the need not only to purchase a gun but to show that gun to his wife.

Jennifer was visibly anxious after months of meetings with lawyers and appearances in court. She'd been prodded, evaluated, doubted, and second-guessed. She'd been cross-examined under oath by her unfaithful husband. Also: the strained pickups and drops-offs, the play-dates and threats, the paramour and the paramour's daughter, the kids being used to manipulate and unbalance. Fotis and Michelle showing up at the New Canaan Country School. The story about the mafia and the baseball bat. Fotis coming at her with the car. His clipped and threatening manner on the phone, his dead-eyed stare in court. The emails and texts, the Instagram posts. And of course the mean little Glock in its mean little case.

Perhaps Dr. Herman caught Jennifer on a few bad days, amid a handful of angry, frustrated moments, and took those moments for the whole, which, if so, was worse than a mistake; it was an injustice. Or perhaps Fotis conned Dr. Herman. Charmed him and fooled him, becoming exactly what the psychiatrist needed him to be—the loving father and abused spouse, the guiltless man facing the challenges of middle age. This had always been Fotis's great talent. He read you, saw what you needed him to be, then became that thing. It's what he did with Jennifer. It's what he did with Michelle. It's what he did with loan officers and potential clients. He operated in that zone where salesmanship becomes psychopathy.

Jennifer's lawyer, Reuben Midler, in seeking to have the psychological evaluation thrown out, described it as flawed and not in accordance with the court's orders.

As soon as Fotis had the report, he used it as the basis to file his own ex parte motion. He demanded immediate custody of the children. In doing this, he seemingly copied Eric Broder's original motion and merely swapped the names. This would serve two functions: first, poetic justice—like retrieving a dud incoming missile, fixing it, and firing it back at the enemy; second, frugality. It would save on legal fees. "I'm afraid for the physical safety and emotional well-being of our minor children," Fotis argued. "I am concerned about Jennifer's well-being, and after Dr. Herman's report and Jennifer's diagnosis, I have a better understanding of what has caused, and continues to cause the acrimony in our lives. She plainly cannot co-parent."

All of which makes what happened next especially puzzling.

Part
FIVE

JENNIFER DULOS BELONGED to an American aristocracy. She lived in a world of private schools, chauffeur-driven cars, five-star resorts. It was an Ivy League world in which everyone was credentialed and approved. When there was a faux pas in this world, it usually involved fashion. When there was corruption, it usually involved illegal donations or bribes. When there was a crime, it was usually white-collar.

Fotis led Jennifer from this world into a low-rent landscape of cheap accountants, storefront attorneys, cut-rate intimidators, and mysterious Europeans. Chief among the questionable characters who traveled in Fotis's circle was the fifty-three-year-old Kent Mawhinney, a small-time lawyer with an office in Bloomfield, outside Hartford. Most of Kent's cases dealt with immigration. He represented hardworking immigrants who needed help with their documents. This was not a moral stand. It was business.

Kent Mawhinney grew up in South Windsor, Connecticut, where he still lives. He is slight but paunchy, with slumped shoulders and a bald head—in the old way, a few dirty-blond strands combed over to cover the damage life has done. His expression is perpetually sour. In pictures, he resembles a fidgety animal that wants to run, and does, but always gets caught. Kent coached youth hockey in his spare time, and earned extra money as a referee, which proves that you never really know who is officiating your kid's game.

Mawhinney represented the Fore Group in several cases, including a suit that had dogged Dulos in 2014. The company was being sued by a client, Oladejo Lamikanra, in what amounted to a contract dispute.

This is the man Fotis dreamed of punishing with a brick dropped from an airplane.

Despite differences in appearance and background, Fotis and Kent had the same problem: both men were plagued by an estranged spouse who was making life difficult. Kent's situation seemed worse. His wife had been granted full custody of his fifteen-year-old twin sons, and he'd been accused of rape, arrested, and charged with sexual assault.

According to the *Hartford Courant*, Monica Mawhinney, a certified public accountant in South Windsor, "accused [her husband, Kent Mawhinney] of raping her repeatedly in the early hours of Jan. 21, 2019. The incidents occurred after he had filed for divorce. They were still both living in their South Windsor home but permanently sleeping in separate rooms." Monica Mawhinney said her husband had forced himself on her in lieu of rent. (Kent settled the case in 2022, striking a deal that left him, according to the Manchester, Connecticut, *Journal Inquirer*'s Alex Wood, "with no rape conviction but with a conviction for violating a family violence protective order issued after he was accused of the rape.")

Fotis and Kent, under the same sort of pressure, perhaps entertained the same sort of fantasy: *Wouldn't it be great if my wife disappeared?* Did they attempt to realize their dreams together? Did they make a Faustian bargain? Was it like the Patricia Highsmith novel *Strangers on a Train? You do mine, I do yours. Criss-cross.* Such questions would tantalize the police.

May 19, 2019. Sunday morning. Light rain. Unseasonably cold. Fotis Dulos called Monica Mawhinney. He said he wanted to talk about

Kent. She agreed to meet at Max's Oyster Bar in West Hartford. They sat in a booth in back. The restaurant was empty. Rain dripped from the awning onto the sidewalk outside.

Fotis told Monica that Kent was sorry for what he'd done, still loved her, and wanted to get back together. He suggested she return with him to 4 Jefferson Crossing, where Kent was waiting to apologize. They could use one of the guest bedrooms to consummate the reconciliation.

Monica rejected this offer, then changed the subject, but Fotis kept insisting she return with him to 4 Jefferson Crossing. "No!" she finally shouted. She'd taken out a protective order for a reason.

Monica called her lawyer and the cops as soon as she got home. According to the police report, "Dulos abruptly paid the bill and left when [Monica] insisted she would not meet Mawhinney." The police report also explained that Monica "felt she was being 'baited' and was uncomfortable with the fact that Dulos kept inviting her back to his residence. She stated that she believed that Dulos was 'indebted' to Mawhinney and that she believed Dulos was working on behalf of Mawhinney to get rid of her. She believed 'Mawhinney wanted her dead.'"

Jennifer had moved into the house she'd purchased at 69 Welles Lane in New Canaan, the $4 million mansion less than a mile from the New Canaan Country School.

By purchasing a house in New Canaan, Jennifer would have been letting Fotis know the move was permanent and that the children's lives would, in some sense, continue without him. The fact the house was in the monied center of Fairfield County, amid Connecticut's Gold

Coast, which Fotis had never really been able to penetrate, must have salted the wound.

Fotis was supposed to pick the kids up at the new house at 4:30 p.m., May 22, 2019. He said he planned to take them to Grace Farms, a cultural center that sprawls across 80 curated acres in New Canaan. Fotis had taken the kids there before. They'd spent afternoons playing soccer at Grace Farms, speaking Greek, and telling stories outside the Zen center, which can be rented for private events. Somehow, suffering through something as sad as the divorce of your parents is worse in a beautiful place. The sublimity, meant to console, highlights the awfulness.

Fotis usually arrived late for pickups at Jennifer's house, sometimes very late. This time, he was early. Per court order, visitations were not to proceed in the absence of a court-sanctioned monitor. Dennis Puebla, who owned the monitoring company, usually sent an employee to handle the task. But Fotis arrived so early that last day that he beat the monitor, a young Black woman named Sidnee Streater, by thirty minutes.

Jennifer told Fotis to leave and come back at the agreed time. She did not want him on the property without the monitor.

The kids were waiting out front when Fotis returned. He parked the car and got out. Fotis had always been proud of his thick, flowing hair. Now it had been shaved. The kids commented on this with astonishment, and ran their fingers across his scalp. It made him look smaller—skinny and gaunt and more than a little like a Fore Group employee, Pawel Gumienny, who shaved his head.

"He did end up looking like Pawel, to the extent that Pawel [seeing Fotis] commented, 'Hey, you look just like me,'" Detective John Kimball said later.

Gumienny, startled when he saw the newly sheared Fotis Dulos, made a joke of it, saying, "Are you trying to be as handsome as me?"

Fotis told Jennifer he'd gone to a candy shop while killing time. He'd returned with chocolate bunnies, which he handed out to the kids. Jennifer told Fotis that she ate chocolate every day, so he smiled and handed her a bunny, too.

He played basketball with the kids in the driveway as the monitor took notes on her phone.

Fotis and the kids left for Grace Farms at 5:00 p.m. They returned fifteen minutes later. Fotis said Grace Farms was closing soon. He asked Jennifer if they could picnic in her backyard instead.

"Jennifer's agreement was partially attributable to the fact that Sidnee Streater—a third party observer and designee of Puebla— would be at the home monitoring Dulos at all times," Lauren Almeida told police.

Fotis had brought ice cream cake for dessert. He wanted to put it in the freezer. Jennifer reminded him that he was not allowed in the house, and put the cake in the freezer herself.

Jennifer and Lauren operated like waiters during the visitation, bringing and retrieving glasses, silverware, drinks, napkins, plates. According to Lauren, they "placed the food out on the rear patio table and locked the rear mudroom door to prevent Dulos from entering the kitchen."

There was salad, bread, and cake. Then the kids sat over their empty dishes playing a game called "Would You Rather . . ."

At 7:07 p.m., Jennifer retrieved one of the older boys for lacrosse practice.

Fotis and the others played basketball until 7:37, when Jennifer— she'd already allowed Fotis seven extra minutes—said it was time for homework and bed. "The kids hugged Fotis, then went inside," Sidnee Streater reported. "At 7:41, Fotis got into his Chevy Suburban and left."

The following sentences appear in the notebook I carried on visits to the house at 69 Welles Lane. I walked the driveway, the yard, and the street with copies of the arrest warrants and testimony in hand. I was trying to retrace Jennifer's steps, and understand what had happened.

1. Did Fotis arrive early so he could case the grounds?
2. Does the fact that Fotis turned up for that last visitation with a shaved head mean he knew what he was going to do even as he handed Jennifer a chocolate bunny?
3. Did Fotis shave his head in an effort to frame Pawel Gumienny?
4. Did the conclusions of the psychological evaluation report being so favorable to Fotis serve as a justification for his actions?
5. Did it trigger him?

Fotis was back in Farmington in time for dinner. He'd organized a small party—Hutch Haines and his wife, Erin, waterski friends, were there, as was another old friend, Steffen Reich, and his wife, Beth, a domestic violence counselor. Fotis stood over the grill, cooking steak in olive oil. He served Greek salad with the steak, raised his wineglass, and toasted "new beginnings."

Kent Mawhinney reportedly stopped by and spoke to Fotis and Michelle on the front steps at 4 Jefferson Crossing. According to Mawhinney, Fotis said he'd made up his mind to deal with Jennifer.

Why, if the police report is right, did Fotis Dulos finally decide to act?

Was there a particular event or circumstance?

Was there a provocation?

Some suggest it was Michelle Troconis. Call it the Lady Macbeth theory. Michelle had grown tired of the headache and distraction and financial drain of Jennifer and the divorce. She had grown tired of waiting for the marriage to end so her life could begin. She'd shown signs of paranoia in these weeks, telling people, according to the police, that she was worried Jennifer would win the case and somehow cause Michelle to lose custody of her daughter, Nicole. Which does not have to mean Michelle actually told Fotis to kill Jennifer, or even knew it would happen. She'd only have to issue an ultimatum: settle it or we're finished.

Or he might've been pushed by the fact that Jennifer had purchased the house in New Canaan, which would've made it clear to Fotis that, if Jennifer was calling the shots, he'd never get back what he'd lost.

Or maybe it was the financial situation. The Fore Group was going under by May 2019. Fotis had accrued a debt he'd never be able to repay. He owed millions to banks and millions to Gloria Farber, who was forcing him into insolvency. Not even his house, which he built but did not own, was safe. Gloria held the title and would be coming for that, too. In this scenario, Fotis feels the self-pity of Prometheus, tied to a rock, his liver picked apart by an eagle. And even if he won the divorce case, what would he get? A few additional hours of custody a week? A few more parental rights? He'd still be broke. And without money, or access to first-class flights and five-star hotels, how long could he realistically expect Michelle Troconis to stick around? It was a fog through which he would see a single light: The trust funds. Two million per kid. Times five. Not enough to make him rich, but enough to satisfy his creditors. Jennifer was the sole executor of those funds, but what if Jennifer were gone?

Jennifer was obsessed with her dollhouse when she was a girl. Life was perfect there: one father, one mother, three kids. Samantha, James, and William. Or Sophia, Sebastian, and Silas. She attempted to build a real-life version of that dollhouse in Connecticut in her thirties. It fell apart in her forties, but she was not destroyed. She was in fact on her way to establishing a new home, a new life, a new house with foundations in the real world, when the pit opened.

Each day is its own kind of challenge for a single mother of five. May 24, 2019, was about traffic control. Too many kids, too many plans, too few adults. Jennifer and Lauren had worked out a schedule the night before. Jennifer would drop the kids at school in the Chevy Suburban in the morning, go home, have breakfast, then take the Range Rover into Manhattan for a doctor's appointment. Jennifer was very clear about this: she would take the Range Rover instead of the Suburban because the Range Rover is easier to park. Lauren, who lived near Farmington, would arrive at the New Canaan house at 11:30 and get four of the kids from school at 12:30, take them home for lunch, and then drive them into the city to meet their mom. The fifth was going on the bus to have a playdate at a friend's house and would join the others later.

Lauren arrived at the house as agreed. Entering through the garage, she sensed something was wrong. Jennifer had made such a point of saying she would take the Range Rover, yet here it was, in the garage, and the Suburban was gone.

Lauren went in through the mudroom. Jennifer's handbag was on the floor. Would Jennifer go to New York without her purse? An unopened granola bar was on the kitchen table next to a full cup of tea. This was out of character. Jennifer did not leave beds unmade or dishes uncleared. It wasn't even enough for her to carry a mug to the sink. She had to rinse it and put it in the dishwasher.

Maybe Lauren was thinking about this as she dumped out the tea and washed the mug. She reached for a paper towel. That's when she realized the rack was empty. She went to get a fresh roll. What she found, she told police, was "incredibly strange." She'd put a twelve-pack in the pantry the day before. Only two rolls were left. "I wondered what had happened last night that they used ten rolls of paper towels," she said.

Lauren got the kids from school at 12:30, brought them home for lunch, then texted Jennifer.

It was 12:43 p.m. No response. Jennifer usually responded to a text within minutes.

Lauren noticed that the door that led to the backyard was unlocked. Weird. Unless the kids were playing out there, that door was always bolted.

Lauren texted Jennifer again. It was 1:10 p.m. She said they were leaving New Canaan and would arrive at Gloria's apartment by 2:30. No response.

Lauren texted again when she arrived at Gloria's. Maybe Jennifer got hung up with the doctor? But no. Nothing. Then she called. 4:00 p.m. The call went straight to voice mail. "Immediately my stomach sank, and I had a feeling that something was wrong," Lauren said. "In the almost seven years that I have worked for Jennifer I NEVER EVER had a hard time reaching her and NEVER had an issue with her phone being off."

When Lauren got to the doctor's office, she was told that Jennifer had never showed up. "My first thought," said Lauren, "was that Fotis did something." Lauren went outside and began making calls: *Have you seen Jennifer? Where is Jennifer?* There was a beat beneath these questions, a basso profundo: FOTIS, FOTIS, FOTIS.

In Washington, Connecticut, there's an inn and spa called the Mayflower. "Jennifer used to go there whenever she needed to get away for a day or two," one of her friends told me. "She did not get massages or manicures. She did not like to be touched in that way. She'd stay in the room, read and write, and order room service. That was her best time. That's where I assumed she was when they said she was missing. That was thought one. When I called the Mayflower and they said Jennifer had not checked in, my mind went immediately to thought two: Fotis."

Lauren Almeida called Laurel Watts, one of Jennifer's oldest friends. Together they decided to contact the New Canaan police. It was the message from Laurel Watts, taken by a desk officer, that marked the start of the investigation. Lauren, who made her own call, told the police that "a mother of five is missing and is going through a divorce with a man that has threatened her in the past and owns a gun."

Fotis had called Lauren that afternoon. He had a visitation scheduled for the next day—Saturday, May 25, 2019—and wanted to make sure the nanny was there on time with the kids. Having ignored this message—she had been scared to answer—Lauren asked the police what to do. *Is it okay to talk to him?* The police told her to wait—they wanted to contact Fotis first. A New Canaan cop called back a few minutes later to tell Lauren it was fine for her to talk to Fotis.

Lauren called at 8:41 p.m. Jennifer had been missing for twelve hours. Lauren later said she was taken aback by Fotis's behavior on that call. It was a day of surprises. "Fotis never asked me how Jennifer was doing, or when I had last heard from her, or showed any concern about the fact that Jennifer was missing," Lauren explained. "He did ask how the kids were doing and asked if I had all the kids at Gloria's apartment."

Fotis reminded Lauren that he "had a visitation with the kids at 11:00 am Saturday morning." It was Memorial Day weekend. "He told me that I needed to make sure I woke up early enough to leave New York so that I was not late. [He said] the kids really needed him right now, that this visitation still needed to happen."

Night at Gloria's apartment. Sirens on Fifth Avenue. Delivery trucks at dawn. Lauren's phone chimed at 5:39 a.m. A message from Fotis: "GM [good morning] Lauren—any news?"

Lauren skipped the visitation, but Fotis continued to text and call, text and call, text and call, demanding to see the children.

The New Canaan Police station is in a brick building at 174 South Avenue. There are columns in front and a sign over the door. If the department seems small, with just forty-five officers tasked with protecting more than twenty thousand residents, that's because New Canaan has always been one of the safest towns in Connecticut. It's where New York City police go when they ascend to cop heaven. The citizens are rich, the kids future-oriented, the domestics documented. Now and then, an entire year goes by without a single violent episode.

The stories of murder in New Canaan are obsessed over because there have been so few of them. In 1969, a ten-year-old named Mary Mount vanished off her New Canaan street, sparking a manhunt unmatched in town until the search for Jennifer Dulos. Mount's body

was found in the South Norwalk Reserve shortly after her disappearance. The killing remains unsolved. On December 10, 1970, a New
Canaan father returned from his job at Hi-Standard Manufacturing
in Hamden, Connecticut, to find four members of his family—wife,
daughter, son, and mother—slaughtered in their house at 93 Mill-
port Avenue. The murder weapons included dagger, hatchet, hammer,
necktie. A surviving son, seventeen-year-old John Rice, was the only
suspect. "The youth, an avid outdoorsman who was to be promoted
to Eagle Scout last night, is about 6 feet tall and weighs 200 pounds,"
the *Hartford Courant* reported. "He has dark brown hair, wears glasses
and has a severe case of acne." Rice turned himself in on December 16,
1970. He was found not guilty by reason of insanity. In 2021, seventy-
seven-year-old Albert Kokoth killed his seventy-five-year-old wife. He
said he shot her by accident. Though the first shot might have indeed
been a mistake, the second, third, and fourth shots probably weren't.

All to say, when the missing persons call came about Jennifer Dulos, the entire department took notice. The investigation, which would
be the most expensive in Connecticut state history, started with a request to Verizon. The police wanted information on Jennifer's phone:
When had it last been used? What cell tower had it "pinged"? When
you make a call, the signal bounces off the nearest tower and up into
space, reaches a satellite, and then rebounds to the phone of the person
you dialed. With basic geometry—these three points (tower, satellite,
receiver) describe an immense triangle—you can determine the location of any cell phone, present or past.

According to Verizon, Jennifer's phone last pinged a tower near
Waveny Park in New Canaan at 11:09 Friday morning, May 24, 2019.

Captain Andrew Walsh and Sergeant Kenneth Ventresca of the
New Canaan Police Department went to Waveny Park on the night of

the disappearance in search of Jennifer's Chevy Suburban. They found it on Lapham Road near the edge of the park at 8:00 p.m. "The tailgate was backed up against this tree," Sergeant Ventresca reported. "The Suburban was not running; keys were not in the ignition. The gear lever was actually stuck in reverse. The doors were locked . . . You could see the cleanup of the blood-like substance all over the passenger side under a flashlight."

Two different New Canaan cops, Officer Matthew Blank and Sergeant Aaron LaTourette, had gone to Jennifer's house at 69 Welles Lane at around 7:00 p.m. They knocked on the door, heavy service belts creaking. Leaf shadows, night noises. No answer. They phoned Lauren Almeida, who gave them the garage door code. They typed the numbers by the glow of the pad. The door opened. The search began by flashlight. There was what looked like blood on the floor and what looked like blood splatter on the Range Rover.

They continued into the house. The record from their police body cam, which was shown at the Stamford courthouse in 2024, resembles footage taken of the interior of a wrecked ship, the ghostly halls and haunted rooms suggesting sudden disaster. There's an Andy Warhol silkscreen of Jackie O.—Jennifer fetishized America's fashionable wives—a picture of the Dulos children, and, on the second floor, closets filled with children's shoes and clothes. A silver C-shaped—Clea-Noelle?—Mylar balloon is tied to a counter in the kitchen. Straining at its tether, this balloon functioned as a clock—according to a company called Balloon Party Palace, "In optimum environments, mylar (foil) balloons will remain full and taut for 3–5 days"—demonstrating the temporal closeness of zero hour.

"In addition to blood evidence in the garage, there was evidence that someone had attempted to clean up blood," the state police detective

John Kimball, who helped oversee the investigation, said later. "There were what appeared to be swirl marks on the sides of the vehicles."

Officer Thomas Patten, who examined the garage more thoroughly the next day, cataloged additional evidence:

- Blood splatter found on the garbage cans
- Blood splatter on the driver's side door
- Swipes where someone tried to clean up concrete floor
- Partial bloody shoe prints
- A quarter sized blood drop on the right fender on the range rover
- The left front fender had been wiped clean

At this point, per procedure, the New Canaan police called in the Major Crimes Unit of the Connecticut State Police, which had been created to work on just such cases. From there, it became a joint investigation, with the state cops supplying high-tech gadgets and expertise, and the local cops supplying on-the-ground knowledge of the town.

Within forty-eight hours, the investigators, using cell phone and internet data, had pieced together Jennifer's last known whereabouts.

Friday, May 24, 2019:

7:50 a.m.: Jennifer Dulos is seen on neighborhood security cameras driving Chevy Suburban down Welles Lane.

7:58 a.m.: Jennifer Dulos is seen arriving in Chevy Suburban at New Canaan Country School.

8:05 a.m.: Jennifer Dulos is seen on surveillance driving toward the house on Welles Lane.

10:25 a.m.: Jennifer Dulos' Chevy Suburban is seen leaving Welles Lane.

10:38 a.m.: Jennifer Dulos' Chevy Suburban is seen on camera near Waveny Park on Lapham Road.

11:09 a.m.: Jennifer Dulos' phone goes dark.

"Did you ever hear of something called luminol?" an investigator asked Michelle Troconis later.

No.

"Luminol is something we use to look at evidence," said the cop. "To see if blood was somewhere. When it hits blood, it illuminates."

For example, said the cop, we covered the inside of Jennifer's garage on Welles Lane with luminol.

Handing Michelle a photo of the garage, the cop pointed out illuminated patches, saying, "It's all that."

"That's blood?" asked Michelle.

Yes, said the cop. "And who do you think that [blood] belongs to?"

In an interview, Kathryn Pinneri, who in 2022 served as president of the National Medical Examiners Association, told me: "When luminol touches a place blood has been, even if the blood's been cleaned up, it turns fluorescent. If there's been hemoglobin on a surface, the luminol turns blue. You have to turn the lights off to see it. There's an eerie glow. It can also show how much blood has been spilled.

"It depends on the age and size of the person, but, on average, we have about five liters of blood in our body. Most people can tolerate losing as many as two liters of that blood. If you lose three liters and don't replace it immediately, you're going to die."

According to Connecticut's chief medical examiner, James Gill, who worked the case, the amount of blood seemingly spilled in the garage probably means Jennifer Dulos sustained an injury or injuries that would have been "non-survivable" without medical intervention.

Fotis seemed detached when the police got him on the phone that first night. Maybe it was the accent, or all that education, but his demeanor was strangely disengaged. You'd expect a man whose estranged wife had just gone missing to be curious, emotional, confused. But no, nothing. "Mr. Dulos never seemed concerned about his wife," an officer on the call said later.

Officer Thomas Patten asked Fotis to come by the New Canaan police station the next day. There was nothing accusatory in this request. It was standard. The police were trying to find Jennifer, and wanted the husband's help. Fotis said he'd be there at around 12:00 p.m., Saturday, May 25.

Fotis did not arrive until 2:47 p.m. He'd asked Jacob Pyetranker to go with him. Like many of Fotis's decisions, this one was halfway smart. "Halfway" because when the police call you into the station a day after your estranged wife has vanished, it's smart to have an attorney, but *only* "halfway" because Jacob Pyetranker is not a criminal lawyer. He's a divorce lawyer, and he seemed beyond his depth from the start. He got in and out of the criminal case fast, but not before watching his client make a critical mistake.

Fotis arrived before Pyetranker. He should have waited for his attorney in the parking lot, but, because he was an arrogant man who always believed he had everything under control, he went into the station by himself. The New Canaan police officer Thomas Patten and the

Connecticut State Police officer Christopher Allegro met him in the lobby. Detective Patten later said Fotis seemed flustered. He had a look that cops recognize—a person trying to maintain composure, trying to hide out in the open.

Fotis spoke first, another mistake. If you are meeting with police, you should volunteer nothing; even your tone of voice can give you away. Let the police start by telling you what they know.

Fotis asked if there'd been any news about his wife.

One cop said no.

The other said that's why Fotis was there; they needed his help finding her.

Then Pyetranker came in. He told the police that his client would "not be cooperating."

The officers said they were "surprised Dulos would not help."

Pyetranker said he and his client would be leaving.

Pyetranker handed something to Dulos.

"Is that your phone?" one of the cops asked.

Fotis said, "Yes."

The cop asked to see it.

As if subject to mind control, Fotis handed his phone to Officer Allegro.

The cop tapped the screen until the security prompt appeared.

"What's the code?" he asked Fotis.

"0—0—0—0."

Officer Allegro typed it in.

Pyetranker protested, saying that the police officers were not allowed to look at Fotis's phone.

"I'm not looking at it," said Officer Allegro. "I'm securing the phone and data it contains." He added that he was putting the phone in airplane mode until he could get a search warrant.

Pyetranker stared at the cop. The cop stared back. Now and then, when someone is thinking very deeply, you can almost hear the gears turning.

Pyetranker said he needed to confer with his client alone. They went outside to talk. A moment later, without saying goodbye to the police, Fotis and his lawyer got in their cars and drove away.

Was Fotis Dulos capable of murder? That was a key question for the police and a stumbling block for friends. Here was a man who had never been arrested, who, as far as anyone knew, had never committed a violent act, not even during the most intense marital squabbles. How could he suddenly become a killer?

I asked professionals, criminologists, cops, and psychiatrists if a person who commits murder is on the same spectrum as everyone else. That is, can an otherwise healthy person become a person who kills, not in self-defense or in the heat of battle, but with cool premeditation? Or are killers different from the rest of us? There is no consensus, but, according to research, nearly 5 percent of the human population can be classified as psychopathic.

For those closest to Fotis, the best defense can be summed up in one sentence: He was simply not capable of murder. Ethan Fry, writing for the *Stamford Advocate* in July 2019, described his interview with Fotis's sister, Rena Dulos Kyrimi: "[She] is an architect in Athens, where she said Fotis still has many friends and family members who do not believe he would be capable of harming his wife." As Fotis was growing up, Rena, who was thirteen years older, had operated as something like a guardian. A child in such a situation really has three parents. "I almost raised him," Rena told Fry. "I know him so very well."

Those who had seen Fotis and Jennifer argue in Farmington disagree. "I was there when they fought on the lawn," a neighbor told me. "I was there when he got angry. I heard his sick revenge fantasies . . . I don't know what he did or did not do to Jennifer, but I did not consider him harmless."

Fotis left messages for Lauren Almeida on the afternoon of Jennifer's disappearance, then left several more that night. He said he was merely checking in, but what he really wanted was the children. If step one had been "Disappear Jennifer," step two was "Get the kids."

Lauren texted back to tell him the kids were healthy and safe.

"Thanks for your response," wrote Fotis. "Please send me updates every three hours. I do not want to feel that I am pestering you, but please understand that I am the father and I am extremely concerned with the situation."

He asked, for the second time, if everyone was together at Gloria's apartment. Lauren did not respond. Then, at noon on Sunday, May 26, Fotis showed up in Gloria's Fifth Avenue lobby. He tried to walk straight to the elevators, but the doorman stopped him. He'd been told to watch for Fotis. If he turns up, the doorman was instructed, don't let him in. "He is unwelcome in Gloria's residence."

For a moment, while arguing with the doorman, the glassy veneer that Fotis wore all through these tragic hours fell away. His eyes were wild. He must've known this was his best and possibly only chance: *Get the kids and go. Argentina. Greece. The world has amnesia. If you stay away long enough, everything will be forgotten. But if you don't escape now, you'll be trapped like a fly in glue.*

He and the doorman argued. Grunts and curses, the shuffle of loafers on waxed marble. Carrie Luft was in the apartment with Gloria, Lauren, and the kids. What were the kids thinking? They loved their father. He was so close, an elevator ride away, and yet, though they could not know it, he was already gone.

Carrie called 911. Cops from the New York Police Department were there in minutes. They broke up the fight, talked to the doorman, talked to Fotis. He told them that his mother-in-law had abducted his children. He was there to take them home. The New York cops called the police station in New Canaan, where an officer said, "Fotis Dulos is prohibited by court order from visiting with his children unsupervised."

The cops told Dulos to leave. *Go away, cool off.* According to the NYPD, "Dulos ultimately complied." That "ultimately" suggests Fotis was not so quick to walk away.

On Tuesday morning, May 28, Fotis's new divorce lawyer—Michael Rose, the third man on the case—filed papers asking that Fotis Dulos be given full custody of the Dulos children.

The timeline:

Jennifer disappears on Friday, May 24.
Fotis shows up at Gloria's building on Sunday, May 26.
Fotis files for full custody on Tuesday, May 28.

Why full custody?
Maybe because he knew Jennifer was never coming back.

Waveny Park is three hundred acres in the center of New Canaan. Bounded by the Merritt Parkway on one side and Lapham Road on the other, it's an oasis of green fields, dark trees, and meandering trails. There are buildings in the park, including parts of New Canaan High School and "the castle," a twenty-thousand-square-foot mansion built by the Texaco co-founder Lewis Lapham in 1912. Lapham's grandson Christopher Lloyd grew up in the mansion. Before he found his way to acting—famous first as New York City hack Jim Ignatowski in the sitcom *Taxi*, a character given Lloyd's own Eastern Establishment background, then as the mad scientist Doc Brown in *Back to the Future*—Lloyd dreamed of being a herpetologist. According to Timothy Dumas, who spoke to Lloyd about the Waveny estate, the future Doc Brown would "roam the grounds with his best friend, a German shepherd named Ricky. He'd catch snakes in the pond (which I assume the cops searched those many years later) and brought them into the house."

The Lapham family bequeathed the property to New Canaan in 1967. The castle, which has appeared in TV shows and movies, including *All My Children* and *The Stepford Wives*, was designed by the architect William Tubby. Its grounds, which are all arbors, vistas, and ivy-covered gazebos, were laid out by the firm Olmsted Brothers, founded by the sons of Frederick Law Olmsted.

At first, the cops believed that Jennifer had been killed in or near Waveny. The Chevy Suburban had been left in reverse and backed into a tree with its running lights on, suggesting Jennifer had been confronted while in the car, then dragged into the park. That meant her body, which, if found, would turn this into a murder investigation, was hidden somewhere in Waveny Park.

State Police from New York and Connecticut joined in the search of Waveny Park. There were drones, helicopters, dogs. Locals were asked to help find the missing mother. Jennifer was not very well known in New Canaan. She'd lived there for only a little over a year, and her kids went to private school, but many women identified with her situation. Jennifer represented the worst-case scenario, what could have happened to them if things in their marriage had gone terribly wrong. They were scared and angry—at Fotis and the courts and the lawyers and the judges and the system that let Jennifer be erased on a beautiful suburban morning.

It was amid this spectacle that *The New York Times* first covered the story, which appeared on the front page under the headline "Mystery in a Wealthy Town: She Dropped Off Her Children, Then Went Missing." It was one of over a dozen Dulos pieces published in the *Times* alone.

According to the FBI database, "482 wives were slain by their husbands in the United States in 2019." According to the United Nations Office on Drugs and Crime, "47,000 women and girls worldwide were killed by their intimate partners or other family members in 2020."

Why does the Dulos case, compared with the large number of other cases, attract so much interest? Why does the name "Jennifer Dulos" still routinely appear in national newspapers?

Some tell you it's the media's obsession with dead white women. Jennifer was pretty and Fotis good-looking; they went to Ivy League schools; Jennifer was white and her daddy was rich; she seemed to have it all.

But the case resonates for other reasons, too: because the quotidian details are disturbingly familiar; because the story says something about our society, which, though placid on the surface, is roiling beneath; because it expresses a terrifying truth—when a bad person is determined, no amount of money, court orders, bodyguards, or security systems can protect you.

The Waveny Park search turned up nothing. Neither did searches of the car, the house, or the property on Welles Lane. In many such cases, the cops give up. It's nearly impossible to prove a murder without a body. How do we even know Jennifer is dead? What if she ran away? She'd done it in 2000 when she quit the Playwrights Collective. Overwhelmed by the conflict of family and writing life, she got in her car and went to Colorado, where she used the name Jennifer Bey and became a Christian. She dropped off the radar like a struck plane, only to reappear months later. What if she'd done it again? What if Fotis is arrested and tried, then, ten years later, Jennifer walks into a police station? How will that look? Cases like Jennifer's tend to end up in the cold case file. If that's not what happened here, it's only because the cops caught a break.

It came as a result of the warrant that let the police search Fotis Dulos's phone.

Investigators had interviewed Fotis and Michelle. Both had an alibi, and both gave accounts that corroborated the alibi of the other. Michelle said she woke up with Fotis at 4 Jefferson Crossing at 6:40 a.m. on May 24. She said she had sex with Fotis in the shower; made breakfast for her daughter, Nicole; dropped Nicole off at Renbrook; and then went to the Stop & Shop in Simsbury, where she took a selfie with the store robot. She had the photo in her phone with date and time. Alibi. Fotis, who agreed about the wake-up time and shower sex, said he spent the rest of the morning in his office at 4 Jefferson Crossing. He said he took a call from his friend Andreas Toutziaridis in Greece at 10:00 a.m.—there'd be a record of that—then went to 80 Mountain Spring Road, where he was rehabbing a house.

The GPS on Fotis's phone backed up the first part of the story, putting him at 4 Jefferson Crossing that morning. It showed him driving to 80 Mountain Spring Road at 2:00 p.m. and staying there until 3:38 p.m., when the phone returned to 4 Jefferson Crossing. The phone was back at 80 Mountain Spring Road at 5:21 p.m., then—and here was the weird part—went down Albany Avenue and into Hartford. Michelle's phone made the same trip. Weird because people like Fotis and Michelle don't go to Albany Avenue in Hartford, a high-crime drug bazaar, a blighted ghetto, and among the most dangerous places in the state. When I told Jeremy Donnelly, a lawyer who represented Kent Mawhinney, that I planned to visit Albany Avenue, he said, "I wouldn't suggest it, not after sundown. If you do go, don't get out of your car. There are drug lookouts and runners on every corner. You'll get into trouble immediately."

Why did Fotis and Michelle go to Albany Avenue in Hartford on the night of Jennifer's disappearance? It didn't make sense to investigators. When they asked Michelle, she said they'd gone because it was near Starbucks. "To be honest, I didn't know where we were," she said. "Fotis was driving. I looked up and noticed it was a funky area, but I was on the phone."

The investigators called the Hartford Capital City Command Center, aka C4, which surveils trouble spots around the state. On a heat map, these areas—the Hollow in Bridgeport, the East Side of New London—would glow red.

They asked if C4 had any cameras on Albany Avenue in Hartford.

Any cameras?

As it turned out, that stretch of road—Albany Avenue between Baltimore Street and Oakland Terrace—was wired. According to the Connecticut State Police analyst Joshua Quint, there were more than a thousand surveillance cameras in the area in 2019. Investigators requested footage taken on May 24 between 7:00 and 8:00 p.m., when Fotis's phone pinged the local tower. Studying this film, the investigators spotted Fotis's truck, a black Raptor—Connecticut plate 910YFC—sharking up and down Albany Avenue. It would disappear from one camera, reappear on another. Now and then, with the back of the truck still visible in one shot, the front would arrive in another, Fotis and Michelle behind the windshield.

The skin of a gecko is transparent, its organs visible beneath. If you trap a gecko on a wall, it freezes. You can see its shiny black eyes and its tiny abdomen rising and falling. It believes itself invisible, though you are looking right at it. It's not stupid; it's dumb. It does not know what it does not know, which makes it arrogant. That arrogance courts ruin. That was Fotis Dulos on camera in his Ford Raptor. He believed he was invisible, but he was in fact on camera nearly the entire time.

This is a story about marriage, divorce, money, class, status, love, resentment, and hate, but it's also about technology. Fotis Dulos planned carefully and executed smoothly, but he could not beat the technology, which was stunning in its capabilities. It's not that Fotis overestimated himself. It's that he underestimated everyone else.

A report on the relevant C4 footage describes Fotis as a man "in light-colored shirt, dark pants and ball cap getting in and out of a truck." Each time he gets out of the truck, he throws a bag of trash into another garbage can or dumpster along Albany Avenue. The following is a summary of the police timeline:

> 7:31:26 PM: Ford Raptor enters Albany Ave.
>
> 7:32:01 PM: Ford Raptor is seen going east on Albany Ave.
>
> 7:32:07 PM: Ford Raptor turns from Albany Ave. onto Milford Street. Several black plastic bags seen in bed of truck. Truck goes off camera for a time.
>
> 7:39:13 PM: Ford Raptor reappears, stops at Albany Ave. and Garden Street. Man gets out of truck, grabs plastic bag out of the back and puts it in trash can.
>
> 7:40:57 PM: Ford Raptor continues east on Albany Ave. to Center Street, where it makes a U-turn. Ford Raptor

bed comes into view. Truck now holds a single plastic
bag.

7:41:24 PM: Ford Raptor stops at Green Street and Albany
Ave. Man gets out, takes last bag from back, shoves it in
garbage can.

7:50:05 PM: Ford Raptor, no more bags, drives down Albany
Ave. out of camera range.

In one shot, Fotis pushes what looks like a FedEx envelope into a
storm drain at the corner of Albany Avenue and Adams Street. In another, he throws away a "large rigid object consistent with WeatherTech
brand rear cargo liner missing from Jennifer's 2017 Chevy Suburban."

Michelle Troconis sits in the passenger seat, mostly talking on her
phone. She opens her door at one point, leans out, and wipes her hand
on the pavement. You can almost feel the grainy concrete. The police
said this footage showed Michelle disposing of evidence, the act of an
accomplice. Michelle says she was in fact wiping gum off her finger.

The investigators made a crucial mistake of their own. They should
have driven to Albany Avenue to examine the cans, drains, and dumpsters as soon as they'd seen the footage. Maybe because it was the start
of a holiday weekend—Memorial Day—they let forty hours pass before
they searched. The garbage was collected from half the dumpsters on
Albany Avenue in that time. Whatever evidence had been in those
bins was taken to a recycling center, where it was lost amid the general churn and incineration of a Hartford County trash facility. But
half the bins and dumpsters remained untouched, and it was in these
that the police found the evidence that would indict Fotis and Michelle. Twenty-two items were retrieved, including blood-soaked paper towels, a broken mop handle, a bloody sponge, black garden gloves,
black Husky gloves, a bloody poncho, a bloody bath towel, an Intimis-

simi bra, and the extra-small Vineyard Vines T-shirt said to be Jennifer's favorite. The bra was so blood-soaked it was hard to tell if it was white or red. Considering the circumstances, the slogan on the T-shirt seemed cruel: EVERY DAY SHOULD FEEL THIS GOOD. According to the state forensic lab, the blood on these items contained Jennifer's DNA.

Most disturbingly, four bloody zip ties were recovered. "There's little reason to zip tie a dead person, so it is reasonable [to conclude] she was alive when she was bound by the ties and [that] they were used to prevent her escape," according to police.

Investigators retrieved the FedEx package from the drain. "Sucked up" was the verb used to describe this process. There was a set of old license plates inside, the sort you are supposed to return when your new plates arrive. Connecticut: 5T6WBU. Using blue tape and clear adhesive, someone had altered them to read: 516WDJ.

"Fotis was so smart that he was stupid," a detective told me. "He dumped all that stuff on Albany Avenue because he figured no one would look there, and, if they did, they'd just say, 'Oh, someone got stabbed in a gang thing.' But, because there's been such violence, the place is plastered with cameras. Albany Avenue was actually the dumbest place to hide evidence."

"He probably figured another set of bloody towels and zip ties would never be noticed on Albany Avenue," one of the lawyers told me. "And if they are noticed, they'll just be blamed on Black gangs."

"Dulos was trying to frame Hartford's entire Black community," a Hartford cop told the local Fox News station.

What the police did not find on Albany Avenue turned out to be nearly as important as what they did. The murder weapon is the story of that forty-hour delay. C4 footage showed a man pulling a bag from the garbage at Albany Avenue and Garden Street. This man, a homeless person named George who was tracked down by police, told the

Hartford Courant that in the bag he found a bloody pillow—and a hunting knife.

"The homeless man took the knife and put the pillow back into the garbage bag," the *Hartford Courant* reported on January 8, 2020. "He said the knife had blood on it that he wiped off. He said he sold it to a guy named Fudge for $10 worth of crack cocaine. Fudge said he sold the knife for food. It's never been found."

Fotis and Michelle were at the Avon ski club when the story broke. Members had greeted the couple warily. Even if they had nothing to do with the disappearance, their hanging out at the pond while the cops searched for Jennifer seemed grotesque.

When Dana Hinman, the co-owner of the pond, asked, "Where is Jennifer?" Fotis started blathering about his divorce and the fact that Jennifer had run up a medical bill for $14,000. When Hutch Haines, the club's other co-owner, told Fotis it was inappropriate for him to be at the pond, Fotis looked straight through him. Clarifying the point, Haines said, "Go home."

Fotis wandered away from Haines but did not leave the pond. He got a drink from a cooler, then stood looking at the water. Michelle had gone to say hello to someone. Just then, everyone's cell phone buzzed. It was a news alert: "Detectives in Hartford have recovered trash bags possibly related to the Dulos case in city garbage receptacles along Albany Avenue."

"Fotis watched the news story and eventually looked up at Michelle and locked eyes with her," Dana Hinman said later.

Investigators searched many more locations, including the house at 4 Jefferson Crossing in Farmington on May 30, 2019. Michelle's mother,

Marisela Arreaza, was in town then, visiting Michelle and Nicole. "Around 5:30 a.m., Arreaza said she and her 12-year-old granddaughter awoke to police officers at the front door," the *Stamford Advocate* reported. Arreaza "claimed she didn't know Fotis Dulos and her daughter were under investigation at the time, but she figured the law enforcement presence had something to do with the disappearance of Jennifer Dulos."

Michelle's attorney Jon Schoenhorn calls the search a fishing expedition. Detectives spent seventy-two hours in the house, taking nearly everything and photographing whatever they did not take, including, according to Schoenhorn, documents covered by attorney-client privilege. Three generations of Troconis women—Marisela, Michelle, Nicole—left the house under armed guard. "It was like the Wild West, if I may use that analogy," said Schoenhorn. "The police escorted them one by one to get their belongings."

Cop cars, marked and unmarked, blocked the road in front of the house. Neighbors stood at their windows. Everyone knew Fotis, the builder who'd designed the subdivision. They knew Jennifer, too. They knew about the separation and the impending divorce. They had seen and heard the fights, some of which had spilled onto the lawn. They'd seen Jennifer running barefoot down the driveway. They knew she was missing and that the police were searching—and still the arrival of this flashing armada came as a shock, like the fall of a dictator or king.

Crucial evidence was found in the trash at the Fore Group office—scraps of paper covered with writing that investigators branded "alibi scripts," a characterization rejected by the defense. Rejected because the name assumed the conclusion. It told you what you were going to see before you looked.

These so-called alibi scripts were seemingly a rundown, in hourly increments, of everything Fotis and Michelle had done on May 24 and

May 25. They memorialized the details that established the alibis. Michelle said she'd written them at the instruction of Fotis's lawyer Jacob Pyetranker, who told Fotis and Michelle to record everything they'd done the day of Jennifer's disappearance before they forgot.

When the investigators were able to prove that the scripts left out key events—there was, for example, no mention of the trip to Albany Avenue in Hartford—Michelle seemed to obfuscate. "Well, it doesn't include everything," she said. Just "highlights." The scripts were correct, she said, except when they weren't. And that was less untruth than omission.

The alibi scripts and Michelle's statements put Kent Mawhinney, whose role investigators had been trying to determine, in the middle of everything. Michelle's assertion that Kent was at 4 Jefferson Crossing the morning of the disappearance was enough to get a search warrant of his phone records, which showed him talking to Fotis Dulos at 7:30 p.m. on May 24, when Fotis was on Albany Avenue. If Kent knew what Fotis was doing on Albany Avenue, it would make him an accessory after the fact.

A good criminal investigator is like a good novelist in that he or she strategically withholds information. You don't reveal what you don't know, and you don't reveal what you do know. Let people assume and, in assuming, reveal the information *they* have.

Kent Mawhinney's answers were vague and contradictory in his first interview with investigators. He said he'd neither seen nor spoken to Fotis on May 24. The cops did not tell Mawhinney they knew about his 7:30 p.m. phone call. They let him assume they knew nothing and watched him talk. In interview number two, when Mawhinney again said he'd neither seen nor spoken to Fotis on May 24, investigators confronted him with the phone record. Seeking to explain his oversight, Mawhinney said he'd fallen down a flight of stairs on May 25 and could remember nothing as a result.

The detectives expanded the search for Jennifer's body. It's not just safety that the police are expected to bring a community, but also the perception of safety. It's not enough to *be* secure—you have to *feel* secure to be comfortable. The people of New Canaan would not feel safe until Jennifer's killer had been identified and arrested, but, without a body, that would be difficult.

Thousands of acres of Fairfield and Hartford counties were searched, as was every Fore Group property, including 80, 84, and 88 Mountain Spring Road in Farmington and 585 Deercliff Road in Avon. Police combed the trails behind 4 Jefferson Crossing where Fotis and Michelle used to ride minibikes. Some of these went all the way down to the Farmington Reservoir. Lakes were dragged, cellars unearthed, septic tanks emptied. According to *Vanity Fair*, the cops "had a yellow Labrador trained to sniff out electronics search the preserve near [Jennifer's] home, hoping to find her phone, which was missing."

One afternoon, a member of the Windsor Rod & Gun Club, a shooting range that Kent Mawhinney helped found in East Granby, Connecticut, happened upon a freshly dug hole on the property. Six feet long, three and a half feet deep, and covered with a tarp. There was a bag of lime—the sort used to speed the decomposition of bodies—inside. The club member who found the hole said it was "100 percent a human grave."

Knowing about the search for Jennifer Dulos—the news was everywhere—the man called the cops, who waited over a month before excavating. The ground had been filled back in by then. "The police searched the hole and the area around it in August, but they never found human remains, signs of the tarp or of lime," *The New York Times* reported on January 9, 2020. "However they reviewed cellphone data that showed that Mr. Mawhinney's phone had been used near the Gun Club on March 29 [2019] and again at about 11 p.m. on May 31 [2019], a week after Ms. Dulos's disappearance." Mawhinney dug the hole; then, hearing that the hole had been discovered, he filled it back in and hid the tarp and lime—that's the best theory.

How did Monica Mawhinney feel when she heard about the hole behind the Windsor Rod & Gun Club?

When she pictured it, did she see her own grave?

Officers from the Connecticut State Police's Western District Major Crime Squad studied surveillance footage gathered from cameras posted on various streets and highways, including the Merritt Parkway and I-84. There are recording devices everywhere along these roads—at exits and entrances, rest stops, gas stations, junctions—though you won't notice them unless you're on the lam. If Fotis did travel from Farmington to New Canaan early on the morning of May 24, he would have driven by dozens of these devices. It was a feat of police work: track down all that footage, comb through the hours of highway blur until you see a glint of gold.

Fotis owned four vehicles—a Ford Raptor, a Chevy Suburban, a Porsche Cayenne, and a Jeep Grand Cherokee—none of which could be found in the footage. But the police noticed another vehicle parked at 4 Jefferson Crossing, a beat-up red Toyota Tacoma pickup truck that belonged to Pawel Gumienny, the Fore Group's project manager.

Gumienny gave his background to a jury in Stamford many months later. He said he came to America from Poland shortly before the 9/11 attacks. The carpentry work he found in Connecticut eventually led to Fotis Dulos, who hired Pawel first to frame a house in Avon, then as a full-time employee. Fotis, Michelle, and Pawel talking together on a suburban lawn after Jennifer's disappearance—three immigrant strivers, each of whom came to America in search of a particular grail.

Pawel said he considered Fotis Dulos a friend. And trusted him. Which is why he felt comfortable leaving the Tacoma, when not using it on the job, in the driveway at 4 Jefferson Crossing with the keys inside. Once the police had modified their search to include this information, they began spotting the Tacoma, its license plates altered, all over the footage. It was seen exiting the Merritt Parkway in New Canaan early on the morning of May 24. It was seen at the Lapham Road turnabout at Waveny Park—this shot was captured by a security camera mounted on the back of a school bus. It was seen getting back on the Merritt later that morning. There was a man behind the wheel, head shaved. The resolution was not great, but it looked like Pawel Gumienny. One theory had Pawel, who'd been working on a house at 61 Sturbridge Hill Road in New Canaan, killing Jennifer on behalf of Fotis. Another had Fotis shaving his head to look like Pawel.

The investigators interviewed Pawel Gumienny multiple times, culminating in an eight-hour session at the state police troop barracks. Pawel was terrified when the police first showed up. He stammered as he spoke—but he did speak, his memory becoming sharper after he'd agreed to an immunity deal with prosecutors.

He said he'd gone to 4 Jefferson Crossing to pick up his truck early on May 24, but it was gone. Fotis had left a message for Pawel to use the Ford Raptor instead. That afternoon, when Pawel went back for his Tacoma—he needed it for the weekend—and still could not find it, he drove to 80 Mountain Spring Road, where Fotis had been working.

Pawel recognized the Tacoma from a distance—the blessing and curse of a red vehicle. He parked the Ford Raptor in the driveway at 80 Mountain Spring Road, then went looking for Fotis.

How do you celebrate a murder?

If there was a person who presented an obstacle to your plans and that person had suddenly been removed, how would you mark the occasion?

Pawel found Fotis, pants around his ankles, fucking Michelle Troconis against the passenger-side door of the Tacoma.

"Fotis and I were against the car, the Tacoma," Michelle told investigators. "Fotis was like behind me. Like physical contact. Pawel arrives. I think Pawel or Fotis says, 'I didn't see anything,' or 'We weren't doing anything.' I think something like a joke."

Pawel backed away as Fotis pulled up his pants. Fotis told Pawel to take the Raptor for the weekend. Pawel said he needed the Tacoma. They argued. Fotis gave in, with a caveat. He wanted Pawel to replace the Tacoma's back seats. Go to the dump, find seats that match, and swap them. And don't use the word "seats" when speaking of this switch, said Fotis. Pawel was to instead refer to them as "hardware."

Michelle shuttled between 80 Mountain Spring Road and 4 Jefferson Crossing all afternoon. On three separate occasions, her arrival at Jefferson Crossing—she was alone in the spooky McMansion—was followed by the appearance of smoke from the living room chimney. Since it was a balmy wind-tossed May afternoon, investigators came to suspect Michelle set those fires for reasons other than warmth.

Fotis "borrowed" the Tacoma again a few days later. When Pawel went looking for it—he was anxious to recover the vape charger he left inside—he found Fotis and the truck gleaming fresh from the car wash. Pawel demanded an explanation for his boss's sudden interest in the tidiness of the truck. Fotis, lip curled in a strange thin smile, said he cleaned it because Pawel was never going to do so. Fotis again said he wanted the seats changed. The seats in there now, Fotis explained, "look ghetto." Fotis told Pawel he would get in trouble if he didn't make the change, and possibly lose his green card.

Pawel talked about the behavior of Fotis and Michelle in the hours after Jennifer's disappearance, comments and exchanges that took on new importance when he realized Jennifer was missing. Pawel had always liked and tried to help Jennifer—he set up the kids' swing set and secretly spirited some of Jennifer's stuff from the Farmington house before the separation. He said Michelle had shown flashes of anger regarding Jennifer, calling her a bitch on multiple occasions. The first such occasion was when Jennifer, according to Michelle, would not let the kids visit Farmington to say goodbye to their dying dog, Beckham. In court, Pawel quoted Michelle as saying, "That bitch should be buried right next to the dog." Another outburst came after Jennifer vanished, which put Michelle and her daughter, Nicole, in the tabloids, exactly where she did not want to be. According to Pawel, Michelle responded by saying, "I'm going to kill that fucking bitch when she turns up."

Pawel said he was present for another conversation that seemed ominous in retrospect. Fotis was talking to a subcontractor, an audio/video expert. Fotis was showing this man pictures of Jennifer's house on Welles Lane in New Canaan. He wanted to know where security cameras would typically be installed on such a property. Pawel warned his boss later, telling him that, with the new tech, a camera can be anywhere. "She can record you with anything," said Pawel. "Just don't do anything stupid."

Investigators showed Pawel pictures of the Tacoma on I-84 and the Merritt Parkway taken on May 24. He was able to identify Fotis at the wheel and the black object in the truck bed. It was the French bicycle Fotis had shipped from Greece—the childhood bike he'd ridden in Athens. According to a 2020 article in the *New Canaanite*, "Gumienny told investigators that Fotis Dulos had asked him months before the murder—in the fall of 2018 or early 2019—to repair the vintage 10-speed bicycle."

Detective John Kimball, of the Connecticut State Police, reported: "Video from a residential surveillance system showed a person riding a bicycle in a northwest direction along Weed Street [the morning of Jennifer's disappearance]. The cyclist appears to be dressed in all dark clothing with a hood pulled down low to hide their face." Looking at the footage, Pawel Gumienny was able to finger the bike and the rider.

At the end of Pawel's first interview, the cops said they were seizing the Tacoma as evidence. Pawel asked if they wanted the original seats, too. Fotis's vehemence about changing them—Pawel had used seats taken from the Porsche Cayenne, which Fotis had wrecked sometime before—had made Pawel suspicious enough to keep the originals under a tarp in his garage. Examining the seats, the cops immediately noticed a dark stain. Tests would later show this was Jennifer's blood.

"Fotis said he spilled coffee," Michelle said when asked about the stain.

"Did you see a coffee cup?" one of the detectives asked.

"No, because I didn't look inside the car."

"Did the paper towel smell like coffee?"

"No, I didn't smell it."

"You don't have to smell it. Coffee just stinks."

"I held the towel, but I didn't smell it."

"But still, you didn't smell coffee?"

"No."

By June 1, investigators had enough facts to arrest Fotis Dulos and Michelle Troconis on charges of tampering with evidence and hindering prosecution. They could not yet charge them with murder, but they could arrest them for the lesser charges, seize their passports, saddle them with GPS monitors, and make them put up bail, all of which would prevent their escape. As a dual national with family and friends in Greece, Fotis Dulos was considered a serious flight risk.

When the warrant was issued, Fotis and Michelle were staying at the Residence Inn by Marriott in Avon, a cookie-cutter hotel with a fire pit in back, a pool tarped half the year, long sad hallways, and a breakfast buffet that served guests every morning until 11:00 a.m. They'd checked in after the police searched 4 Jefferson Crossing. A house that's been searched is a house that's been violated. You seek anonymity in the aftermath, a room where you can close the door, crank the AC, and vanish.

Fotis did not protest when the police arrived at 11:15 that night to arrest him and Michelle. He'd hired a criminal attorney, Norm Pattis, a tall, charismatic, attention-seeking barrister with round glasses and a gray ponytail, a self-described friend of the banished and champion of lost causes. Pattis had warned Fotis of the arrest, and told him to go quietly.

Fotis was taken to Garner Correctional Institute in Newtown, Connecticut, where he spent just two days, but which, according to his sister, was enough to traumatize him. "Among other indignities," Fotis was "forced to stay naked, in a cold cell, with spotlights trained on him," Rena Dulos Kyrimi told *CT Insider*'s Lisa Backus in 2021. This sounds less like truth than accusation, but Rena insisted the experience left Fotis determined to stay out of jail no matter the cost.

The public got its first look at this new Fotis Dulos, shackled at the wrists in an orange jumpsuit, as he entered the Stamford courthouse on June 11. He was small but looked even smaller flanked by beefy guards. The stubble on his face was as long as the stubble on his head, and his saucer eyes were those of a lost child.

He was greeted at the defense table by his legal team. There was Norm Pattis, whom Fotis was meeting in person for the first time. Pattis towered over Fotis and looked down at him benignly. There was Pattis's colleague Kevin Smith, who was short and thick. His dark hair was swept into a ponytail that seemed like a tribute to Pattis. Smith smiled at Fotis, chucked him on the shoulder, and said, "How ya doin', buddy?" There was Patrick Nugent, a legal intern who'd be working for Pattis through the summer. Pattis introduced him to the court as a young student "who will stand before the bar and get his feet wet at the law." There was Rich Rochlin, a West Hartford lawyer whom Pattis had hired partly for his office's proximity to the Dulos residence. Rochlin's first task was to gather the documents necessary to arrange bail. When Fotis turned his wide, fear-struck eyes to Rochlin, Rochlin said, "Don't look at me. Look at the judge."

Pattis asked the judge to set bail at $100,000. In arguing this, he cited the fact that Fotis had never been in trouble with the law and was accused of no more than evidence tampering, though you'd never know it by reading the newspapers, which cast him as a dubious character from the beginning. The *Hartford Courant*'s first piece on the Dulos case (May 30, 2019) quoted Jennifer's divorce filing, which presented the husband with the paramour as a dangerous man: "I believe [Fotis] to be highly capable and vengeful enough to take the children and disappear."

At Fotis's arraignment on June 11, Pattis delivered a stem-winder in the mode of Clarence Darrow:

> Mr. Dulos has been tried and convicted in the court of public opinion for a crime that he's not yet been charged with and

candidly I have doubts can be brought and can withstand a probable cause inquiry. Indeed, from my perspective it's somewhat surprising he's here at all. What we know is that Jennifer went missing sometime in the early morning of the twenty-fourth and was reported missing by late day. We've been able to account for Mr. Dulos's whereabouts with independent evidence for almost all of that time, including an early-morning meeting at his home with an attorney [Kent Mawhinney]. He received a call from Greece. We don't yet have verified phone records, but we know who the person is and have spoken to them. We believe that Ms. Troconis was in and out of the house with him from a period roughly from about 9:30 until about 1 p.m., when he next reliably surfaces in the search warrant at 1:33. So he's up in Farmington for some period of three to four hours, which on the state's theory, apparently, or the public's theory, would have given him time to drive down, commit a vicious crime, dispose of the body, get rid of the car, and drive back up to Farmington. It's possible, I suppose, as a matter of mathematics, but as a matter of experience it's a ludicrous suggestion . . .

We don't know where Jennifer is. We don't think the state knows where Jennifer is. We think that this bond and these arrests were an attempt to pit the two of them—Ms. Troconis and Mr. Dulos—against one another in a classic prisoner's dilemma that was designed to give the first person to speak a get-out-of-jail-free card on charges that are flimsy at the outset for information about the body . . .

Mr. Dulos would have had no motive. The custody battle was turning in his way. The court had made adverse findings about his soon-to-be ex-wife. And among those findings were conclusions about her stability and her mental health that we will not put on the record at this time but simply say that we are aware of those.

The prosecution's case was made by the chief state's attorney Richard Colangelo, who lived with his wife and children in Easton, Connecticut, twenty miles up the Merritt Parkway from New Canaan. I wrote about Colangelo's role in *Air Mail* on March 7, 2020:

> His work on the case can be seen as machinations at the highest levels of state—and also as one Fairfield County parent investigating the demise of another. It's perfect that Colangelo, a graduate of Westhill High in Stamford, Norwalk Community College, UConn, and Quinnipiac school of law, would become the engine of justice. This is a story of upper-crust people. Jennifer's uncle helped found Liz Claiborne—her wildly wealthy father attended shul alongside Michael Bloomberg. In her 20s, she ran with an elite Manhattan crowd that, according to an acquaintance, included Calvin Klein's daughter, Marci. Michelle Troconis skied with celebrities in Tierra del Fuego and mingled with aristocrats on the Arabian Peninsula. As for Fotis . . . well, the contrast could not be more stark. Whereas Fotis graduated from Brown and Columbia, skinny and handsome, in love with women, fun, resort life, and big projects, the man who brought him down is a beefy, gray-haired 53-year-old community-college graduate.

In arguing for a higher bail, Colangelo pointed out the severity of the possible crime and hinted at charges to come. The judge set bail at $500,000 and required Dulos to wear a GPS tracking device on his ankle. He would be allowed neither to leave Connecticut without permission nor to see or talk to Michelle Troconis. Fotis paid $50,000 in cash, money advanced by several old Brown friends who'd wagered on his guilt or innocence. (Those who bet on his innocence agreed to pay a percentage of his bail if he was convicted.) The balance was covered by a bail bond.

Fotis glanced at the courtroom gallery on his way out. He was looking for Michelle. She was there, awaiting her turn before the judge. Her hair was combed back. She wore a blue button-down polo shirt. She was looking straight ahead but seeing nothing. She had what war correspondents call a thousand-yard stare. Fotis caught her attention. What was he trying to say with his eyes? *I will always love you. None of this matters. We have eternity.* Or, *Keep your mouth shut. If we both say nothing, we walk.*

Michelle had been arrested in her pajamas in front of her daughter, Nicole, and driven south to New Canaan for her first encounter with police. She began cooperating, or trying to, soon after. In explaining herself, she said, "I'm, like, so innocent!" Her interrogation continued through several meetings, the tone of which went from light and chummy to hard and mean. Detective Kimball laughed when Michelle described the color of Pawel Gumienny's Tacoma pickup truck as "Bordeaux." He became serious when he said, "Fotis lies to everybody, and the reason he lies to everybody is because he only cares about one person in the world—and that's himself. He didn't care about his first wife, didn't care about his second wife, and doesn't care about you."

If you consider Michelle's interview sessions in composite, you see just how bad she was as a witness. At first she stuck to the story in the alibi scripts: she woke beside Fotis at 6:40 a.m. on May 24; had sex in the shower; dropped Nicole at school; went to Stop & Shop; returned to the house, where she saw Kent Mawhinney in the office;

spent the afternoon cleaning 80 Mountain Spring Road; then went home for dinner.

When asked about Albany Avenue—*Why didn't you include that in the scripts?*—she said, "I know it looks bad, but I was really just writing down the highlights."

By the end of the second interview, the police had gotten used to watching her dissemble. When presented with a new piece of evidence, she simply came up with a new story to explain it.

Where were you on the morning of Jennifer's disappearance?

I was with Fotis at 4 Jefferson Crossing.

What time did you wake up?

6:40 a.m.

Is that when both you and Fotis woke up?

Yes.

Why does Fotis's phone show his alarm going off at 4:20 a.m., then being shut off at 4:21?

Okay, fine. Yes. So, maybe he wasn't home the entire morning.

When investigators said they had evidence that Fotis hadn't been home at all, Michelle, who seemed increasingly anxious, put her face in her hands, sobbed, and said, "Okay. Okay. He wasn't home."

Michelle's first lawyer, Andrew Bowman—whom she replaced with Jon Schoenhorn—tried to reel her in, but she blew right past him. It was as if she needed to talk. Clips of these sessions were released to the press; the full six hours were later played in court. Michelle looks flustered at one point, pulls her hair, bangs herself in the head, and cries, "What do you want? I'll tell you whatever you want. I didn't do this."

She said she'd seen Fotis and Kent Mawhinney together at the Fore Group office that morning. Then she said she had not actually seen them but had only heard their voices. Then said that it was she—not Fotis—who met Kent at 4 Jefferson Crossing. Fotis was gone but had left his phone behind. It was sitting on a table in front of her when it rang. Kent told her to answer. It was Fotis's old friend Andreas Toutziaridis calling from Greece. Andreas had been with Fotis when he ran into Jennifer at the Aspen airport all those years ago. It was Andreas who'd encouraged Fotis to pursue Jennifer, the beautiful heiress, even though Fotis was already married. The olive-skinned, gray-haired Andreas works in the hospitality industry in Athens, as president and CEO of a food services company called Intercatering. As per police theory, Fotis had tasked Andreas with calling his—Fotis's—cell phone on the morning of Jennifer's disappearance to establish an alibi. Michelle took the call. She talked to Andreas for maybe twenty seconds. She did not in fact see Fotis until 2:00 p.m., when he arrived at 80 Mountain Spring Road in the Tacoma. Asked if there'd been tension between her and Fotis, she said, "We fight all the time." She said most of the fights were about Jennifer. She said that Fotis cursed Jennifer, saying, "Sometimes I hope she disappears."

The police never lost interest in Andreas Toutziaridis. His cell phone, a Samsung Galaxy, was seized by federal agents when Andreas came through customs at Newark Liberty International Airport on June 25, 2019, a month after Jennifer went missing. He was on his way to Farmington to see Fotis.

According to the *Stamford Advocate*, "Dulos texted Toutziaridis around 10:25 p.m. the night before Jennifer vanished—a WhatsApp message, written in Greek—instructing him to call 'the next morning.'" And according to NBC Connecticut, a special agent with the Department of Homeland Security who searched Andreas's phone said this: "Almost two hours after the call to Dulos' iPhone and by the time authorities believed Jennifer Dulos was already dead, Toutziaridis, via WhatsApp, sent a link to a common internet meme video to Dulos that depicts a man being posed a question by a female off-camera who asks 'All right, you have two choices. A) You can live the rest of your life with your wife or B) . . .' at which time the male on camera interrupts and yells 'B' and the video ends."

Fotis stepped out of the courthouse into a press swarm after that first arraignment. "I've never seen anything like it," said Rich Rochlin, the lawyer assigned to drive Fotis home to Farmington. "It was like a movie, millions of cameras and reporters, all of them screaming questions."

The networks were there with sound trucks, boom mics, and helmet-haired anchorpeople. It was the wealth and privilege, the beauty of the participants, that made it tabloid fodder. The mansions, the money, and the unsolved mystery: Where is Jennifer?

Fotis was the perfect villain: a foreigner, a playboy, an inhabitant of the upper reaches who'd fallen into the jaws of public opinion. "He's been convicted by innuendo," Norm Pattis told the media. "I'm hoping for better from a jury."

Rich Rochlin pushed Fotis through the crowd and into the front seat of "the [Rochlin] family Honda." The cameras closed in. Fotis can be seen in the video, a small man in a bucket seat who sits there and sits there, then smiles. It's inscrutable: *Why is this man smiling?* People can be forgiven for reading meaning into that smile, for seeing in it evidence of psychopathy. Like the whiteness of the whale, or the dark side of the moon, or the rings of Saturn, it's the inexplicableness of Fotis's smile that makes it chilling.

As a condition for bail, Fotis was required to turn over all his passports. In the way of a drug dealer, he had many versions of the same document: Greek and American, expired and current. A court officer retrieved them in Farmington. A state trooper, sent to guard the scene, let the officer into 4 Jefferson Crossing. While looking for the documents, the officer claims he came across the novel Jennifer had once been working on. (Few have ever seen the manuscript.) It's called "Tear Me Open." It's about a woman who disappears and whose husband is accused of murdering her.

July 2, 2019. Fotis sat down for the only in-depth interview he'd give about the case. He probably did so for reasons of publicity. Hundreds of news stories had already been published. Fotis was portrayed as a blackhearted villain in nearly every one. The people reading those pieces would make up the jury pool. To win the case, he'd have to show them he was not a murderer, but a victim.

The interview was done in the kitchen at 4 Jefferson Crossing in Farmington. Fotis was seated on the right side of the shot, and the interviewer, Sarah Wallace from NBC 4 New York, on the left, but your eyes kept searching the background, the kitchen of the possible killer, the marble countertops and white cabinets, the stainless steel appliances with their nickel finish. There was evidence of Hilliard Farber's money everywhere: a $1,500 cappuccino maker, a $5,000 Viking stove. The room was as clean as a surgical theater. Count on a con man to crave the appearance of order.

Fotis wore a blue-and-white checked shirt and blue jeans. His brown hair was turning gunmetal gray. He appeared laid-back, calm. Coldness was the impression many took away. His detachment was unsettling.

Sarah Wallace, a local television news veteran—blond hair, silver earrings, red nail polish, a necklace with a round pendant (like an amulet worn to ward off the evil eye)—deftly turned the interview into something close to a real conversation.

"How do you think the public looks at you?" she asked.

Dulos paused as if searching for the answer, or pretending to search because he knows that that's what the innocent do, then said, "It depends. I think that the people that do not know me, they probably look at me as a monster . . . And that is because of the information that has come out. And I cannot speak about what happened. So, they take the narrative that they see from the arrest warrants and what is being reported in the press and they draw their own conclusions, so I have already been convicted in their mind."

Asked if he had a message for Jennifer's family, Fotis said, "I send my prayers. I had my differences with Jennifer, like many people do when they go through a marriage. It didn't work out for us. But that doesn't mean I wish her ill in any way."

"Where do you see this going for you?" Wallace asked.

"I try to go day by day," Dulos answered. "When it first started I seriously pinched myself a couple of times and I said, 'This cannot be true. I'm dreaming this. I'm wearing orange, and I'm in a cell six feet by nine feet. And this cannot be true.' So, it's a day by day—I'm hoping we'll get through this."

He said he understood why people questioned his innocence. He said he knew that, in 90 to 95 percent of such cases, "it's the spouse."

Pressed to respond to that conventional wisdom, he bristled. "It's *ninety* percent," he said. "It's not a hundred percent. I'm in the five or ten percent category."

No one knows what they want from an accused killer, but it's probably not percentages. Sarah Wallace underscored how strange it was for Fotis to resort to the odds: *There's a ten percent chance I did not murder my wife.*

"I know what I have done and I know what I haven't done," said Fotis.

Close watchers noticed what he did not say: *I did not kill Jennifer.*

Fotis shifted and looked away when asked about his relationship with Jennifer. In Vegas, they call this a tell. He spoke of Jennifer in the past tense, as if he knew she was dead while deflecting blame from himself, as if he believed her death was her own fault. "As you know," he told Wallace, "we *were* in a very contentious divorce that was fueled by *her* attorneys."

Wallace interrupts, and you can see she's nervous. She's felt a chill. She suddenly knows who she's talking to.

"You're not allowed to have contact with the children at all . . . How is that for you?" she asked.

"It's heartbreaking . . . This is a very tough time. I'm sure they have a lot of questions. I'm sure they're missing their mom. And I'm sure they're missing their dad. And I'm here. I'd be able to support them and help them through this time."

When asked about those who speculated that he wanted Jennifer "out of the way," Fotis said, "Well, that's ludicrous, because I never wanted Jennifer out of the way. Even if I could get sole custody, I would still not take it because I would want my children to have a relationship with their mother because I care about the children."

"But that is interesting," said Wallace, "I mean, because the perception is, contentious ugly divorce and a motive clearly to do something."

And there it is once more: the inscrutable smile.

"My motive has been for the past two years to move on with my life," said Fotis. "I have five beautiful children. I had Michelle and I had a profession that I loved."

Here were are again, in the past tense. At some level, Fotis knows he's already dead. What's more, the sentence meant to argue his innocence—"My motive has been for the past two years to move on with my life"—can just as easily be taken as a rationalization for his guilt.

Asked to offer proof of innocence, he said, "You have to look at who is most badly affected by this situation."

"And you're saying that's you?"

"Yes."

"'Emotionally distancing' is the term I would use," said Judy Ho, a clinical and forensic neuropsychologist, after watching the video of Fotis's interview with Wallace. Ho cautioned that she did not personally evaluate, diagnose, or treat Fotis, but she did add, "Why wasn't Fotis more fired up? The fact that he showed no emotion, positive or negative, is a sign that something might be amiss."

On *Access Hollywood*, Stan Walters, a body language expert who is known as the "Lie Guy" and who trains police and FBI agents in the art of interrogation, talked about how calm Fotis remained throughout. The detachment, the cold answers—it's as if he based his performance on psychopaths he'd seen in movies. Fotis remained physically still for every moment of the interview but one, said Walters. "He fidgeted when Wallace asked: Are you worried about Jennifer?"

Walters concluded, "The entire interview was only twenty-three minutes long. Dulos was asked about concerns he has for Jennifer and all he does is talk about how terrible it is for him."

Here is *CT Insider* on Fotis's champion Norm Pattis, whom it described as the region's "most colorful and controversial lawyer":

For more than 20 years, Pattis has roamed the state's halls of justice looking for trouble. In that time, he's been called everything from "attorney Slash and Burn" to "the P.T. Barnum of the courtroom." Combative, whip smart, fast on his feet, provocative to the point of incendiary, Pattis specializes in cases that make most people cringe. He's defended everyone from child murderers to rapists—he admits to being particularly drawn to homicide cases. If the allegation is heinous and the defendant reviled, chances are pretty good Pattis is involved.

According to *CT Insider*, Pattis is "well-known—and not liked—for turning legal arguments into lectures aimed at judges and lawyers he sees as inexperienced, and often publicly criticizes them in his blog."

Though Pattis looks like the late crusading liberal attorney William Kunstler, he actually occupies the libertarian right of the political spectrum. He's probably most notorious for representing Alex Jones, the podcaster who was sued—and found liable—for claiming the Sandy Hook massacre was a hoax. Pattis said he took the case to champion the First Amendment. Other Pattis clients have included Tony Moreno, a father convicted and sentenced to seventy years for dropping his baby off a bridge, and Jermaine Richards, a nurse convicted and sentenced to life for killing and dismembering a college student. "I like a fight," Pattis told *CT Insider*. "I'm 64 years old and I have a ponytail. I have issues with authority. If I take a case and it pisses off the other 7 billion people on the face of the Earth, that's their problem, not mine."

Asked why he represented the state's most hated people, Pattis cited his childhood, when he, too, was loathed and felt abandoned. Pattis grew up in Detroit in the 1960s. His father ditched his mother, who took up with a violent drunk who terrorized the young Norm Pattis:

Pattis . . . found himself unwelcome in his own home and would only return after his mother and the man went to bed. At one point, he tried sleeping in the woods, only to get extremely sick.

It is those two traumatizing experiences—abandonment and being unwelcome and loathed in his own home—that drive him. He understands what it's like to be hated and forsaken, giving him empathy for the accused who are reviled and the downtrodden, and he's driven to come to their aid.

For Pattis, job one was to change the public perception of the Dulos case. This could be done in two ways. First, improve Fotis's image. That's what the Sarah Wallace TV interview was probably about. Second, muddy up Jennifer. Pattis would do that by making innuendos and floating baseless theories. Same facts, different story. Possible facts, alternative theory. You don't have to know the truth to pose the question, especially if it's done in the media. If you change the mind of the public, you pressure the prosecutor, who is already going to have a hard time getting a murder conviction without a body. In this way, you may force the prosecutor to downgrade or even drop the charges.

Pattis implemented his strategy via counterfactual narrative, as in, *Maybe it happened this way* . . . Some of it was done at press conferences, some of it in off-the-record conversations with reporters, and some of it in legal motions.

For example, Pattis used a medical bill—Jennifer had been charged $14,000 by a doctor less than a year before her disappearance—to wonder if she'd received a terminal diagnosis, and perhaps had only months or weeks to live, and therefore decided to destroy Fotis in the little time she had left. She might have done this by killing herself in a way that framed Fotis, suggested Pattis, who called it the "revenge suicide hypothesis."

At another point, Pattis cited Jennifer's youthful move to Colorado to suggest that she had run away. In this case, he mentioned a medical bill that arrived at her house *after* her disappearance. Though it was a typical delay—she saw the doctor in May, and the invoice arrived in July—Pattis used it to argue for proof of life. "If Ms. Dulos herself did, as the bill suggests, receive medical services on July 7, 2019, she is obviously alive, if not necessarily well."

Pattis also referenced Jennifer's unfinished novel, the manuscript she'd worked on over the years, to pose the so-called *Gone Girl* theory. Pattis wondered if Jennifer, like the heroine of the Gillian Flynn book, had faked her own death to punish her husband. He claimed it had all been laid out in Jennifer's work in progress.

This theory gained traction—there was something stirring about the notion of Jennifer Dulos, who'd never made it as a dramatist, turning her own life into a cinematic thriller. "We defy the state to prove she is in fact dead," said Pattis. "There is no body that we're aware of, and I'm sick and tired of hearing about it."

The *Gone Girl* theory was especially hurtful. It had Jennifer abandoning her mother and her kids, who were the purpose of her life. It added insult (defamation) to injury (murder). And it made no sense. In Flynn's novel, the husband is innocent and the wife is alive. In the real world, the wife has almost always been murdered and it's almost always the husband who did it.

Gillian Flynn herself issued a statement:

> I have been following the story of Jennifer Dulos's disappearance. This situation is so incredibly painful, I can't imagine

what her children, her family, and all those close to her are going through. I am deeply sorry for Jennifer and her loved ones.

I've seen in recent coverage that Jennifer's husband and his defense attorney have put forward a so-called "Gone Girl theory" to explain Jennifer's disappearance. It absolutely sickens me that a work of fiction written by me would be used by Fotis Dulos's lawyer as a defense, and as a hypothetical, sensationalized motive behind Jennifer's very real and very tragic disappearance.

Pattis responded to Flynn in court: "As to the *Gone Girl* references: I've not shared with the public the 551-page novel [Jennifer] wrote, but Joan Gillian [*sic*], the author of *Gone Girl*, says she's sickened by what I have to say? I'm not going to sit back and let a popular author do that to me or my client. My response is, 'Be gone, girl.'"

Norm Pattis took shots at the prosecutor Richard Colangelo at every opportunity. Colangelo and his assistants responded by quietly building their case. Working with state and local police, they tracked down dozens of cell phone records, financial records, and video files. Much of the case would be based on technology: what could be seen on surveillance, what could be proved by emails and bank statements.

Though it seemed nearly certain that Fotis Dulos was the killer, the prosecutors still had to answer several crucial questions.

One: How involved was Kent Mawhinney? Was it a wrong place/wrong time situation? Or was he an accomplice? He stopped by 4 Jefferson Crossing the night before the murder and spoke by phone to Fotis as Fotis trashed evidence on Albany Avenue. What are the odds of all that being coincidence? There was also Fotis's lunch with Kent's wife at Max's Oyster Bar and the freshly dug grave at the Windsor Rod & Gun Club.

Two: What about Andreas Toutziaridis, the Greek friend whose timely call had given Fotis an alibi? Had Andreas known why he was calling? If so, did that make *him* an accomplice? Perhaps Andreas knew what happened to Jennifer's body. A request was made to the Department of Homeland Security, which issued a subpoena for Andreas's phone.

Three: Could Fotis Dulos really have pulled off such a crime without assistance? According to most theories, he killed Jennifer and hid her body by himself, then made it back to Farmington by the early afternoon. Was that possible, or had someone else helped him kill Jennifer or hide her body? Fotis might have handed Jennifer off to such a person after the murder. You catch glimpses of the investigators' search for an unidentified accomplice in the warrants, notes, and records. Maybe a friend from Greece flew in, participated, and was back on a plane before Lauren Almeida had called the police.

When I asked around about the possibility of a second man, a name kept coming up: Christos. "The police are very interested in finding him," one of the attorneys told me. "He was a friend of Fotis's from Greece, and the cops see him as a possible accomplice. How did Fotis get rid of the body? For a while, the detectives believed he must have had help."

"Pawel [Gumienny's] truck was an unreliable heap," another attorney said. "Three times out of ten, it wouldn't even start. No way Fotis would use it to drive Jennifer's body all the way back to Farmington."

I asked Kevin Moynihan, New Canaan's first selectman, what he knew about the case.

"The police wouldn't tell me anything," he said, "but I did pick up an interesting detail from a member of the town's ground crew. There's a huge mulch pile next to Waveny Park beside the Merritt. You can see it steaming in the winter. A truck goes in there and turns it all over at intervals. The guy who drives that truck told me that he saw a black Suburban drive *into* the pile that morning. It parked there, stayed there, then drove away. There is no road back there—that means that truck went through a field. Whoever was driving it was there to throw something away."

Fotis Dulos was arrested for the second time, again for evidence tampering, on September 4, 2019—three months after his first arrest. He'd spent most of that time either confined to his house, in court, conferring with lawyers, tending to his failing business—he visited worksites, looked at properties, pitched potential clients—or riding his scooter on Jefferson Crossing. He was not allowed to see or speak to his children. He pressed his lawyers to appeal this court order, but they said forget it. *Fotis, you have bigger problems.* Like what? *Like life behind bars.*

He was always waiting for police lights to appear in the front window. Then it happened. Marched away in cuffs, head down—a picture of defeat. They processed him at the Connecticut State Police barracks in Bridgeport. Newspaper photos show him stepping through a doorway, moving from sunlight into darkness. He is wearing a sports shirt and shorts in these pictures (showing off his tan), along with leather shoes and an ankle monitor.

Michelle Troconis, who was cooperating, had not been arrested that second time. But the investigators were increasingly frustrated with how little she was giving them, which suggests either that she was withholding information or that she truly didn't know what had happened to Jennifer.

There was hardly a time when Fotis Dulos did not have a girlfriend or a wife. He often had both at once. He apparently could not stand being alone. His vanity required a mirror. He needed to see himself as he was himself seen. Without regular intakes of admiration, he would dry out like drought-stricken turf.

There had been the first wife, the second wife, the paramour. What now? He was not allowed to see or speak to Michelle Troconis since their arrest on June 1. Though surrounded by attorneys, he was, in a sense, all alone. He would turn brittle if he did not find company, but what woman would enter his life at this point?

Fotis did have charisma, a charm that drew people like moths to flame—which first illuminates, then incinerates. Even those who distrusted Fotis acknowledge this. "He was a very charismatic and charming person," Carrie Luft told CBS News. "He was very handsome. He was smart and funny."

"He had an incredible way with women," said Rich Rochlin. "He was very charming, very handsome, in unbelievably great shape, small but with six-pack abs, and certain women could not resist him. He spoke with a thick Greek accent, was smart and funny, but it was a kind of frat house humor. He'd give you a lot of ribbing."

Charisma is characteristic of psychopathy. There are no boring psychopaths. They hum with electricity. Like the globe in junior high science class, they are lit from within. How else could they work their magic? Decisions that seem inexplicable in the abstract—marrying a man one month after his divorce, following him to Connecticut—make sense in the presence of that electric glow.

To diagnose psychopathy, doctors consult the Hare Psychopathy checklist, developed in the 1970s by the psychologist Robert Hare and later revised:

1. Glibness / superficial charm
2. Egocentricity / grandiose sense of self-worth
3. Proneness to boredom / low frustration tolerance
4. Pathological lying and deception
5. Conning / lack of sincerity
6. Lack of remorse or guilt
7. Lack of affect and emotional depth
8. Callous / lack of empathy
9. Parasitic lifestyle
10. Short-tempered / poor behavioral controls
11. History of promiscuous sexual relations
12. History of early behavioral problems
13. Lack of realistic, long-term plans
14. Impulsivity
15. Irresponsible behavior
16. Frequent marital relationships
17. History of juvenile delinquency
18. Revocation of conditional release
19. Failure to accept responsibility for own actions
20. Many types of offense

If his apparently psychopathic traits didn't make Fotis appealing enough, add the fact that he was in serious legal peril, out on bail, suspected of murder, and possibly facing a life sentence. Such a doomed character will be irresistible to a person who is attracted to partners for the same reasons Norm Pattis is attracted to clients. They want the doomed, forsaken, damned, and dangerous. They want the excitement of the headlines and the charge of life in the eye of the storm.

Anna Curry met Fotis Dulos in the early 2000s when they worked together at Capgemini. Not much about her is publicly known. Did she hook up with Fotis back then or were they just friends? Did they stay in touch during the intervening years or did she reach out only after she read about him in the news?

Anna arrived late on the scene. The *New York Post* dubbed her the "mystery woman" and described her as Fotis's "latest girlfriend—an attractive brunette financial executive who bears a striking resemblance to both the wife he was accused of killing, Jennifer Dulos, and the former gal-pal . . . Michelle Troconis."

What is known about Anna comes largely from social media. She was born in North Carolina and graduated magna cum laude from Duke University, had a successful career in wealth management in New York, returned to North Carolina, and then appeared alongside Fotis Dulos in Farmington after his arrest. The fact that Anna looks more than a little like Jennifer, with delicate features, wide-set eyes, and high cheekbones, was unsettling.

What did Anna Curry want?

Why did she come to Fotis's aid with such generosity so late in the day?

People are a mystery. Maybe it was love. Maybe it was friendship. Maybe she saw a colleague abandoned by the world and went to him as naturally as a parent goes to a child standing too close to the train tracks. Maybe it was thrill-seeking, a desire to be in the middle of a real-life murder case. According to Wikipedia, J. G. Ballard's 1973 novel *Crash* is the story of "car-crash fetishists who become sexually aroused by staging and participating in car accidents."

The house at 4 Jefferson Crossing was desolate when Anna Curry arrived in the fall of 2019. Jennifer was gone. The Dulos kids were living with their grandmother. Michelle and Nicole had left. The toys, which included thousands of Legos, were all that remained, along with Kleopatra Dulos's cat, Madonna, who had outlived so many.

Fotis spent most of his time alone, away from the paparazzi. When he was spotted—in court, at the supermarket, riding his scooter on Jefferson Crossing—it was usually in the company of Anna Curry. He insisted the relationship was platonic. Hooking up with another woman while Jennifer was missing and Michelle was out on bail was not a good look to present to potential jurors. Anna was an old friend who'd come to offer support—that's how he played it. "They said they were not *together* together, but no way that was true," said a legal adviser who had dinner with Fotis and Anna. "They were all over each other. She fed him off her fork." The adviser then showed me a picture from his phone: Fotis and Anna from the waist down, legs intertwined. Fotis wears shorts and leather shoes with his GPS monitor. Anna wears green pumps. This image—hairy and smooth, ankleted and bare—looked like the cover of a Harlequin romance.

Gloria Farber was eighty-two when Jennifer disappeared. Her husband was dead. Her older daughter, Melissa, was in no position to take care of Jennifer's five children. This left Gloria to face grim reality essentially alone. She had money, but at such moments you realize money is nothing. Now and then, Gloria's picture appears in the tabloids. In one story, published in June 2019, a photo shows her holding her phone, its cover decorated with a portrait of her grandkids. They've become her purpose. Protect them, raise them.

The court awarded Gloria full custody of her grandchildren shortly after Jennifer vanished. Gloria's civil case against Fotis, which she pursued to the end, reached the courtroom in December 2019. Documents found in discovery showed that Fotis was more than $4 million in debt. The divorce had been costing him thousands a month. He was spending thousands more on travel with Michelle. Gloria was seeking repayment of $1.7 million loaned to the Fore Group by Hilliard. Fotis insisted the money had been a gift. Gloria won the suit.

Additional documents showed that Hilliard had set up a trust fund for each grandkid. In total, these funds were worth around $10 million. In the event of divorce, the funds would be controlled by Jennifer. In the event of Jennifer's death, they would apparently be controlled by Fotis.

Fotis spoke to a reporter outside the Hartford courthouse—that's where the civil trial took place—on December 19, 2019. In the last interview he would ever give, his words seemed so insincere it seemed like taunting. "All I want to say," Fotis told the reporter, "is that I wish Jennifer and her family a happy holiday and I just pray that they give my kids my love and my best wishes."

Rich Rochlin was at the Stamford courthouse on January 7, 2020, when Judge John F. Blawie issued a warrant, signed the day before, to arrest Fotis Dulos for murder. Rochlin called his client. He told him to be ready. *They're coming.*

Why did it take police so long to arrest Fotis for murder?

Jennifer had been gone for nearly seven months. Every bit of evidence had pointed to Fotis from the start—blood, DNA, phone records. But, because there was no body, the prosecutors had to be especially meticulous. They had to build a case that Norm Pattis could not puncture. By early January, they believed they'd done so. Much of the case relied on electronic surveillance, scraps of footage that, when pieced together, played like a movie about one terrible day.

While assembling this puzzle, investigators were on the lookout for four vehicles—a black Chevy Suburban, Fotis's regular ride; a white Jeep Cherokee Laredo, a car Fotis shared with Michelle; Fotis's black Ford Raptor; and Pawel Gumienny's red Toyota Tacoma pickup. Searching for these vehicles amid the tidal flow of traffic was like looking for a pattern in the stars.

Investigators were eventually able to account for nearly every key moment of the morning and afternoon of May 24, 2019. Imagine a Hollywood storyboard, with sketches filling a series of panels. In one the Tacoma ghosts through Farmington, desolate at dawn. In another, the Raptor is parked beside a dumpster on Albany Avenue in Hartford, night creeping in. The moments were assembled into a timeline:

> 5:35 a.m. The Tacoma exits the driveway at 80 Mountain
> Spring Road in Farmington, a property the Fore Group
> was preparing for sale. The sun is fiery red on the
> horizon. Distant hills reflect its glow. The pickup turns
> left onto Farmington Avenue, and heads south.
> 6:36 a.m. The Tacoma speeds past the Fairfield rest area on
> the Merritt Parkway, a brick structure with bathrooms
> and a Dunkin' Donuts. From above, this all looks
> like woodland, but beneath the trees are houses and
> towns. The Long Island Sound is five miles south. With
> windows open and wind blowing, you can smell the sea.
> 7:03 a.m. The Tacoma exits the Merritt Parkway at the New

Canaan rest area. Almost ninety minutes have elapsed since it left Farmington.

7:31 a.m. The sun is up, the New Canaan streets beneath it as orderly as circuits in a computer. A man in a black hoodie cinched to hide his face rides a bike—a black French Mercier with ram's-horn handlebars—along Weed Street. Its passing is captured by an electronic fish-eye lens. It's a twenty-minute ride from Waveny Park to 69 Welles Lane.

7:40 a.m. The southern edge of Waveny Park is seen from a camera mounted on the back of a yellow school bus. You can almost hear the kids screaming. As the bus turns, the world reels and Lapham Road comes into view. The Tacoma is parked on the shoulder.

8:05 a.m. Jennifer Dulos, having dropped her kids off at the New Canaan Country School, is recorded by a neighbor's surveillance camera as she drives her Chevy Suburban back to the house at 69 Welles Lane.

8:05–10:25 a.m. The picture goes dark. Two hours and twenty minutes of nothing. The key scene has played out off-camera. This is when the murder happened, and possibly when the body was hidden. It's like the black hole at the center of the universe, the vortex that spaghettifies everything. From the arrest warrant: "At some point between Jennifer's arrival home and 10:25 AM the crimes occur in the garage and the residence. Dulos packages Jennifer using plastic zip-ties and places her inside her own 2017 Chevrolet Suburban . . . Dulos cleans the garage using supplies he finds in the garage and paper towels from the kitchen."

10:26 a.m. The garage opens, the Chevy Suburban exits. Jennifer's house has become a crime scene. Her phone sends out its last signal as it arrives at Lapham Road, where the Tacoma is waiting.

11:12 a.m. The Tacoma passes the Merritt Parkway's New Canaan rest area on the northbound side. In the bed of the truck is a black bike with ram's-horn handlebars.

11:25 a.m. The Tacoma passes the Fairfield rest area. It took twenty-six minutes going, thirteen minutes coming back. The difference is the result of traffic or stress. The driver is speeding.

11:40 a.m. The Tacoma takes the Bridgeport exit onto Route 8, then heads north. The seat beside the driver is piled with garbage bags. Jennifer could be in one of those bags. She weighed just 110 pounds at the end. She'd lost much of the blood in her body, making her even lighter. She would have been easily handled, bundled, carried away.

12:00 p.m. The Tacoma is on I-84 North near Waterbury.

12:22 p.m. A surveillance camera shows the Tacoma turning in to 80 Mountain Spring Road. Six hours and seventeen minutes have elapsed. The Tacoma has returned to its point of departure.

1:36 p.m. Two vehicles pull into 80 Mountain Spring Road, the white Jeep Laredo and the black Chevy Suburban. Michelle Troconis is driving the Jeep. She arrives with cleaning supplies—bucket, sponge, Clorox. She said she intended to clean the house in preparation for sale. When told she had in fact been destroying evidence, she told the police, "That makes me hate him even more."

2:24 p.m. The Jeep Laredo leaves 80 Mountain Spring and heads north.

3:55 p.m. The Jeep Laredo returns to 80 Mountain Spring Road. Another period of darkness—one hour and thirty-six minutes off-camera. Pointing to the timeline, a cop might say, *Maybe they got rid of the body right here.*

5:29 p.m. Fotis and Michelle drive to 4 Jefferson Crossing. Then the Ford Raptor, its bed filled with trash bags, goes back down Jefferson Crossing, takes a right on Deercliff Road, a meandering tunnel of sumac and pine, and heads east on Albany Avenue toward Hartford.

There are various degrees of murder, each with its own nature and punishment. *Involuntary manslaughter* is the result of a negligent but accidental action. If Fotis had gone to Welles Lane with only the intention of confronting Jennifer, gotten into an argument, and shoved her such that she accidentally hit her head and died—that would have been involuntary manslaughter. If convicted, Fotis would have served no more than five years in prison. *Voluntary manslaughter* is a murder that comes in the heat of passion, unplanned, instantly regretted. If Fotis had gone to Welles Lane with only the intention of confronting Jennifer, gotten into an argument, and, in the course of that argument, lashed out with ill intent and killed Jennifer, that would have been voluntary manslaughter. If convicted, Fotis would have spent no more than twenty years in prison.

Second-degree murder is a murder committed during the commission of a crime. If Fotis had broken into the house at Welles Lane to steal a personal item and Jennifer had surprised him in the act, and

273

he panicked and shot her and she died—that would have been second-degree murder. If convicted, Fotis would have spent life in prison. *First-degree murder* is a murder that is done intentionally, with forethought. The fact that Fotis committed murder in the first degree is evident from the tremendous effort he took to create an alibi and cover his tracks.

Leaving his phone at 4 Jefferson Crossing so that the records would show he was far from the scene during the crime; arranging for a call to be made to that phone by his friend Andreas Toutziaridis; arranging to have that call answered by Michelle Troconis to further prove he was nowhere near New Canaan; shaving his head so that he would resemble Pawel Gumienny on electronic surveillance; using Pawel's truck and altering the license plates; parking the truck on Lapham Road and continuing to Jennifer's house by bike; leaving Jennifer's car on Lapham Road with the running lights on and shifted into reverse so that it would look like she had been the victim of a random crime; carrying the evidence north and dumping it on Albany Avenue in Hartford; insisting that Pawel replace the seats in the Tacoma—all of this is evidence not merely of premeditation but of careful planning.

But Fotis Dulos made two mistakes. First, he took his phone with him to Albany Avenue—if the cops had not found the zips ties, bloodstained towels, and clothes in the trash (the phone having led them there) they would never have been able to charge Dulos. Second, he grossly underestimated the investigators and the technology available to them. He knew he'd be on camera part of the time. That's why he shaved his head, took Pawel's truck, and changed the license plates. He did not know he'd be on camera much of the day.

Even so, he was able to hide Jennifer's body in a place that has not, to date, been found. This is the mystery that remains. In trying to solve it, investigators focus on two gaps in the timeline: 10:25 to 11:12

a.m., and 2:24 to 3:55 p.m. Jennifer's body must have been disposed of during one of those intervals, either in the morning, in which case she was dumped in or near New Canaan, or in the afternoon, in which case she was dumped in or near Farmington.

Fotis Dulos was taken into custody at 10:00 a.m. on January 7, 2020. A telling photograph shows him being led from his mansion in handcuffs—a fall that steep must've been dizzying. A state trooper holds him by the left bicep. A detective holds him by the right bicep. His graying hair has grown in to the point of being tousled. He wears jeans and a T-shirt, and looks less like a killer than like a model in a Gap ad.

Michelle Troconis was arrested and charged with conspiracy to commit murder the same day. Kent Mawhinney, having allegedly helped Fotis secure an alibi, was also charged with conspiracy to commit murder. Michelle surrendered without incident, but Kent ran. As in a cop show, an all-points bulletin was issued. He was captured by gun-waving troopers near Tolland, Connecticut, on I-84.

Kent was the only conspirator who did not make bail, at least not right away, which had been set at $2 million. He had neither the money nor the collateral to secure a bond. He looked terrible in every picture, a slight, balding middle-aged man marked by ruin. He spent several months in detention. At one point, trying to work with prosecutors, he apparently shared information that tightened the focus on Michelle Troconis.

Here's what Kent Mawhinney reportedly said: The night before the murder, when he stopped by 4 Jefferson Crossing, Fotis told him that he planned to get rid of Jennifer in the morning. Kent said he argued with Fotis, and, in the end, convinced him, or believed he'd convinced him, to call it off. Kent did not learn otherwise until the following evening, when Fotis called from Albany Avenue to say, "It's done." For a time, it looked like Kent would work out a deal to become a witness for the state. But no agreement was reached. He is, as of this writing, awaiting trial.

At his arraignment on January 8, 2020, Fotis's bail on the murder charge was set at $6 million. "To get bonded out a defendant must post 7% of the bond in cash," the *Hartford Courant* reported. "With a $6 million bond, Dulos needed $420,000." He was able to secure his release with the help of Anna Curry, who put up $147,000 and agreed to pay the remaining amount in fifteen installments. That was enough for a bail bond, which Fotis backed with a collateral of Fore Group properties that he valued at $10 million.

Then, on January 9, Fotis was back at 4 Jefferson Crossing. He was confined largely to the house. The world was bleak outside the windows, the lawns first faded, then covered in snow.

Did he lie awake in bed at night, staring at the ceiling, wondering where he'd gone wrong?

Leaving the house had become torturous. Fotis was pointed out in stores and denounced on the street. He symbolized everything evil about a bad marriage—the cheating, the power imbalance, the coercive control. Many women knew it from their own experience, had lived all of it except the murder. Jennifer had become a martyr to some people, not only because a bad marriage killed her but also because she'd believed in the holiness of marriage so unflaggingly.

Makeshift memorials began to appear. It happened spontaneously, a natural outpouring of pain and sorrow. People left pictures of Jennifer along with messages, ribbons, candles, notes, and flowers. Two such memorials were erected in New Canaan, one downtown and one in Waveny Park. Another sprang up in Farmington, a few dozen feet from 4 Jefferson Crossing. Fotis could not return from his lawyer's office without being confronted by the collection of items. He saw it not as a tribute to Jennifer, but as a personal insult. It was not about her, but him—an accusation, a slur. On January 17, 2020, he stopped beside the Jefferson Crossing memorial, got out of his car, walked over, and ripped the display apart, pulling off the notes and flowers. He was caught on camera and hauled back to court. "This was no ordinary memorial," Norm Pattis said in his client's defense. "It was a means of taunting him."

Pattis went on: "Imagine you woke up one night in the face of a missing loved one, a missing loved one with whom you may have been engaged in some court related hostilities. The world thought you were responsible for the missing loved one's disappearance and they began to place items on your lawn or close to your home. Do you leave them there and say all is fair in love and war, or do you remove them?"

Every time Fotis played victim, you could not help but imagine the last morning of Jennifer's life, as I do whenever I think about those terrible hours.

She was up by 6:00 a.m. to get the kids ready for school. Breakfast. Backpacks. Homework that still had to be done. She dealt with the morning chaos alone; the nanny, Lauren Almeida, would not be arriving until later. Everyone scrambled for the best seat in the car, the short drive to New Canaan Country, laughter in the Suburban.

The kids were at school by 7:55 a.m. Jennifer looked at her watch.

She'd have just enough time to go home, have a quick breakfast, and switch cars to drive into the city for her doctor's appointment. She turned onto Welles Lane and went past the manicured lawns and the beautiful houses, the gardens bursting with hyacinths and peonies, tall ornamental grasses bending in the breeze. Her street, her town. No more bodyguards. No more arguments. No more guns. She'd finally begun to settle in. She looked in the rearview mirror. She was gaunt, gutted. That's what life can do.

As she turned in to the driveway, she pressed the button to open the garage. It was huge inside. She'd never really gotten used to the size of suburban life. She was a Brooklyn girl at heart. She parked the Suburban next to the Range Rover, shut the engine, closed the garage. There was a shadow. Something slipped beneath the door. Or had she imagined it?

She entered the kitchen through the mudroom, put the kettle on the stove, got a granola bar from the pantry. She'd come to subsist on almost nothing. For the last few years, fear and anger had been all that kept her going.

She made tea, carried the mug to the table, and sat with the unopened granola bar looking out at the yard and the trees, and at the shadows under the trees. The divorce would end and time would pass. There is nothing more powerful than the tidal flow of everyday life.

She looked up, and there he was, knife in hand—a hunting knife with a pearl handle that folded in two. She stared at the knife, then gazed into his eyes, astonished. He dragged her out to the garage. She had never learned to fight. But she could scream. So she screamed. It was a scream that echoed all her other screams, only this time there was no one other than Fotis to hear it. She cried as he hit her, bound her wrists with zip ties, and pushed her down into the oil stain beside the Range Rover.

He knew exactly how much time he had before Lauren Almeida would arrive, and he used all of it, shouting at first, making the case he'd never been allowed to make in court, then stabbing her until the blood was on the cars and on the walls and on the floor.

Her last thoughts were of her parents and her children. Then she was stepping through the red doors and Hilliard was on the other side in a tuxedo and everyone was applauding and throwing rice.

There was more blood than Fotis expected. He soaked it up with whatever he could find, paper towels from the pantry, bathroom towels from the closet. He cut away the zip ties, put her body in a bag, and loaded the bag into the Suburban. He washed his hands in the kitchen and wiped down the sink but missed a single drop of his own blood. He checked the garage one last time. It looked okay to Fotis, who did not know about luminol and its profound message: *There is no hiding; everything will be revealed.*

IS THE INNOCENCE of Fotis Dulos a possibility?

Norm Pattis was preparing to argue it. He could not explain Jennifer's disappearance, but he did not need to. He needed only to create a reasonable doubt in the minds of the jurors. Maybe Jennifer's not even dead. And even if someone had killed her, why did it have to be Fotis? The divorce had been turning his way. He had filed for sole custody. What was the motive?

The evidence found on Albany Avenue was troubling, but Pattis had an explanation: Fotis had come home on the night of Friday, May 24, 2019, to discover the bags filled with bloodstained items on his front steps. Knowing how bad it would look, he drove them down to Hartford in a panic.

Pattis implied that Fotis had been framed and said he could even identify the probable culprit. "It's someone known to this court," said Pattis, who was not ready to name the person, though it was most likely Pawel Gumienny, whom Fotis had seemingly been setting up from the start. "If Mrs. Dulos is in fact dead," Pattis continued, "we have reason to believe she met her end at the hands of a third party unrelated to Mr. Dulos and without his knowledge."

~

January 28, 2020. Fotis received a call that morning. There was an issue with his bail. "The state sought to revoke the bond because the Palmetto Surety Company was now saying it could no longer guarantee the loan because the collateral used to secure it wasn't sufficient," Dave Altimari reported in the *Hartford Courant*. "Palmetto underwrote the bond with six pieces of real estate—but two of them, including the Jefferson Crossing home—are in foreclosure and a third is significantly overvalued."

Fotis was required to make up the difference—several hundred thousand dollars—or return to jail. He was ordered to appear in court at noon. He sent Anna Curry to the Farmington branch of the People's Bank to see how much money was in his account ($92.70), then spent the rest of the morning trying to secure funding. At 11:00 a.m., he spoke to a bail bondsman, Mark Motuzick, who later told police that Fotis sounded "like he was in a rush, or out of breath, like he was working out."

Fotis had planned to meet Anna Curry later at court. A police officer called her shortly after noon to say Fotis had not shown up. Anna called Kevin Smith at Norm Pattis's office and asked him to call for an ambulance while she contacted the Farmington Police.

Two officers were sent to 4 Jefferson Crossing for a wellness check. They knocked on the front door. No answer. They went to the garage. "I looked in the window of the door and saw that the windows of the [Chevy] Suburban were fogged up and suspected that someone was inside the vehicle," wrote Lieutenant Sean P. Bailey. "I could see a haze in the garage that appeared to be vehicle exhaust."

An officer got into the garage through the house. A hose fixed with duct tape had been run from the car's tailpipe to the passenger window. The gaps beneath the garage door had been sealed with Styrofoam, and a carbon monoxide detector had been removed.

An officer got Fotis out of the car and onto the driveway. "[His] skin was gray," Lieutenant Bailey reported. "He was not breathing, and appeared lifeless."

"He wanted to do this," Anna Curry told the police.

"Obviously, the potential for a bond revocation was devastating news to him, but throughout he has been a fighter and resolute," said Norm Pattis. "In our review of the discovery we very much liked our options for trial and we very much liked our possibility of success. So this development comes as stunning news to me."

"Officers removed him from the vehicle and performed CPR in the driveway—a dramatic scene that was captured by aerial footage," the *Stamford Advocate* reported. "As the scene was unfolding, family members of Fotis and Jennifer Dulos were notified that he had died."

The report of Fotis's death was premature. Doctors at the University of Connecticut Health hospital in Farmington detected a faint heartbeat. Fotis was flown by Life Star helicopter to Jacobi Medical Center in the Bronx, which has a hyperbaric chamber, the only known treatment for carbon monoxide poisoning. Fotis spent three days in medical purgatory, drifting between worlds.

In an interview with NBC Connecticut conducted while Fotis lay in critical condition, Norm Pattis said:

> He was held out to the world as a man believed to have murdered his wife and every possible inference was drawn against him in every forum whether it be social media, a court, walking to and from court, in the street, in stores. I think the weight was difficult to bear. I don't know that people who have

not been accused can appreciate the savageness of the criminal justice system. We have a presumption of innocence in this country for a reason. And all the folks who harped on Mr. Dulos can obviously take some grim satisfaction in today's event. But my message to each and every one of them is shame on you.

For many, it was a suicide attempt that seemed like a confession.

"To those who contend Mr. Dulos' [actions reflect] a consciousness of guilt, we say no," Pattis later told the media. "We say it was more a conscience that was overborne with the weight of a world that was too busy to listen and wanted a story more than it wanted the truth."

Rena Dulos Kyrimi believed it was the fear of returning to jail that caused her brother to check out. "Fotis was an easy target," she said. "They accused him of murder from the beginning. He didn't have any strength to fight anymore."

The police searched 4 Jefferson Crossing the day after Fotis's suicide attempt. There were pictures of the children on the dashboard of the car and a note on the passenger seat.

> All,
>
> If you are reading this I am no more. I refuse to spend even an hour more in jail for something I had NOTHING to do with. Enough is enough. If it takes my head to end this, so be it. I want it to be known that Michelle Troconis had nothing to do with Jennifer's disappearance. And neither did Kent Mawhinney. I ask the State to let them free of any such accusations. I also ask the State to stop harassing my friends; Andreas Toutziaridis, and Anna Curry. They are honorable people. Please let my children know that I love them, I would do anything

to be with them, but unfortunately we all have our limits. The State will not rest until I rot in jail. My attorney can explain what happened with the bags on Albany Avenue. Every thing [*sic*] else is a story fabricated by the Law Enforcement. I want to thank all my family and friends that stood by me this difficult time [*sic*]. Above all Anna Curry. I am sorry for letting you down and not continuing the fight.

> Fotis

"His suicide note must be the most narcissistic suicide note I've ever read," Daphne de Marneffe, author of *The Rough Patch: Marriage and the Art of Living Together*, told me. "It's like a suicide note written by Donald Trump. It's everyone's fault but his own."

"He figured he'd never get out of jail and so killed himself," said David Adams, the co-founder of Emerge, a counseling program for men who abuse women. "He left a note and everybody expected it to be a confession and an explanation—this is where her body is—but instead it basically says, 'I'm innocent. The system drove me to kill myself.' It's typical of the behavioral profile of a psychopath. No remorse. These are people who see the world through the filter of narcissism—no matter what, they are the victim."

"Everything a psychopath does is guided by self-concern," Dr. Judy Ho said of psychopaths in general. "They take their own life so they won't be arrested or don't have their day in court or because they don't want to die in jail. They don't want their fate determined by a judge or jury. That is what makes them suicide risks. You would think somebody so egotistical would not kill themselves, but they will if it's to protect their ego and self-image, which to them is more important than living."

On January 29, 2020, Gloria Farber brought her grandchildren to Jacobi Medical Center in the Bronx to see their father for the last time.

He'd possibly been kept alive for just this purpose, sustained like a prop, because, at this point, attention had already turned to the survivors.

I do not know what was said. I can never know. In entering this room even in my mind, I have entered a holy place. I understand that. I won't try to describe the scene; I simply note its existence: the mother killed at the hand of the father, the father dying by his own hand, the grandmother and grandchildren waiting for an explanation that will never come.

In those first days after their father's death, the Dulos children lived on the Upper East Side with Gloria Farber. Some would attend Poly Prep, a private school in Dyker Heights, Brooklyn, favored by elite athletes. Theodore and Petros are said to be outstanding lacrosse players. Some would attend Jennifer's alma mater, Saint Ann's. Much of their day-to-day care is seen to by Lauren Almeida, who started as a nanny and became more like a parent. When Gloria dies, I've been told, Lauren will assume full custody and have access to much of the Farber family fortune.

Why did it happen? Because the parents forgot their role as parents? Because the parents became fixated on each other and who would win and who would lose, and in that fixation let their children become chips in a game they played all night? Or simply because Fotis Dulos was a psychopath who followed a twisted psychopathic logic all the way to the end?

Fotis was removed from life support on January 30, 2020, and died an hour later. Rena Dulos Kyrimi wanted to bury him in Connecticut, but, worried the grave would be desecrated, shipped his body to Greece instead.

In 2020, the Connecticut General Assembly passed a bill that expanded the definition of "domestic abuse" to include coercive control. It's called Jennifer's Law. Jennifer was not officially declared dead until January 2024, more than four years after her disappearance. Her body has not, to date, been found.

Starting with her first arrest in 2019, Michelle Troconis's case made a long, tortuous, Odysseus-like journey through the legal system. She tried different lawyers and different strategies but never stopped insisting on her innocence. She sought to recast herself from accomplice to victim. "As a mother, I am saddened for the loss that these 5 children have suffered," she wrote on social media. "Based on what I have learned in the last year, I think it was a mistake to have trusted Fotis Dulos & the ppl around him."

Michelle claims complete ignorance regarding Jennifer's fate. Jailed, defamed, saddled with a GPS anklet, demonized online and in the media—Michelle believes she should be seen as one of the tragedy's biggest losers, aside from Jennifer. Asked why prosecutors continued to pursue Michelle even after Fotis was gone, her attorney Jon Schoenhorn responded in writing: "When Fotis Dulos takes his life & they have spent millions of dollars they were not going to pursue the charges against Michelle Troconis but now they have to justify millions of dollars."

Michelle set up an Instagram account to restore her public image. When not swearing to her innocence, she has implied that Fotis, if he actually did anything to Jennifer, and maybe he didn't, was provoked by aggressive attorneys and a relentless soon-to-be ex-wife. Michelle wrote about her work with animals and the disabled on Instagram, and posted a picture of herself whispering to a horse. She took swipes at the prosecutors, including the chief state's attorney Richard Colangelo, who was forced to resign from office in a nepotism scandal in 2022. She wondered if Fotis was framed, possibly by an employee. "Schoenhorn reveals that DNA from a hoodie thought to be linked to the 'suspicious cyclist' in fact . . . throws a wrench into the state's THEORY of the crime," she wrote in one post. It "has Pawel Gumienny DNA a Fotis Dulos employee."

When I asked Schoenhorn about Michelle's Instagram account, he told me he didn't believe his client was involved, suggesting it was operated by family members. But Michelle herself wrote me from the account, sending a picture of *Personals*, the collection with Jennifer Farber's essay "Window-Shopping for a Life," and asking to be put in touch with Tom Beller, who edited the book.

I passed this request along to Tom Beller. He rejected it with disgust.

Michelle Troconis went on trial for several charges, including conspiracy to commit murder and tampering with evidence, at Stamford Superior Court in January 2024. The early days of the trial were interrupted by the state's first blizzard in three years. That is, the trial began in winter. By the time it ended twenty-seven bruising days later, it felt like spring.

In the course of those twenty-seven days, the entire heartbreaking epic was strung before the jury like a panoply, a circus parade. Michelle's sisters were there, as were her mother and father, who, at the end of many sessions, stood in front of the cameras outside the court to denounce the injustice of the process. The Dulos kids were there, too, not every day but often enough to remind reporters, gawkers, and jurors that this was a tragedy measured in lost relationships and crippled lives, that its price is exacted more from the living than the dead.

The jury was shown Jennifer's blood-soaked Intimissimi bra; her bloody Vineyard Vines T-shirt (EVERY DAY SHOULD FEEL THIS GOOD); and the bloody zip ties, bloody paper towels, and blood-soaked sponges. The prosecution's case began with Lauren Almeida, the nanny who looked so much like the young Jennifer, and ended with eighty-eight-year-old Gloria Farber, who shamed just about everyone else who took the stand with her beauty, grit, and class. She'd lost her husband in 2017 and her daughter in 2019, but here she was, on March 1, 2024, smiling when she probably wanted to curse, staring across the room at Michelle Troconis, the woman whose appearance at the waterskiing club in Doral, Florida, set the whole train in motion.

Here's how I reported these events in *Air Mail*:

> Michelle, in shawl and slacks, her long rust-colored hair swept back, reading glasses on her head, face frozen in an expression that my grandmother would have called *Farbissina punim*, listened carefully to the closing arguments. Now and then, she reached out to touch one of her sisters, who sat in the first row. Tall and slender, these beautiful sisters had entered the court side by side, like ninjas, shoes going clickety-clack, as if ready to do battle. Their father, Dr. Carlos Troconis, a cardiologist in Miami, white-haired, balding, and dressed like a British banker, sat next to them, the patriarch trying to contain a situation that already had spun out of control. Like Gloria, there must've been moments when he felt he had lived too long.
>
> Michelle turned to the jury when Schoenhorn began his close. They looked into her eyes, as if trying to read her inner nature. She stared back, blank. The room had become muggy. The seats were filled with women from New Canaan, Avon and Farmington, blonde and symmetrical, rows of colored sweat-

ers. They traded glances, whispered during breaks. A picture of the Dulos children was shown on-screen. They are young in the picture, smiling, gathered around a smiling Fotis. They are not so young in the court, and they do not smile. Everything is a clock. The time between this moment and that moment does not exist for Jennifer.

The defense's job was to re-cast Michelle: from paramour to victim, just another person who'd fallen victim to Fotis's charm.

According to Schoenhorn, the state had failed to connect Michelle to the crime and should in fact view her as a casualty, second only to Jennifer. The man she fell in love with, the man smiling in the picture, did not exist—she was deceived. The case is entirely circumstantial, he explained, based on coincidence, on "supposition on supposition on supposition."

The judge called for a short recess before the prosecution got its last 30 minutes. I followed the crowd into the hall, which was suddenly jammed with lawyers, cops, spectators, family members. It was the intimacy, the multiplicity of fates, the ant-farm quality of life on the fourth floor in Stamford, that resonated.

At 11:54 A.M., the two oldest Dulos children were amid the crush, discussing the case with a gray-haired man as the cop who interrogated Michelle Troconis looked on, while, just down the hall, behind a door marked RESERVED, Michelle Troconis sat with her phone in her lap, eyes big, dark, and wild. I have seen that look on the faces of friends who have realized they are screwed.

A few days later, Troconis stood as decisions on each of the six counts were read. Here's how that would have sounded to her: Guilty, Guilty, Guilty, Guilty, Guilty, Guilty. Michelle put her face in her right hand, sat down, and dropped her head to the table. Her shoulders rose and fell. One of her attorneys rubbed her back. She wore a beautiful white sweater . . . Long hair spreading across the table and falling to her knees, Michelle was bent like a comma when the marshals arrived with the cuffs to lead her away.

The main players returned to court on May 31 for Troconis's sentencing. She had come straight from jail. Her clothes were plain, her wrists bound. The handcuffs were removed. She had her hair in a pony tail, which she adjusted nervously, fingering the braid like a rosary.

Gloria Farber made a statement, as did friends and family of the perpetrator and victim. Killer and killed—they are bound together, as in a web, for eternity. Most devastating were the statements of the Dulos kids. "My mother was everything to me," Petros told the court, "but during the divorce I became very bitter with everyone around me, especially my mom. The defendant's actions mean I will never be able to tell my mom how sorry I am for not being a better son when she needed me."

Theodore spoke next. "My life now is nothing like it used to be," he said. "I no longer have my mother, my hero. I'll never talk to her again. I'll never do my homework with her again. I'll never ask her for advice again. I'll never go on an errand with her again. She will never see me graduate high school. She will never see me graduate college. She will never see me get married."

Then, turning directly to Troconis, who was sitting at the defense table in a white sweatshirt, eyes bloodshot and filled with tears, Theodore said, "Five kids lost their mother. Michelle, you caused this damage. On May 24, 2019, you not only knew about but conspired to murder a daughter, sister, friend and a mother of five kids. That day you took away five children's source of comfort, of protection. You showed no remorse and have yet to show any to this day . . . You expected to get away with it because you believe you are above the law. You thought no one would suspect you and all suspicion would fall on my dad. Unfortunately you underestimated law enforcement and the justice system in our country that day and in the days and months following. You were caught red-handed and are shocked. You will spend the next however many years behind bars and this will give you the time to think about what you have done. Every day you will wake up in a small cell with not much to do. You will have many years to contemplate what you know you have done. If you have just a least bit of humanity I suggest you let us know exactly what happened that day and where my mother is."

Judge Kevin A. Randolph called a recess, as if to give the families and people in the court time to absorb the surge of emotion that seemed at the point of overflowing. He was composed when he returned. Raised high on his platform, rocking gently in his high-backed chair, the judge explained the reasoning behind the sentence, which, in the way of a dramatist, he withheld for a few extra beats. Fotis had gone, leaving Michelle to face justice alone. She stood with shoulders back when the sentence was finally announced. Toughness had been expected, but the terms still came as a shock: Fourteen and a half years in prison. Her eyes had gone glassy by the time the judge adjourned, as if she was already steeling herself for what came next.

I went to Farmington to meet Lisa Nkonoki in the winter of 2024. Lisa believes she is the only person who spoke to Jennifer *and* Fotis near the end. Worried that some might accuse her of inventing these discussions—Lisa has had her own legal problems—she showed me the texts that have her scheduling meetings with Fotis and Jennifer, admonishing and offering advice to both.

Lisa lives on one of those rhythmically hilly Farmington roads that suggest just how beautiful this land must have been before the towns, factories, grist mills, and mansions. It's what Fitzgerald meant when he wrote about "a fresh, green breast of the new world."

As Lisa stood on the front step of her house—the Purple Palace— she gave me a neighborhood tour from afar. Across the street is the fifty-thousand-square-foot mansion that belonged to 50 Cent after it belonged to Mike Tyson. She then led me through her own house, showing off the hundreds of Black Santas she has collected, Christmas trees, Christmas lights, and pictures of herself with various celebrities—keepsakes from the public relations work she did before becoming a life coach. There were framed posters in which Charlie Brown, Linus, and Lucy—the whole Peanuts gang with the exception of Snoopy—were Black.

We sat in the dining room. She talked about Fotis and Jennifer and divorce in Fairfield County. When asked if there was a lesson in this tragedy, she said yes, the lesson is that sometimes it's better to be poor. "If you're poor and there is no money for a psychiatrist and a GAL, there is no psychiatrist or GAL and the case is just settled."

When I asked about her theories on Jennifer's body, Lisa said, "Fotis knew what he was doing. He knew when the garbage in Hartford would be picked up and knew where it would go—to the incinerator. You know [that] that trash is turned into fossil fuel, into dust. It's hard to find somebody from dust. It's no accident he did it on the Friday before Memorial Day. He knew that would slow everything down. He was probably thinking nobody's going to look into this for twenty-four hours. He'd have the kids by then, and the money would follow the kids. As for Jennifer, by the time the police finally got to Albany Avenue—if they ever did—she'd be gone. And if they did find her? He's thinking, well, it's an urban area. He's not thinking there's cameras. He figured the cops would think a minority domestic that used to work for the family had robbed and killed Jennifer."

Then Lisa took me on a ride. She has an SUV. It's said you can learn a lot about a person from the way they drive. Fotis drove like a maniac. Lisa drives like a Buddha—with detachment, authority, calm. We followed Mountain Road to High Street, continued to Mountain Spring Road, then Ely Road, which brought us to the top of Fotis's hill, where we stopped at Jefferson Crossing. It was midwinter, but the sun beat down, lighting up the redbrick Dulos mansion, porches, and porticos. We continued on to Albany Avenue, turned right, and then went past the Renbrook School, where parents sat in their cars, queued for the afternoon pickup. Ahead of us, way across the valley, we could see Hartford, dark and smoky in the distance.

Jennifer, who'd been sparklingly alive to everyone who knew her, who had the wrong dream and followed it into a dark corner, who pursued that dream with an intensity so hot it burned blue, became no more than a problem for a medical examiner at the end, the cause of the manhunt, the body in the shallow grave, or in the cement that is the foundation of the spec house, or at the bottom of the pond that is perfect for waterskiing. If a body survives without a soul, perhaps a soul can survive without a body. That's the object of every prayer.

A Note on Sources

This narrative is constructed of several reportorial strands. The majority of the material—facts, dates, biographical material, and quotes—comes from primary sources gathered by police, prosecutors, and detectives, government and private; court officers and judges; and family members, witnesses, and friends in the course first of the Dulos divorce and then of the police and prosecutorial work aimed at explaining Jennifer Dulos's disappearance and bringing her killers to justice. It amounts to thousands of pages of transcripts and depositions, police reports, search and arrest warrants, interview notes, legal filings, court decisions, crime scene reports, lab reports, and blood and DNA test results. There are text and email exchanges between Jennifer and Fotis, MP3s of calls between Fotis and his kids, JPEGs of family photos and home movies, Instagram and Twitter posts that carried coded information about the affair that led to the divorce.

Most of this material is public and can be found in the Stamford courthouse. Some was given to me on the sly by friends and attorneys in hopes that its publication might lead to reform in the divorce court, which many blame for playing a part in the tragedy, heating up what should've been cooled down. I have tried to use only the material that concerned the adults—not the kids—and steered clear of anything that was protected or needlessly intrusive, though I was of course informed by all of it.

I've enriched this primary data with other sources. I interviewed cops, lawyers, detectives, and psychiatrists involved in the divorce, and I spoke to friends and colleagues who'd known and worked with Jennifer and Fotis throughout their lives. I read newspaper and magazine articles that covered Jennifer's disappearance and the police investigation as it unfolded; I read Jennifer's work as an essayist and her articles on *Patch*. I attended the trial of Michelle Troconis, or as many days as I could manage, which I reported on for *Air Mail*. Much of the detail about Jennifer's childhood, college years, New York years, and years of motherhood and married life comes from her own writing. What she did not write she discussed under oath on the witness stand during her divorce proceedings.

Most of the people I spoke to are named in the text. A few asked for anonymity in fear of jeopardizing their relationships or careers; I agreed. I visited the places Jennifer worked and lived: houses, schools, and streets. I visited the homes Fotis built and the pond where he and his kids water-skied. I retraced the routes taken by Jennifer and Fotis on Jennifer's last day. I watched the news interviews—Fotis only really sat for one—and breaking reports that tracked the case. I listened to the Dulos true crime podcasts and watched the Lifetime movie *Gone Mom*. For the more general issues addressed in the book—from the difficulty in proving murder without a body, to the task of a medical examiner, to the question of psychopathy—I spoke to experts in the field and read their books.

This process and my access to court records gave me the dialogue that appears in these pages. If it's in quotes, it's verbatim. The sources of particular quotes and other factual information are identified in the endnotes. The amount of detail in the records, including the granularity of the status markers, was overwhelming.

Notes

INTRODUCTION

4 *"I know that filing for divorce"*: This statement appears in Jennifer's response to the response Fotis Dulos had filed in riposte to Jennifer's ex parte motion, which, filed on June 20, 2017, requested the court to issue a temporary restraining order to grant Jennifer full custody of the children until a settlement could be reached.

4 *Fotis Dulos was Greek, born in Turkey*: Though there are many sources on Fotis Dulos's biography, I relied heavily for details on Fotis's own testimony about his background, which he gave, under oath, at the Connecticut Superior Court in Stamford (hereafter Stamford courthouse) during a custody hearing on June 28, 2017.

4 *a fifty-two-year-old builder of luxury homes*: On the Fore Group, see the company's own promotional material, which is still online. Also see Fotis's testimony in the Stamford courthouse. Jennifer also testified about the business dealings of the Fore Group, as did Lauren Almeida, the family nanny who began as a Fore Group employee.

4 *Raised in Argentina, Venezuela, Chile, and Miami*: For the biography of Michelle Troconis, I relied on Fotis's and Michelle's own testimony in court and during depositions. Some of the details were also laid out in the warrant the police issued for Troconis's first and second arrests.

5 *Her father was rich, her mother was brilliant*: On the Dulos family background and the connection to Liz Claiborne, see Douglas Martin, "Arthur Ortenberg, a Liz Claiborne Founder, Dies at 87," *New York Times*, February 5, 2014. Also see the book Arthur Ortenberg wrote about his family, his wife, his life, and the business, *Liz Claiborne: The Legend, the Woman* (Taylor Trade Publishing, 2009). This same ground is covered in several newspaper and magazine stories.

6 *"She did not look like the woman in the newspaper"*: This and other facts, quotes, and observations about Jennifer during the divorce come from my interview

with Jennifer's divorce lawyer, Eric Broder, conducted at his office at 55 Green Farms Road in Westport, Connecticut.

6 *Fotis was waiting for Jennifer when she returned home*: For details on the crime scene, the best sources are the detailed warrants issued in the winter of 2020 for the arrests of Fotis Dulos, Michelle Troconis, and Kent Mawhinney.

7 *"Successful people don't live in Farmington"*: This statement, which has been widely reported, appeared in the contempt-of-court motion Fotis Dulos filed against Jennifer Dulos on November 3, 2017.

PART ONE

13 *New Canaan served as a lab*: On the Harvard Five and the history of New Canaan, see the website ConnecticutHistory.org. Also see Mary Louise King, *Portrait of New Canaan: The History of a Connecticut Town* (New Canaan Historical Society, 1981), and William D. Earls, *The Harvard Five in New Canaan: Midcentury Modern Houses by Marcel Breuer, Landis Gores, John Johansen, Philip Johnson, Eliot Noyes, and Others* (W. W. Norton, 2006).

13 *With just over twenty thousand residents*: On the wealth and demographics of Connecticut towns, see New Canaan Equity Profile at Data Haven (ctdatahaven .org) as well as statistics from the U.S. Census Bureau.

14 *she'd always valued*: On exclusive clubs and Jennifer's love of all things Wasp and the world her father called "Bank," see her essay "Window-Shopping for a Life" (published under her maiden name, Jennifer Farber), which appeared in *Personals: Dreams and Nightmares from the Lives of 20 Young Writers*, ed. Thomas Beller (Houghton Mifflin, 1998).

15 *more expensive than most universities*: For details on the history, mission, and cost of the New Canaan Country School, see the school's website (country school.net) and *The U.S. News & World Report Guide to Private Schools*.

15 *Tuition for the Dulos kids*: On the details surrounding Jennifer and the New Canaan Country School, see the testimony Jennifer gave in court on various occasions, but most extensively at the Stamford courthouse hearing on May 30, 2017.

15 *a prewar redbrick apartment house*: Details from Jennifer's childhood in Brooklyn and her time at Saint Ann's come from her essay "Window-Shopping for a Life," and her testimony at the Stamford courthouse in the summer and fall of 2017.

15 *a victim of her own naïveté*: For details on Jennifer's car and driver as well as the ways in which she was sheltered, I relied on my interviews with members of the Playwrights Collective, including Colette Burson, Kate Robin, Tim Cunningham, Eduardo Machado, and Dan Rybicky. I also talked to Tom Beller and Steve Garbarino, who both spent time in the limo.

16 *Lauren Almeida, a University of Connecticut graduate*: Information on Lauren Almeida comes from court testimony from Fotis, Jennifer, and Lauren herself, as well as notes taken by police and prosecutors during various interviews with Lauren in the course of the investigation. Lauren also supplied the details of Jennifer's day-to-day routines.

17 *The New Canaan police gathered footage*: The story of the surveillance foot-

age comes from the search and arrest warrants, which include a moment-by-moment breakdown of the crime as well as images from the footage itself. See also Dave Altimari, "Timeline: How State Police Used Video to Track a Truck They Believe Fotis Dulos Was Driving the Day Jennifer Farber Dulos Went Missing," *Hartford Courant*, September 9, 2019.

17 *Gloria Farber grew up in Newark*: Gloria Farber's family background, as well as the details of her childhood and education, come mostly from Ortenberg, *Liz Claiborne*. Gloria filled in more of the details herself when she appeared on the talk show *Charlie Rose*. She also spoke about childhood education, her specialty. See also Martin, "Arthur Ortenberg, a Liz Claiborne Founder, Dies at 87."

19 *She earned a bachelor's degree at Rutgers*: Additional details about Gloria Farber's background come from Hilliard Farber's private obituary (January 8, 2017) as well as newspaper articles and social media.

20 *"I saw your mother and I knew, just knew"*: Jennifer's characterization of her parents' marriage appears in her essay "Window-Shopping for a Life."

20 *He'd been raised in Rahway*: The facts on Hilliard Farber's background come from the obituary his family printed when he died, as well as a handful of stories that appeared in *The Wall Street Journal* and *The New York Times*, which covered his exploits at Chase Bank in the 1970s.

21 *"I wanted to be the pure, fresh Ivory girl"*: See Jennifer's essay "Window-Shopping for a Life."

22 *the U.S. Securities and Exchange Commission*: For facts behind Hilliard's exit from Chase Manhattan, I relied on newspaper articles, including "Chase Manhattan Accepts Finding by S.E.C. on Inadequate Controls," *New York Times*, September 21, 1976, and "Banks' Problems Create Controversy," *New York Times*, October 7, 1974.

22 *People who knew Hilliard*: Descriptions of Hilliard Farber and his personal magnetism come from many interviews—it was a recurring theme, almost a leitmotif—including those with members of the Playwrights Collective as well as Jennifer's friends from college. While testifying, Fotis Dulos described his father-in-law as a very powerful man.

22 *"a large man, once slim, tall and dark-haired"*: See Ortenberg, *Liz Claiborne*.

22 *Their first child, Melissa*: Descriptions of Melissa Farber and her mental condition come from court transcripts and documents. Fotis Dulos spoke of it several times, including in a February 4, 2019, filing in which, citing a history of Farber family mental illness, he asked that Jennifer be drug-tested and no longer allowed to drive the kids. Many of Jennifer's friends spoke in interviews about Melissa, her mental health crisis, her illness, and her role in the family. Many details come from friends of Jennifer who knew Melissa at different points in her life, starting in high school.

23 *She enacted her fantasies with her dollhouses*: On Jennifer's love of dollhouses, see her essay "Window-Shopping for a Life."

23 *Gloria at first refused to buy the perfect little dollhouse*: See Jennifer's essay "Window-Shopping for a Life."

25 *"an exclusive racquet club"*: See Jennifer's essay "Window-Shopping for a Life."

26 *Once religiously affiliated, Saint Ann's*: For Stanley Bosworth and the history of Saint Ann's, I made use of the school's website as well as magazine and newspaper stories, including Ariel Levy, "The Devil and Saint Ann's," *New York*, April 30, 2004, and John Leland, "An Elite School, a Boy's Suicide and a Question of Blame," *New York Times*, July 2, 2023.

27 *Hilliard Farber donated large sums*: The entire record of the Farbers' donations, including those made to Saint Ann's and Brown, is public and can be found online. See, for example, a year-by-year record of the Gloria and Hilliard Farber Foundation tax filings at ProPublica.

27 *Beller, who'd been taken in by Saint Ann's*: Tom Beller has chronicled his expulsion from Riverdale and his life at Saint Ann's and Vassar in essays and short stories. For an early reportorial take, see Dahlia Dean, "Peeping Tom," *WWD*, May 22, 1995.

28 *"the way men turn to the Sports Page"*: See Jennifer's essay "Window-Shopping for a Life."

30 *Brown did in fact seem to have a special relationship*: In the wake of the recent Supreme Court ruling that struck down affirmative action in college admissions, *The New York Times* has run several stories about the tight relationship between East Coast prep schools and the Ivy League. See, for example, Aatish Bhatia, Claire Cain Miller, Josh Katz, and Stuart Schmill, "Study of Elite College Admissions Data Suggests Being Very Rich Is Its Own Qualification," *New York Times*, July 24, 2023, and Aatish Bhatia and Claire Cain Miller, "Explore How Income Influences Attendance at 139 Top Colleges," *New York Times*, September 11, 2023.

30 *Jennifer said she liked Fotis okay*: This comes from several sources, including Jennifer herself.

31 *Jennifer Farber was a book person*: Descriptions of Jennifer at Brown come from several college friends, including Hugh Warrender.

31 *Her first college boyfriend*: Information on Jennifer's romantic life at Brown, including her relationship with Rich Yelland, comes from college friends. She apparently dramatized her relationship with Yelland in several plays and wrote about it in "Window-Shopping for a Life."

31 *Rich's friend Hugh Warrender*: Hugh Warrender was kind enough to talk about Jennifer to me and share the memoir of her visit with him included in the text.

34 *So why did she break up with Gunnar*: The man Jennifer disguised as "Gunnar Graham" runs like a ribbon through her life and correspondence. Her failure to love and commit to him is one of the main subjects in "Window-Shopping for a Life."

34 *a private club in Scarsdale*: It's interesting that Jennifer, despite her love of "Bank," names Quaker Ridge, which was founded in 1916, the days of the gentleman's agreement, as a golf club that gave Jews a place to play. Winged Foot, Quaker Ridge's Westchester rival, was restricted into the 1970s. See "Numerous Sport Clubs in New York Are Closed to Jews and Negroes," *Jewish Telegraphic Agency*, July 14, 1959.

35 *Most of the people enrolled*: For information on the NYU graduate dramatic

writing program as well as Jennifer's particular experience, I relied on interviews with several of Jennifer's classmates as well as her professor, the playwright Eduardo Machado, and information from the school's own website and promotional material.

36 *One Fifth Avenue*: For information on One Fifth, see Christopher Gray, "Streetscapes: 1 Fifth Avenue; A Good Joke Not Well Retold," *New York Times*, October 4, 1992, and Michelle Duncan, "Why One Fifth Avenue Is Still One of NYC's Most Star-Studded and Desirable Buildings," *Architectural Digest*, October 7, 2002.

37 *She could see Washington Square Park from the window*: For the details on the apartment and Jennifer's life there, I relied on several of Jennifer's friends, including Colette Burson, Tom Beller, and Steve Garbarino, all of whom spent time there.

39 *"Armando was on to something real"*: Carrie Luft was intensely involved with the Playwrights Collective, until she wasn't. She is an honest critic of Eduardo Machado and his practices. She also became a spokesperson for Jennifer, Gloria, and the Dulos kids after Jennifer's disappearance. I spoke with her while writing my stories for *Air Mail*, then met her in person while working on this book, though she did not agree to a formal interview.

42 *They introduced themselves with a manifesto*: On the Playwrights Collective, I made use of various interviews with former members, and, of course, with Eduardo Machado as well as the archive at the Rose Collection of the New York Public Library, where I found old flyers, programs, show bills, donor lists, and the articles cited in the text, many of which are not online.

46 *The first was called* The Red Doors: As far as I've been able to determine, no copies of these plays exist, nor do audio or video recordings of the performances. Aside from the stage bills, the loss is complete. It's as if they never existed. The details and dialogue given in the text come from people who either acted in or worked on the productions.

49 *Rob was like Jay Gatsby*: On Rob Bingham, I relied on the reminiscences of his friends and *Open City* publishing partners, Tom Beller and Daniel Pinchbeck, as well as Lee Smith, who considered Daniel his best friend, and Gerry Howard, Rob's editor at Riverhead Books. Details of his life and relationship with Jennifer appear in the Dulos divorce documents. See also Daniel Pinchbeck, "Cast Your Magazine upon the Waters," *New York Times*, February 22, 1988; Tina Kelley, "A Life of Comfort, Lived Hard; A Writer Is Remembered for His Promise and His Failings," *New York Times*, December 10, 1999; Vanessa Grigoriadis, "Boy, Interrupted," *New York*, January 3, 2000; and Marie Brenner, *House of Dreams: The Bingham Family of Louisville* (Random House, 1988).

51 *it may be best remembered for the parties*: On *Open City*, see Tom Beller's introductions to the publication's various collections as well as the journal itself, back issues of which can be purchased at its website (opencity.org). See also Daniel Pinchbeck's books about his life and adventures with hallucinogens, *Breaking Open the Head: A Psychedelic Journey into the Heart of Contemporary Shamanism* (Broadway Books, 2002) and *2012: The Return of Quetzalcoatl*

(Tarcher/Penguin, 2006). See also Joyce Johnson, *Minor Characters: A Beat Memoir* (Houghton Mifflin, 1983). As for the parties, some of these memories are mine.

53   *He was already succeeding in literary New York*: Information on the young Tom Beller comes from the middle-aged Tom Beller—we are friends and spoke several times in the course of my reporting—as well as his owns essays and stories, his life being a primary subject of his oeuvre. See also the newspaper and magazine articles that have greeted the publication of each of his books.

61   What Party? *opened in March 1997*: In discussing *What Party?* I relied on information gleaned from interviews with many of the participants as well as the archive at the Rose Collection, which includes programs, cast lists, and show notes. I exchanged emails with Charles McNulty of the *Los Angeles Times*; he reviewed the play for *The Village Voice* but hardly remembers it now.

66   *"The person you are looking for"*: Several people told me a version of this story. This particular version comes from Jennifer's playwriting friend Colette Burson.

66   *In 1994, Jennifer purchased a dog*: Jennifer wrote about her dog in personal essays and again in her posts for *Patch*, which she began when she was living in Canton and Farmington, Connecticut. See Jennifer Dulos, "The Best Part of My Night," *Patch*, March 5, 2012.

67   *Aspen was a nineteenth-century boomtown*: On the history of Aspen, Colorado, see the websites for the Aspen Chamber Resort Association (aspenchamber .org) and the Aspen Historical Society (aspenhistory.org), as well as Western Mining History (westernmininghistory.com). On the 10th Mountain Division, see Peter Shelton, *Climb to Conquer: The Untold Story of WWII's 10th Mountain Division* (Scribner, 2003), and Maurice Isserman, *The Winter Army: The World War II Odyssey of the 10th Mountain Division, America's Elite Alpine Warriors* (Houghton Mifflin Harcourt, 2019). This was all supplemented with personal reporting, meaning trips to Aspen, including one in 2004 for *Rolling Stone* magazine, which sent me to the Hotel Jerome to interview Hunter S. Thompson.

68   *Jennifer worked on a novel in Aspen*: The documentation of Jennifer's time in Aspen in sparse. It is a sort of blank area in the otherwise well-chronicled story of her life. What I did learn comes from interviews with friends, especially the writer Lee Smith. More information came from the Duloses' custody battle.

69   *It was Hilliard who encouraged in Jennifer tastes that were not just Waspy*: This is my read based on interviews with Jennifer's friends and the evidence of her writing. Tom Beller, who describes Jennifer as strong-willed and self-made, thinks one might as easily blame or credit all the Cheever and Fitzgerald she read at Saint Ann's.

70   *Jennifer had used an alias while modeling at Brown*: The story of Jennifer's modeling days and her use of a fake name was covered in court testimony as well as her personal essays. Lee Smith talked about it, too, presumably learning the stories from Jennifer herself. The story of her alias comes up again and again, and appears in a personal letter, which is included in the court file. Several of Fotis Dulos's defense lawyers also spoke of Jennifer's trip to Aspen and her use of a different name as they argued she might have done this again and still in

fact be alive and living as someone else out there in the world. For a time, she even used the other name—Jennifer Bey—as an email address.

70 *she converted to Christianity and started wearing a cross*: I first heard this story from Lee Smith, who visited Jennifer in Aspen. It was later corroborated in the court transcripts by Fotis Dulos, who used the conversion, and the fact that Jennifer had never told Hilliard and Gloria, as a way to attack Jennifer's character.

70 *Jennifer didn't tell her New York friends about the conversion*: I was the person who first told several of Jennifer's friends, including Tom Beller, about Jennifer's Christianity. There is a phrase that has become a go-to cliché for journalists and public officials in reacting to unexpected events: shocked, but not surprised. That's how many of Jennifer's old colleagues said they felt when I shared the news.

PART TWO

75 *Jennifer was on a plane, returning to L.A.*: This story comes from Lee Smith. I was able to confirm the flight and track its course in articles from 9/11 and records from the Federal Aviation Administration.

76 *Fotis Dulos spotted Jennifer as he walked to baggage claim*: This story is multi-sourced. I heard it from Lee Smith, who spoke to Jennifer soon after. Jennifer and Fotis herself both spoke about it in the course of the custody battle. Jennifer also wrote about it in her posts on *Patch*.

76 *Fotis was traveling with his oldest friend*: The name Andreas Toutziaridis comes up in newspaper articles and police reports and even in the files of U.S. Immigration and Customs Enforcement, agents of which issued a warrant to seize his phone. In their reports, police speak of him in the way old-time movie writers speak of a possible third man. What he did or did not know—these are questions that have remained impossible to answer. Jennifer spoke about Andreas in court on May 2, 2019.

77 *Hilary Aldama graduated from Brown*: Though Hilary Aldama has kept a low profile, information on her is available online at the website of her law firm and on the sites of various charities and boards on which she has served. Fotis spoke about her at some length in his own court testimony. Aldama commented on men with "dreamer personalities" on *Loving Living Local*, a TV show that airs on KTAL News in Shreveport, Louisiana. She talked about her third marriage—to the illustrator William Joyce—on the same program..

78 *"She's too young for me"*: Jennifer and Fotis each gave their own version of Fotis's first marriage, and how news of it came out, in court.

79 *Fotis Dulos was born in Turkey*: See Vanessa Grigoriadis, "Fates and Furies," *Vanity Fair*, October 15, 2020. Fotis's biography is also included in Fore Group promotional material and the testimony of Fotis and Jennifer.

79 *Petros Dulos had been born in 1912*: Details on Fotis's parents, Petros and Kleopatra Dulos, come from, among other places, Fotis's sister, Rena Dulos Kyrimi, who provided details in interviews she gave to local papers when Fotis was under house arrest.

81 *waterskiing seems less sport than activity*: I learned about waterskiing and Fotis's life in the water from people he skied with in Avon, Connecticut, including Hutch

Haines, who is skiing royalty in that part of New England. See also Robert Reichart, *Hit It! The 80 Year History of Water Skiing in the Upper Midwest* (Xlibris, 2003).

81 *"I wanted to get exposed to societies and cultures"*: This quote, and other quotes from Fotis's personal essay, appear in Grigoriadis, "Fate and Furies."

81 *Brown was as much about status as education*: For Fotis's life at Brown, I relied on several of his classmates, including Hugh Warrender, who was a frequent guest at Fotis's off-campus apartment. Additional information comes from the court testimony and interview notes with Jennifer and Fotis. I spoke to several other people from the same graduating class, or nearly, to get a general feel for the atmosphere on campus at the time.

83 *He took a position at the multinational consulting firm Capgemini*: On Fotis's professional life after business school and before he met Jennifer, I relied on my own interviews. See also Grigoriadis, "Fates and Furies," as well as the newspaper stories in the bibliography, including Dave Altimari and Edmund H. Mahony, "North Carolina Woman Paid $147,000 to Help Fotis Dulos Post His Bond," *Hartford Courant*, January 29, 2020.

83 *He credited this dream to his sister, Rena*: On Rena Dulos Kyrimi, see the interview she gave to Erin Moriarty in a CBS special that appeared on February 12, 2021. See also the testimony of Fotis and Jennifer; the coverage by Dave Altimari in *The Hartford Courant*; and Larry Noodles, "Dulos Tied Up Jewish Wife with Zip Ties Before Murder," LarryNoodles.com, January 8, 2020.

84 *"It happened very, very fast"*: This quote appears in Timothy Dumas's outstanding article "Where Is She?," *New Canaan–Darien & Rowayton*, September/October 2020.

85 *"Jen was quirky and smart"*: I have spoken to and become friends with with D. J. Paul in the course of reporting.

86 *"[She] went out immediately after the ceremony"*: The person who gave me this quote is one of the few people who asked to be cited anonymously in this book, for reasons of personal safety. I have agreed.

88 *her dress hiked above her knees*: Jennifer's wedding was described by several attendees. For the history of the Metropolitan Club, see "Inside 10 of New York City's Most Exclusive Private Clubs," *Business Insider*, October 26, 2015. Also see the club's website (metropolitanclubnyc.org). As for the layout, I know the joint because I've been to a wedding there myself.

89 *Canton sprawls across twenty-five square miles*: For Canton's history, I made use of the information on the Canton Historical Museum's website (cantonmuseum.org) as well as my own visits to the town. See also the National Register of Historical Places and the demographic information from censuses, present and past.

90 *Jennifer didn't even get to choose her own home*: Jennifer testified about her life in Canton and Farmington at the Stamford courthouse in the spring and summer of 2017. I've made use of transcripts of those hearings. See also Jennifer's posts on *Patch* and interviews with friends and acquaintances from her years in and near the town.

91 *"I'd like to live on the water"*: This quote appeared in the personal essay Fotis

wrote for business school. Fotis further repeated the sentiment to Jennifer, a fact reported by both of them during court testimony.

91 *Fotis called his business the Fore Group*: For details on the Fore Group, see the documents Fotis filed with the court during the custody battle and fight over restraining orders. See also the documents and testimony collected during the civil suit Gloria Farber filed against Fotis Dulos on March 2, 2016.

93 *What could not be processed in words, she burned off with exercise*: For the quotes in this paragraph, see the following articles by Jennifer Dulos: "Blow Drying My Hair—Yes, This Is a Topic," *Patch*, January 16, 2012; "Morning Run," *Patch*, June 19, 2012; and "What We're Not Doing This (New) School Year," *Patch*, September 14, 2012.

95 *"Fotis drove like an absolute maniac"*: This quote appears in Dumas, "Where Is She?"

95 *Jennifer went straight to the most expensive option*: This comes from my interviews and research, including Jennifer's own writing.

95 *"The period after the engagement but before the marriage"*: Dr. Herman's report on the Dulos marriage remains sealed. He spoke with me on the condition that we speak about his work in general and not the particulars of the Dulos case.

98 *He'd believed Fotis had agreed*: The details of the religion, and the fight over how the children would be raised, was a topic of discussion in court and appears in the transcripts of the hearing at the Stamford courthouse. The issue came up in conversations with friends of the couple, talking on and off the record.

98 *"My in-laws were very upset"*: Fotis said this, and explained the fight, at the Stamford courthouse on July 11, 2017. His exact words appear in the court transcript.

99 *Fotis picked up a chair and threw it at Hilliard*: Friends of Jennifer told me the story during my reporting.

99 *Gloria, though a doting mother close to both her daughters*: For Jennifer and Gloria, I relied mostly on Jennifer's own testimony and writing as well as my interviews with Jennifer's friends.

102 *Fotis began taking the older twins*: Information about the Old Farms Skiers and Fotis's life at the pond as a parent and a skier comes from members of the club, including Dana Hinman, who agreed to speak with me only in generalities about skiing and the life and history of the sport and the club. The subject of waterskiing is also a constant topic of discussion in the court documents, interviews with court officers, and even interviews with police. Fotis and Jennifer both wrote about waterskiing and their life at the club in the emails they sent back and forth, to which I had access.

103 *"I feel [the children] are suffering"*: This quote comes from testimony Jennifer gave in court on May 30, 2017.

103 *The Duloses had one of those Santa sleighs*: The Dulos family's Christmas yard display, which made an annual appearance, was described to me by a neighbor who asked to remain unnamed.

104 *Jennifer heard the commotion*: The manner and details of Kleopatra Dulos's death appear in the police report written at the time. The tragedy and its greater

import were discussed by Jennifer and Fotis in court and by several family friends to me in the course of my reporting.

106 *"If that's the case"*: Jennifer actually mused on some of these arguments, and the question of names, in "Blow Drying My Hair—Yes, This Is a Topic." She discussed it in more detail in court.

106 *Her fifth child was christened Cleopatra-Noelle*: The details of the christenings were described to me by a family friend.

106 *"They let us out of the hospital"*: See Jennifer Dulos, "Goodbye, Charlotte Court," *Patch*, February 17, 2012.

110 *Giants games her father took her to*: See Jennifer Dulos, "Post Game Glow," *Patch*, February 6, 2012.

110 *"The master bedroom suite"*: This language is from Zillow circa July 2020. Sales copy being what it is, it's subsequently changed and will presumably soon change again.

111 *With twenty-five thousand residents*: On the history of Farmington, Connecticut, plus its demographics, see the town's website (www.farmington-ct.org). Also see the U.S. Census Bureau profile of Farmington (data.census.gov/profile/Farmington _town,_Hartford_County,_Connecticut?g=060XX00US0900327600); and the page on Farmington at ConnecticutHistory.org (connecticuthistory.org/towns -page/farmington/).

111 *Lisa Nkonoki, a Farmington mother*: My information on Lisa Nkonoki comes from time I spent with her at her house, the Purple Palace, in Farmington, and phone calls and emails that followed. See also Mickey Rapkin, "The Socialite Soprano and the Life Coach," *Town & Country*, January 20, 2016, and Robert Marchant, "Greenwich Police Charge 59-Year-Old 'Life Coach' with Illegally Practicing Law in Divorce Case," *Greenwich Time*, March 17, 2022.

112 *In the articles that followed*: See Jennifer Dulos, "Camp Monk," *Patch*, March 6, 2012, and "More Sleep, No More," *Patch*, April 26, 2012.

113 *"My mother-in-law used to say"*: See Jennifer Dulos, "A Farmington Mother of Five Gears Up for the Birthday-Heavy Month of October," *Patch*, October 3, 2012.

115 *the developer who created Levittown*: On the McMansion and modern suburbia, I built on reporting I did for a story I wrote about William Levitt, the creator of the modern American suburb; see Rich Cohen, "La Belle Simone," *New York*, November 8, 2013. See also David Brooks, *Bobos in Paradise: The New Upper Class and How They Got There* (Simon & Schuster, 2001), and Eric Pace, "William Levitt, 86, Pioneer of the Suburbs, Dies," *New York Times*, January 29, 1994.

115 *There was something phony about the Fore Group*: Details on the finances and operating procedures of the Fore Group are voluminous. See the documents that were produced in discovery during Gloria's civil suit against the Fore Group to recover funds. See also the documents Fotis filed with the court during the early portions of his custody battle. All of these, which are greatly detailed, can be found at the Stamford courthouse. The issues were discussed and analyzed by several newspapers and magazines (see bibliography).

116 *"He always said the goal is Fairfield"*: This quote, as well as the description of the Fore Group's overall long-term strategy, was given by Jennifer in a hearing at the Stamford courthouse on May 30, 2017.

118 *If Fotis needed help*: On Lauren Almeida and her life with the family, I made use of her own court testimony as well as the testimony of Fotis and Jennifer, both of whom talked about her at length. I also had access to emails Lauren wrote to Jennifer in 2017. Some of these were clearly meant to memorialize misbehavior by Fotis.

118 *She was a student at the University of Connecticut*: I verified details about Lauren Almeida's time at the University of Connecticut on the school's website (uconn.edu). Most of my information comes from the testimony of Fotis and Jennifer, and also the testimony of Lauren herself.

120 *"What's a sandbagger?"*: Jennifer talked about accusations of cheating and the specific term "sandbagger" in court on January 31, 2018. Fotis responded and defended himself on cross-examination that same day.

121 *He began traveling several times a year to Miami*: Fotis testified about his waterskiing life in Miami, including details about the club and the boat, at the Stamford courthouse on April 26, 2018. Details were filled in by family friends, including people who were closely connected to those trips.

PART THREE

125 *Michelle Troconis is a jock*: For the biography of Michelle Troconis, I relied on newspaper coverage and magazine articles (see bibliography). More recently, Michelle, seemingly in an effort to improve her image, has begun telling some of her own life story via Instagram. Much of this material was also covered in court and can be found in the transcripts, which are public.

127 *Jennifer regularly checked Petros's phone*: Jennifer testified at the Stamford courthouse about her experience with Instagram and just how she found out about the affair between Fotis and Michelle. Details are also mentioned in her various filings against Fotis for contempt. I heard versions of the same stories from a handful of Jennifer's friends, who had either spoken to her at the time or heard the details later, when they reconnected during the divorce.

128 *signed his father onto Houseparty*: Jennifer spoke about the affair, how she found out about it and how Petros had been made an unwitting accomplice, including his recommendation of the Houseparty app, in testimony given at the Stamford courthouse on October 9, 2018.

129 *the counselor could not be Jewish*: Fotis and his feelings about Jewish doctors and lawyers runs like a ribbon through court transcripts and notes. See, for example, the court transcript from June 27, 2017.

129 *Jennifer and Fotis engaged Mark Lucyk*: This information emerged during the testimony Jennifer gave on the stand on January 31, 2018, when she was being cross-examined by Fotis.

129 *"I was trying to work on our marriage"*: Jennifer spoke about her father's illness and decline in court testimony given on May 30, 2017. It is a subject that comes up again and again.

130 *"My father isn't going to live much longer"*: Jennifer made this summary of her feelings on the stand at the Stamford courthouse on May 30, 2017.

130 *Hilliard was eighty-three*: Jennifer spoke about Sweet's syndrome and Hilliard's decline in court transcripts.

130 *He'd retired in 2008*: For details on the sale of Hilliard Farber's company and its financials, see Tradeweb.com. Also see "Tradeweb Acquires Hilliard Farber," *American Banker*, November 6, 2008.

130 *After collapsing during a vacation*: Fotis recalled Hilliard's illness and collapse in St. Barts in an email to Jennifer dated October 31, 2017.

131 *The funeral service was at Temple Emanu-El*: Details on the funeral service at Temple Emanu-El appear in Hilliard Farber's obituary. I also spoke to a few people who were at the synagogue that day.

132 *To Gloria, that must have seemed like appeasement*: This information comes mostly from a handful of interviews after the first draft of this book was finished. This included talks with Jennifer's friends, and some of the people involved in the case.

133 *Three days into the Aspen trip*: The details of the trips to Aspen and Miami in the spring of 2017 were given by Jennifer in court on May 30, 2017.

134 *An old email had made Jennifer suspicious*: This information was expanded on in testimony given by Lauren Almeida during the trial of Michelle Troconis. See Pat Tomlinson, "3 Takeaways from Day 4 in the Michelle Troconis Trial in Jennifer Dulos Disappearance," *Stamford Advocate*, January 18, 2024.

134 *He and Jennifer had not had sex in years*: This information came out in several places, including the Stamford court, where, on January 18, 2018, Fotis asked Jennifer, who was on the witness stand, "Is it the truth that for the last six years our sexual relationship has been virtually nonexistent?"

135 *"Easter is a big holiday for us"*: This quote and the details in this section, many of them, come from the testimony Fotis gave at the Stamford courthouse on June 28, 2017.

136 *Buckingham Palace*: Both parents described the trip to Buckingham Palace, each from their own point of view, at the Stamford courthouse on May 30, 2017.

138 *a handful of fights*: Jennifer and Fotis both described and argued over the nature of the big fights that marked the end of their life together at the Stamford courthouse on May 30, 2017, and again in testimony over the course of the summer that followed.

138 *"Things are different because we are breaking up"*: This quote comes from testimony Jennifer gave at the Stamford courthouse on May 30, 2017.

140 *"[Jennifer] looked terrified"*: The quotes from this section comes mostly from the court testimony of Jennifer Dulos and Lauren Almeida given at the Stamford courthouse on June 28, 2017.

141 *Fotis became agitated*: The housekeeper, Kazimiera Kaminski, testified in court on June 28, 2018.

148 *Jennifer and Lauren used the occasion to pack*: Details on the hasty move from Farmington have been widely covered in the press. I myself covered it for *Air Mail* in 2020. Details about the moving company appear in several articles (see bibliography), including Dumas, "Where Is She?"

150 *"They wouldn't pick up"*: This quote and the following ones are from the testimony Fotis gave at the Stamford courthouse on June 27, 2017.

150　*He said he was worried about their safety*: This information as well as the quoted phrase—"does pot"—appear in the transcript of the testimony Fotis Dulos gave to Judge Thomas Colin in Stamford, Connecticut, on June 28, 2017.

PART FOUR

153　*Fotis would not be allowed to contact Jennifer*: The quotes and details in this section come from my own meetings with various attorneys involved in the divorce case, as well from the documents themselves: the application for an ex parte motion, Fotis's response, and Jennifer's response to the response, all filed in court, as well as the testimony from both parties in the hearing about the ex parte order that followed.

155　*The police confiscated Fotis's Glock the same day*: The story of the Glock, how Fotis showed it to Jennifer, how it was locked, how she photographed the serial numbers, and how it was seized appears in the warrant the Connecticut State Police filed to search the house in Farmington in 2020. These details and the story were also testified to in court during the discussion about the ex parte motion and the temporary restraining order.

156　*Jennifer had signed a twelve-month, $300,000 lease*: The details of Jennifer's living arrangements, including her lease in New Canaan, were testified to at the Stamford courthouse on June 27, 2017.

157　*Stamford, Connecticut, is the capital of contentious divorce*: On the realities of the Stamford divorce court, I relied on interviews with several lawyers and guardians ad litem who have served in the court, as well as on the newspaper articles listed in the bibliography and the evidence from the most notorious cases themselves, which can be found in the court's database.

157　*Over half a million Americans split every year*: On divorce in America, see "Marriage and Divorce," U.S. Census Bureau (www.census.gov/topics/families /marriage-and-divorce.html); "Marriage and Divorce," CDC (www.cdc.gov/nchs /fastats/marriage-divorce.htm); and Kaia Hubbard, "Here Are the States Where Your Marriage Won't Last," *U.S. News & World Report*, December 8, 2020.

158　*Bobby Bonilla, who battled for assets*: See Ikimulisa Livingston, "Hidden-Ball 'Trick' by Bonilla," *New York Post*, June 1, 2010.

158　*Montel Williams, whose wife*: See Cathy Burke, "Montel's Wife Dumps His Duds," *New York Post*, April 11, 2000.

166　*a GAL is a neutral party*: For the responsibilities, tasks, and methods of the guardian ad litem, I relied on interviews with several present and former GALs, as well as on "Guardian Ad Litem (GAL) or Attorney for a Minor Child (AMC)," State of Connecticut Judicial Branch website (www.jud.ct.gov/family/gal_amc.htm).

167　*Michael Meehan, a bald, middle-aged graduate*: On Michael Meehan, see his biography on the MeehanLaw website (www.meehanlaw.com/attorney/meehan -michael-t), as well as his social media pages and news articles in which he has been described. I tried to reach Meehan several times. In the end, when he finally responded, he said the legal code of ethics made it impossible for him to talk to me. I came away from my research believing he did as well as anyone could have done in what seemed an impossible situation.

167 *though the signs of depression went disregarded by Fotis*: Jennifer testified about this exchange, as well as her search for doctors for her son, at the Stamford courthouse on July 28, 2017.

167 *Fotis had problems with Dr. Lopez*: The quotes and details surrounding the work of Dr. David Lopez and his decision to stop treatment come from court testimony by all major parties: Jennifer and Fotis, Michael Meehan, and even Dr. Lopez himself. Much of this information was also covered in the press when the story broke.

168 *Whenever Jennifer confronted Fotis*: For the story of the OurFamilyWizard app and the many fights over visitation and custody rules, I made use of the court filings for contempt, the counterfilings, the court testimony, and the hundreds of emails and texts that passed between Jennifer and Fotis, to which I had access.

169 *Jennifer was driven to distraction*: This post and Jennifer's reaction to it are included in Jennifer's court filings. I have also seen the photo, the post, and the emails that went back and forth between Jennifer and Fotis as a result.

170 *Fotis persisted in denial*: Fotis was working as his own lawyer during this testimony. At one point, making a mistake known to all watchers of TV court shows—never ask a question you don't know the answer to—Fotis asked Rob Artus if he, the private eye, had photographic evidence of Fotis's arrival at Ski Sundown with Michelle and the kids, then expressed something like astonishment—"You do?"—when Artus answered in the affirmative. This exchange appears in the court transcripts.

171 *Veterans of the company met in the city*: The story of Jennifer's reunion with the members of the Playwrights Collective was told to me by many of the people who were there, including Dan Rybicky and Colette Burson.

179 *Jennifer ran to the house*: Lauren Almeida told police about this terrifying incident after Jennifer's disappearance. Timothy Dumas wrote about it as well, in "Where Is She?" It was reported by Elisha Fieldstadt on the NBC News website ("Jennifer Dulos' Husband Once Tried to Run Her Over with Car, Nanny Told Police") on January 16, 2020.

182 *"I just think being in the house"*: This quote and the others in this section come from Jennifer's testimony, given at the Stamford courthouse on June 8, 2018.

187 *Fotis got Jennifer on the witness stand*: See the court transcript from January 31, 2018.

194 *he had consulted Norman Heller*: Fotis filed a motion to have Judge Heller removed from the case on May 19, 2018. The incident was covered in Dumas, "Where Is She?"

194 *Fotis and Michelle toured the New Canaan Country School*: The quote in this passage, and the details surrounding Michelle's visit to the New Canaan Country School, appear in testimony given by Michael Meehan and the other principals at the Stamford courthouse on July 12, 2018.

196 *Pyetranker, who attended Fordham and St. John's*: On Jacob Pyetranker, see the biography on his law firm's website (www.pyetrankerpc.com) as well as his LinkedIn and other social media pages. Also see his own testimony in the course of the case and the several articles that appeared in the press. He makes

a brief cameo in Fotis's arrest warrant. I reached out to him several times. In the end, he told me he could not talk about his involvement in the case.

197 *he did a good job pretending*: Many of the facts and arguments to follow come directly from the email correspondence between the attorneys.

199 *"To the contrary"*: This ruling appears in a finding on Jennifer Dulos Second Application for Emergency Custody filed by Judge Heller on March 1, 2018.

203 *When a proceeding becomes debilitatingly contentious*: The aura and realities of Middletown were explained to me by Jennifer's first divorce lawyer, Eric Broder.

PART FIVE

211 *Kent Mawhinney grew up in South Windsor, Connecticut*: On Kent Mawhinney, see the detailed warrants for his arrest, which unpack his background, his relationship with Fotis, and his previous legal troubles. He was described in additional detail in the police interrogation of Michelle Troconis.

212 *was being sued by a client, Oladejo Lamikanra*: Details surrounding the lawsuit that Oladejo Lamikanra filed against the Fore Group as well as the company's financial problems appear in the notes and transcripts of the civil case Gloria Farber filed against Fotis and the Fore Group on March 2, 2016, which came to trial in June 2018.

212 *Kent settled the case in 2022*: See Alex Wood, "Ex–Dulos Lawyer Avoids Rape Conviction, Sentenced for Violating Protective Order," *Journal Inquirer* (Manchester, Connecticut), June 20, 2022.

213 *"Dulos abruptly paid the bill and left"*: For details on this encounter, see the police report filed after the incident, the police report compiled after Jennifer's disappearance, and the press coverage, including Dave Altimari, "Michelle Troconis, the Girlfriend of Fotis Dulos, Goes from Possible Alibi to Key Witness Against Her Boyfriend in His Estranged Wife's Disappearance," *Hartford Courant*, September 6, 2019.

213 *the house she'd purchased at 69 Welles Lane*: After the apparent murder of Jennifer Dulos, the address of this house was legally changed to 71 Welles Lane.

214 *"He did end up looking like Pawel"*: Detective John Kimball said this in court during the trial of Michelle Troconis in 2024. Commenting further, Kimball added: "That goes along with the planning and that goes along with creating a diversion." Fotis apparently shaved his body as well as his head. No hair means less chance of leaving DNA behind. Michelle told police she'd helped Fotis shave his hair.

215 *Fotis told Jennifer he'd gone to a candy shop*: For details of the last visitation, see the report filed afterward by Dennis Puebla's designated visitation specialist; the testimony given by Lauren Almeida, who was there; the police reports; and the press coverage, including Dave Altimari, "The Story of the Last Time Fotis Dulos Saw His Children: Chocolate Bunnies, a Haircut, a New Basketball Hoop and an Outdoor Picnic," *Hartford Courant*, February 18, 2020.

215 *Jennifer told Fotis that she ate chocolate every day*: The chocolate bunnies, and Jennifer's response to them, appeared in the police report, then came up again during testimony at the Michelle Troconis trial. See Taylor Hartz, "Troconis

Jury Hears from Parental Supervisor on Dulos' Visit with Kids Before Wife's Disappearance," *Hartford Courant,* February 1, 2024.

216 *Fotis was back in Farmington*: The scene at the dinner party was described to the police later by Michelle Troconis. It was also described by by several people, at length, during the trial of Michelle Troconis.

217 *The trust funds*: At one point, while they were living apart but still married, Fotis, having received a check payable to Jennifer in the mail, forged his wife's signature and deposited the funds in his own account. This detail, which appears in the court records, suggests the mendacity of Fotis Dulos. To me, it means he'd have no moral issue with forging signatures and falsifying documents to get his hands on the money in those trust funds.

218 *Jennifer and Lauren had worked out a schedule*: The details in this section come from the police timeline, the police report, and the arrest warrants, which were based on the cooperation of Lauren Almeida and Jennifer's other friends.

219–20 *Jennifer had never showed up*: This information comes from several sources, including Lauren Almeida's testimony at the trial of Michelle Troconis. See Taylor Hartz, "Nanny Details Contentious Relationship of Fotis Dulos and Jennifer Farber Dulos at Troconis Trial," *Hartford Courant,* January 17, 2024.

221 *a ten-year-old named Mary Mount vanished*: On the disappearance of Mary Mount and other notorious Connecticut crimes, see Erika Grey, *The Wind Cries Mary: Murders That Shook a Power Town* (PeDante Press, 2009), and "Body Identified as Mary Mount's; Connecticut Police Certain They Found Missing Girl," *New York Times,* June 19, 1969.

222 *seventeen-year-old John Rice, was the only suspect*: On the John Rice case, see Paul L. Montgomery, "Hunt Pressed in New Canaan Killings," *New York Times,* December 12, 1970.

222 *seventy-seven-year-old Albert Kokoth*: On the Albert Kokoth case, see Pat Tomlinson, "New Canaan Man Not Able to Stand Trial in Wife's Killing," *Stamford Advocate*, September 28, 2022.

222 *Jennifer's phone last pinged a tower near Waveny Park*: The search information, including the phone records and the details on the home search and the interrogations, is included in the police report and Fotis Dulos's arrest warrant.

223 *"In addition to blood evidence in the garage"*: This quote is taken from the interview Detective John Kimball gave to Erin Moriarty of CBS News on February 12, 2021. By the time I reached out to Kimball and the other detectives, they had been told to stop talking to the press. Kimball said he might or might not be able to talk after the last loose strands of the case were finally tied up.

224 *"Blood splatter found on the garbage cans"*: This list and the other facts in this section come from Fotis Dulos's arrest warrant, which was made public and is available as a PDF online.

226 *Connecticut's chief medical examiner, James Gill*: The facts around the autopsy were released in a statement from the State of Connecticut's Office of the Chief Medical Examiner.

227 *Fotis asked if there'd been any news about his wife*: This information, and a paraphrase of the exchange between Fotis Dulos, Jacob Pyetranker, and the officers at the New Canaan police station appear in Fotis Dulos's arrest warrant.

227 *Pyetranker handed something to Dulos*: This detail comes from the police report. It was not, and maybe never will be, clear why Jacob Pyetranker had Fotis Dulos's phone.

228 *nearly 5 percent of the population*: This statistic appears in the article "Prevalence of Psychopathy in the General Adult Population: A Systematic Review and Meta-Analysis," by Anna Sanz-Garcia, Clara Gesteira, Jesus Sanz, and Maria Paz Garcia-Vera, *Frontiers of Psychology*, August 3, 2021.

229 *"I was there when they fought on the lawn"*: The person quoted asked me to disguise his identity. I have done my best to do that.

229 *"Thanks for your response"*: This quote is from the interview Lauren Almeida gave to the police after Jennifer's disappearance, which is widely quoted in Fotis's arrest warrant.

230 *Waveny Park is three hundred acres*: For maps and information, see the Waveny Park website (wavenyparkconservancy.org).

233 *He said he took a call from his friend*: See Lisa Backus, "Fotis Dulos Asked Friend to Make 'Alibi Call' Morning Wife Vanished, Search Warrant Shows," *Stamford Advocate*, July 31, 2022.

233 *The GPS on Fotis's phone backed up the first part of the story*: The police included a moment-by-moment timeline of Fotis and his vehicle, as captured by GPS data and surveillance cameras, public and private, in their report and on the arrest warrant. That is where all the information regarding locations and times comes from.

234 *Albany Avenue between Baltimore Street and Oakland Terrace*: According to Joshua Quint, Albany Avenue surveillance was discussed by police officers and lawyers at the trial of Michelle Troconis, January 2024. See Taylor Hartz, "Troconis Jury Sees Surveillance Videos from Hartford, Altered License Plates Pulled from Storm Drain," *Hartford Courant*, January 22, 2024.

236 *Michelle Troconis sits in the passenger seat*: The police included still images in their reports and warrants related to the cars, the trucks, and the people driving them. Some of the video, which shows Michelle leaning out of Fotis's truck on Albany Avenue, was also released and has been shown online and on TV.

236 *The investigators made a crucial mistake of their own*: This mistake, along with its importance, was described to me by several investigators who either worked on or followed the case, including several who worked for Fotis Dulos.

237 *The bra was so blood-soaked*: The bra, the Vineyard Vines T-shirt, the Husky gloves, and the bloody poncho were shown to the jury at the trial of Michelle Troconis in January 2024, where the shock of seeing these items in three dimensions registered as audible courtroom gasps. Carrie later released the following statement on behalf of the family: "Witnessing Jennifer's blood-soaked clothing, knowing that was the shirt, the bra, she wore on the last day of her life, made us imagine, again, what she must have endured on May 24, 2019. She died a tragic death, and her loss is felt beyond what words can express."

238 *When Dana Hinman, the co-owner of the pond, asked*: These quotes, and the facts about Fotis in the days after Jennifer's disappearance, come from the arrest warrants.

239 *Jon Schoenhorn calls the search a fishing expedition*: This information comes from statements and filings Schoenhorn has made in court as well as Michelle Troconis's Instagram, where she has argued her innocence.

240 *Kent Mawhinney's answers were vague and contradictory*: The information in this section comes almost entirely from Kent Mawhinney's arrest warrant as well as newspaper articles that covered the case (see bibliography).

243–44 *the blessing and curse of a red vehicle*: The lurid details in this passage were reported by the officers who interviewed Pawel Gumienny; they were then included in Fotis's arrest warrant for murder.

245 *The seats in there now, Fotis explained, "look ghetto"*: This version of the exchange comes from Pawel Gumienny, who shared it during his testimony in the Michelle Troconis trial. See Pat Tomlinson, "Michelle Troconis Said She'd Kill Jennifer Dulos 'When She Turns Up,' Pickup Truck Owner Testifies," *Stamford Advocate*, February 6, 2024.

245 *Pawel also spoke about the behavior of Fotis and Michelle*: This information comes from testimony given by Pawel Gumienny—who spent over six hours on the stand—at the trial of Michelle Troconis in Stamford in 2024. When asked to comment by the press gathered on the street in front of the courthouse, Michelle's lawyer Jon Schoenhorn said he considered it a "win" for the defense, seeing as, to make such a statement in the futue tense—"I'm *going to* kill that fucking bitch"—Michelle had to believe Jennifer was still alive. "As far as I'm concerned, that is certainly the dispositive factor when it comes to the charge of conspiracy to commit murder," Schoenhorn said.

245 *Pawel said he was present for another conversation*: All this information, including the quotes, comes from testimony given by Pawel Gumienny at the Michelle Troconis trial in 2024.

246 *"Gumienny told investigators"*: See Michael Dinnan, "Fotis Dulos Employee Emerges as Key Figure in Murder Case," *New Canaanite*, January 13, 2020.

246 *which Fotis had wrecked*: See Pat Tomlinson, "Owner of Truck Linked to Dulos Case Was Found 'Soaked in Sweat,' Detective Says in Troconis Trial," *Stamford Advocate*, January 30, 2024.

247 *staying at the Residence Inn by Marriott in Avon*: See "Drone Video Shows Police Investigating Dulos Case at Farmington Home Friday," Fox61, June 7, 2019. I have actually stayed in that Marriott and know the hotel and area well from my career as a hockey parent.

247 *where he spent just two days*: See Lisa Backus, "Jail Conditions Contributed to Fotis Dulos Suicide, Sister Says," *Stamford Advocate*, February 4, 2021.

248 *There was Norm Pattis*: On Norm Pattis and the members of his legal team, in this section and in those that follow, see the numerous articles cited in the bibliography. I spoke to several lawyers who have argued against Pattis, as well as detractors and admirers, including reporter Dave Altimari, formerly of the *Hartford Courant*. Pattis himself is legally forbidden from discussing the case, as is his partner Kevin Smith. Pattis's quotes here and throughout—most of them, anyway—were taken from Zoom sessions of his court appearances, which are archived, or videos from newscasts of press conferences.

251 *Brown friends who'd wagered*: This information comes from an old college

friend, one of the bettors, who is in regular contact with the other classmates who made the wager, all of whom live in Europe.

251 *Fotis glanced at the courtroom gallery on his way out*: All of these courtroom sessions were recorded and can be found online.

251 *Michelle had been arrested in her pajamas*: The information and quotes from this section have been taken from the trial of Michelle Troconis at the Stamford courthouse, January–February 2024, which I attended.

251 *Detective Kimball laughed*: This fact as well as other information from the interrogations comes from several sources, including testimony given by Detective John Kimball and other interrogating officers at Michelle Troconis's trial.

253 *"Sometimes I hope she disappears"*: This quote comes from an affidavit Michelle Troconis gave to the Connecticut State Police. It appeared in Dave Altimari, "A Rare French Bike, a Bloody Doorknob and Jennifer Farber Dulos' DNA on Zip Ties Among New Evidence Against Fotis Dulos," *Hartford Courant*, January 8, 2020.

253 *"Dulos texted Toutziaridis"*: See: Lisa Backus, "Warrant: Fotis Dulos Asked for 'Alibi Call' Day Wife Vanished," *Stamford Advocate*, January 31, 2022.

253 *"Almost two hours after the call"*: See Shannon Miller, "Court Documents Reveal Dept. of Homeland Security's Involvement in Dulos Case," NBC Connecticut, August 4, 2022.

259 *"For more than 20 years"*: This quote and the following *CT Insider* quotes about Norm Pattis, as well as several details about him given in the text, can be found in Chris Hoffman, "Attorney Norm Pattis: Defender of the Despised," *CT Insider / Connecticut Magazine*, February 18, 2020.

259 *Pattis is "well-known—and not liked"*: See Danlie Tepfer, "Clients like Alex Jones, Fotis Dulos Court Disfavor for Attorney Norm Pattis," *ctpost*, January 22, 2019.

260 *Jennifer had been charged $14,000*: For details surrounding Pattis's legal strategy, see Dave Altimari, "The Psychiatrist Who Examined Fotis Dulos, the Estranged Husband of Missing New Canaan Mother Jennifer Farber Dulos, Concluded He Is 'Confident and Gregarious," *Hartford Courant*, September 3, 2019.

261 *the so-called* Gone Girl *theory*: Pattis posed the *Gone Girl* theory in court. See WFSB 3, "Courtroom Video: Fotis Dulos Appears in Stamford Superior Court," YouTube, August 9, 2019 (www.youtube.com/watch?v=dc1F3HQ-CxA).

261 *Gillian Flynn herself issued a statement*: See Vanessa Wojtusiak, "Author of 'Gone Girl' Issues Statement Regarding Jennifer Dulos' Disappearance," News8, WTNH.com, July 5, 2019.

265 *"He was a very charismatic and charming person"*: This quote comes from the interview Carrie Luft gave to the CBS show *48 Hours*; see Erin Moriarty, "What Does the Other Woman Know? The Disappearance of Jennifer Dulos," CBS News, February 13, 2021 (www.cbsnews.com/video/what-does-the-other-woman-know-the-disappearance-of-jennifer-dulos/#x).

265–66 *Hare Psychopathy checklist*: See "Hare Psychopathy Checklist (Original) (PCL-22)," at Psychology Tools (psychology-tools.com/test/pcl-22).

267 *The* New York Post *dubbed her*: See Laura Italiano, "Alleged Wife-Killer Fotis

Dulos Had a 'Type'—Brainy, Pretty Brunettes," *New York Post*, January 31, 2020.

267 *What did Anna Curry want?*: I tried to contact Anna Curry on several occasions, reaching out to her via social media, email, and work addresses. I eventually tracked down her cell phone number, or what I was told had been her number. I called and texted. I received a few cryptic messages in return, one that asked me what sort of book I planned to write, and what and how much I knew. I tried to arrange a meeting, but my follow-up texts went unanswered. Anna did resurface briefly in a legal case, in which she was seeking the return of money she had put up for Fotis Dulos's bail. See Alfred Branch, "Woman Involved in Fotis Dulos Case Wants Bail Money Back: Report," *Patch*, May 12, 2021.

268 *thousands of Legos*: The detail about the Legos was covered by various newspapers. Gloria Farber's attorney, Richard P. Weinstein, spoke about them to Pamela K. Browne and Cynthia Fagen, on "Murder in the Morning: The Jennifer Farber Dulos Story," *Killing Time* (podcast), 6 episodes, spring 2024 (killingtimethepodcast.com/).

268 *In one story*: See Louise Boyle, "Elderly Mother of Missing Connecticut Woman Is Seen in New York After Filing for Custody of Her Five Grandchildren—Lovingly Displayed on Her Phone Case—as Their Father Is Charged in Connection to Their Mom's Disappearance," *Daily Mail*, June 6, 2019.

269 *Hilliard had set up a trust fund for each grandkid*: The trust funds and other financial details are discussed by Gloria Farber's attorney, Richard P. Weinstein, on "Dead Men Can't Talk," episode 5 of Browne and Fagen, "Murder in the Morning."

269 *a reporter outside the Hartford courthouse*: See "Fotis Dulos Wishes Missing Wife Jennifer Dulos 'Happy Holidays' in Shocking Message at Civil Trial," CBS New York, December 4, 2019.

270 *assembled into a timeline*: The facts presented in this timeline can be found in the police reports and the arrest warrants as well as the timeline that appeared in the *Hartford Courant*. I filled out the timeline with details and quotes—as well as atmospheric details—from other parts of the warrants.

273 *murder committed during the commission of a crime*: See Brian Duignan, "What Are the Differences Between First-, Second-, and Third-Degree Murder?," Britannica (www.britannica.com/story/what-are-the-differences-between-first--second--and-third-degree-murder).

276 *"To get bonded out"*: See Zach Murdock, "Attorney Norm Pattis, Law Partner Barred from Speaking About Jennifer Farber Dulos Case for 40 Years Under Agreement to Settle Estate of Fotis Dulos," *Hartford Courant*, July 14, 2021.

277 *"This was no ordinary memorial"*: See Dave Altimari and Nicholas Rondinone, "Judge Orders Fotis Dulos, Charged with Killing Jennifer Farber Dulos, to Strict Home Confinement Amid Questions He Removed Items from Estranged Wife's Memorial," *Hartford Courant*, January 23, 2020.

277 *you could not help but imagine*: I hope I have made this clear: the section that follows, the murder from Jennifer's point of view, is an invention, a product of my own imagination in consideration of the known facts.

278 *a hunting knife with a pearl handle*: This is the knife that was pulled from the trash on Albany Avenue as captured on a surveillance camera and described by the homeless man who found it. That man traded it to someone named Fudge for $10 worth of crack cocaine.

279 *There was more blood than Fotis expected*: This is from the police report, the arrest warrant, and the report of the Connecticut medical examiner.

AFTERWORD

281 *Norm Pattis was preparing to argue it*: I spoke to several lawyers who have argued against Pattis as well as detractors and admirers, including reporter Dave Altimari, formerly of the *Hartford Courant*. I tried to talk to Pattis himself, but he is legally forbidden from discussing the case, as is his partner Kevin Smith. Pattis's quotes here and throughout—most of them, anyway—were taken from Zoom sessions, which are archived, of his court appearances or video from newscasts of press conferences.

281 *Pattis implied Fotis had been framed*: See Dave Altimari, "Defense Attorney: Fotis Dulos Found Piles of Bloody Clothes at His Home the Day His Estranged Wife Disappeared. Revelations Come as Judge Agrees to Drop Murder Charges Against Dulos," *Hartford Courant*, March 3, 2020.

282 *"The state sought to revoke the bond"*: See Altimari and Mahony, "North Carolina Woman Paid $147,000 to Help Fotis Dulos Post His Bond," *Hartford Courant*, January 29, 2020.

282 *"like he was in a rush"*: See Emily Brindley and Dave Altimari, "'He Wanted to Do This!': Police Report Details Fotis Dulos' Last Hours in Farmington as He Prepared to Take His Own Life," *Hartford Courant*, May 23, 2020.

282 *"I looked in the window of the door"*: This and the following quote from Lieutenant Bailey are from Brindley and Altimari, "'He Wanted to Do This!'"

283 *"Obviously, the potential for a bond revocation was devastating news"*: See "Attorney Norm Pattis Reacts to Fotis Dulos' Suicide Attempt," NBC News Connecticut, January 28, 2020.

283 *"Officers removed him from the vehicle"*: See: "Jail Conditions Contributed to Fotis Dulos Suicide, Sister Says," *Stamford Advocate*, December 12, 2019.

283 *In an interview with NBC Connecticut conducted while Fotis*: See "Attorney Norm Pattis Reacts to Fotis Dulos' Suicide Attempt," NBC Connecticut.

284 *"To those who contend"*: See Associated Press, "Fotis Dulos, Accused of Killing His Missing Wife, Dies After Apparent Suicide Attempt," *USA Today*, January 30, 2020.

285 *Gloria Farber brought her grandchildren to Jacobi Medical Center*: See Dave Altimari, "Police Say Fotis Dulos in Critical Condition After Attempted Suicide," *Hartford Courant*, January 28, 2020.

286 *the Dulos children lived on the Upper East Side*: This information comes from family friends as well as from members of the faculty of both schools, who have spoken to me in confidence. Petros Dulos has a lacrosse scouting page online (imlca.sportsrecruits.com/athlete/petros_dulos). On a local TV interview,

Richard Weinstein, Gloria Farber's attorney, discussed the home remodel done to accommodate the kids.

286 *When Gloria dies*: This information is from my interviews with several people close to the family who want to remain nameless.

287 *It's called Jennifer's Law*: The law is named not only for Jennifer Dulos but also for Jennifer Magnano, who was murdered by her husband in 2007. See Zach Murdock, "Survivors of Domestic Violence Urge Connecticut Lawmakers to Pass Reforms Named for Jennifer Farber Dulos, Jennifer Magnano," *Hartford Courant*, March 24, 2021. From the article: "The ambitious package was first introduced last year in the wake of the high-profile disappearance and suspected murder of Jennifer Farber Dulos and would build on a bill of the same name that passed after the murder of Jennifer Magnano—at her husband's hands in front of her children—more than a decade ago."

287 *Jennifer was not officially declared dead*: See Joseph Wilkinson, "Jennifer Farber Dulos Declared Legally Dead, More Than 4 Years After Disappearance," *New York Daily News*, January 9, 2024.

287 *saddled with a GPS anklet*: See Alfred Branch, "Michelle Troconis, Defendant in Dulos Case, Wins Removal of GPS Device," *Patch*, April 6, 2023.

287 *Jon Schoenhorn responded in writing*: See Tata O'Neill and John Moritz, "Attorney: Troconis Prosecution Used to Justify 'Millions' Spent on Jennifer Dulos Search," *CT Insider*, December 3, 2021.

289 *Here's how I reported these events in* Air Mail: See Rich Cohen, "The View from Here," *Air Mail*, February 3, 2024, and "Murder in Fairfield County," *Air Mail*, March 2, 2024.

291 *The main players returned to court on May 31*: The sentencing session was streamed by various outlets, including Court TV. It can be seen in its entirety at Court TV on YouTube at https://www.youtube.com/watch?v=wS-X4CDME8U.

293 *Lisa has her own legal problems*: According to Marchant, "Greenwich Police Charge 59-Year-Old 'Life Coach' with Illegally Practicing Law in Divorce Case," Lisa Nkonoki "was served an arrest warrant at Greenwich police headquarters on Sunday, charging her with illegal practice of law and first-degree criminal attempt at larceny, which are both felonies." The Greenwich police lieutenant Martin O'Reilly said of the charges, "She allegedly acted as a legal adviser, when she's not a legal adviser."

Bibliography

BOOKS

Adams, David. *Why Do They Kill? Men Who Murder Their Intimate Partners.* Vanderbilt University Press, 2007.

Beller, Thomas. *How to Be a Man: Scenes from a Protracted Childhood.* W. W. Norton, 2005.

———. *The Sleep-Over Artist.* W. W. Norton, 2000.

———, ed. *Before & After: Stories from New York.* Mr. Beller's Neighborhood Books, 2002.

———, ed. *Personals: Dreams and Nightmares from the Lives of 20 Young Writers.* Houghton Mifflin, 1998.

Beller, Thomas, and Joanna Yas, eds. *They're at It Again: Stories from Twenty Years of Open City.* Open City Books, 2011.

Bingham, Robert. *Lightning on the Sun.* Anchor Books, 2001.

———. *Pure Slaughter Value.* Doubleday, 1997.

Brenner, Marie. *House of Dreams: The Bingham Family of Louisville.* Random House, 1988.

Brooks, David. *Bobos in Paradise: The New Upper Class and How They Got There.* Simon & Schuster, 2001.

Chandler, David Leon, with Mary Voelz Chandler. *The Binghams of Louisville: The Dark History Behind One of America's Great Fortunes.* Crown, 1989.

de Marneffe, Daphne. *The Rough Patch: Marriage and the Art of Living Together.* Scribner, 2018.

———. *Maternal Desire: On Children, Love, and the Inner Life.* Scribner, 2004.

Earls, William D. *The Harvard Five in New Canaan: Midcentury Modern Houses by Marcel Breuer, Landis Gores, John Johansen, Philip Johnson, Eliot Noyes, and Others.* W. W. Norton, 2006.

Farber, Jennifer. "Window-Shopping for a Life." In *Personals: Dreams and Nightmares from the Lives of 20 Young Writers*, ed. Thomas Beller. Houghton Mifflin, 1998.

Federal Bureau of Investigation. *FBI Handbook of Crime Scene Forensics: The Authoritative Guide to Navigating Crime Scenes.* Skyhorse, 2008.

Flynn, Gillian. *Gone Girl.* Crown, 2012.

Grey, Erika. *The Wind Cries Mary: Murders That Shook a Power Town.* PeDante Press, 2009.

Hobson, Laura Z. *Gentleman's Agreement.* Simon & Schuster, 1947.

Johnson, Joyce. *Minor Characters: A Beat Memoir.* Houghton Mifflin, 1983.

Isserman, Maurice. *The Winter Army: The World War II Odyssey of the 10th Mountain Division, America's Elite Alpine Warriors.* Houghton Mifflin Harcourt, 2019.

Kiehl, Kent A. *The Psychopath Whisperer: The Science of Those Without Conscience.* Broadway Books, 2014.

King, Mary Louise. *Portrait of New Canaan: The History of a Connecticut Town.* New Canaan Historical Society, 1981.

Levin, Ira. *The Stepford Wives.* HarperCollins, 1972.

Luft, Carrie. *Cool Guys Don't Go Out with Smart Girls and Other Revelations: A Collection of Five Short Plays.* Baker's Plays, 1991.

Moody, Rick. *The Ice Storm.* Little, Brown, 1994.

Ortenberg, Arthur. *Liz Claiborne: The Legend, the Woman.* Taylor Trade Publishing, 2009.

Pinchbeck, Daniel. *Breaking Open the Head: A Psychedelic Journey into the Heart of Contemporary Shamanism.* Broadway Books, 2002.

———. *2012: The Return of Quetzalcoatl.* Tarcher/Penguin, 2006.

Reichart, Robert. *Hit It! The 80 Year History of Water Skiing in the Upper Midwest.* Xlibris, 2003.

Shelton, Peter. *Climb to Conquer: The Untold Story of WWII's 10th Mountain Division.* Scribner, 2003.

Skehan, James W. *Roadside Geology of Connecticut and Rhode Island.* Mountain Press, 2008.

Snyder, Rachel Louise. *No Visible Bruises: What We Don't Know About Domestic Violence Can Kill Us.* Bloomsbury, 2019.

Stark, Evans. *Coercive Control: How Men Entrap Women in Personal Life.* Oxford University Press, 2009.

Stout, Martha. *The Sociopath Next Door.* Broadway Books, 2005.

Tremain, Derek, and Pauline Tremain. *How to Solve a Murder: True Stories from a Life in Forensic Medicine.* Harper Element, 2021.

NEWSPAPER, MAGAZINE, AND JOURNAL ARTICLES

Allan, John H. "Chase Manhattan Reports $34-Million Overvaluation." *New York Times,* October 3, 1974.

———. "Banks' Problems Create Controversy." *New York Times,* October 7, 1974.

Allon, Janet. "Streets of Dreams; When You're Asleep, New York Becomes Another World." *New York Times,* July 5, 1998.

Altimari, Dave. "Attorney Accuses State Police of Illegally Taking Partially Nude Photos of Michelle Troconis." *Hartford Courant,* March 16, 2020.

———. "Attorney for Fotis Dulos Questions Whether Missing New Canaan Woman Jennifer Farber Dulos Was Ill or May Have Been Undergoing Pregnancy Testing." *Hartford Courant*, September 10, 2019.

———. "Attorney for Missing New Canaan Mother Says Fotis Dulos Had a 'Factual Lobotomy' in Filing for Dismissal of Divorce Case." *Hartford Courant*, January 2, 2020.

———. "Death of Fotis Dulos Ends Contentious, Protracted Divorce Case Against Estranged Wife, Jennifer Farber Dulos." *Hartford Courant*, February 4, 2020.

———. "Defense Attorney: Fotis Dulos Found Piles of Bloody Clothes at His Home the Day His Estranged Wife Disappeared. Revelations Come as Judge Agrees to Drop Murder Charges Against Dulos." *Hartford Courant*, March 3, 2020.

———. "Family of Fotis Dulos Says He Was 'in a Dead-End Where He Saw Taking His Own Life as the Only Way to Be Granted Peace." *Hartford Courant*, February 3, 2020.

———. "For 90 Minutes, Fotis Dulos' Jeep Was Unaccounted For on the Day Jennifer Farber Dulos Disappeared; Did He Use That Time to Hide Her Body?" *Hartford Courant*, June 1, 2020.

———. "Fotis Dulos Says Mother of Missing Wife Owes Him More Than $1 Million." *Hartford Courant*, December 20, 2019.

———. "'I'm Not Charles Manson': Court Transcripts Show Escalating Tension and Anger in Two-Year Dulos Divorce." *Hartford Courant*, July 7, 2019.

———. "'Her Great Joy in Life Is Her Children': Friends of Jennifer Farber Dulos Dismiss 'Gone Girl' and 'Revenge-Suicide' Theories by Estranged Husband's Defense Attorneys." *Hartford Courant*, July 8, 2019.

———. "Kent Mawhinney, Accused Accomplice in Jennifer Farber Dulos Murder Case, Loses Custody of Children as He Sits in Jail." *Hartford Courant*, January 24, 2020.

———. "Kent Mawhinney, Fotis Dulos' Former Attorney, Released from Prison to Visit Ailing Father After Bond on Conspiracy Charges in Death of Jennifer Farber Dulos Is Reduced." *Hartford Courant*, October 19, 2020.

———. "Lawyer for Fotis Dulos Says Prosecutors Are 'Desperate' to Link His Client to Jennifer Dulos' Disappearance and Are Ignoring Other Possible Leads." *Hartford Courant*, August 27, 2019.

———. "The Luxury Connecticut Home of Jennifer Farber Dulos and Fotis Dulos Goes on the Market for $1.75 Million; Furniture, Rugs and Kitchen Items to Be Auctioned Online." *Hartford Courant*, October 24, 2020.

———. "Michelle Troconis Issues Statement Saying She Never Should Have Trusted Fotis Dulos, Doesn't Know What Happened to Jennifer Farber Dulos." *Hartford Courant*, March 21, 2020.

———. "Michelle Troconis, the Girlfriend of Fotis Dulos, Goes from Possible Alibi to Key Witness Against Her Boyfriend in His Estranged Wife's Disappearance." *Hartford Courant*, September 6, 2019.

———. "New Documents Show Fotis Dulos Had More Than $4 Million in Financial Liabilities Weeks Before His Estranged Wife Jennifer Farber Dulos Disappeared; Dulos Says the Documents Are Misleading." *Hartford Courant*, December 3, 2019.

———. "The Psychiatrist Who Examined Fotis Dulos, the Estranged Husband of Missing New Canaan Mother Jennifer Farber Dulos, Concluded He Is 'Confident and Gregarious.'" *Hartford Courant*, September 3, 2019.

———. "A Rare French Bike, a Bloody Doorknob and Jennifer Farber Dulos' DNA on Zip Ties Among New Evidence Against Fotis Dulos." *Hartford Courant*, January 8, 2020.

———. "The Sister of Fotis Dulos, Estranged Husband of Missing New Canaan Mother Jennifer Farber Dulos, Says 'He Is Not the Person They Say He Is.'" *Hartford Courant*, July 1, 2019.

———. "State Police Continue Search of Avon Property for Body of Jennifer Farber Dulos, Near Where Fotis Dulos Lived." *Hartford Courant*, July 11, 2020.

———. "The Story of the Last Time Fotis Dulos Saw His Children: Chocolate Bunnies, a Haircut, a New Basketball Hoop and an Outdoor Picnic." *Hartford Courant*, February 18, 2020.

———. "Timeline: How State Police Used Video to Track a Truck They Believe Fotis Dulos Was Driving the Day Jennifer Farber Dulos Went Missing." *Hartford Courant*, September 9, 2019.

———. "Video Cameras Are Everywhere—and Investigators Are Using Them Extensively in the Case They Are Building Against Fotis Dulos." *Hartford Courant*, September 8, 2019.

Altimari, Dave, Amanda Blanco, and Emily Brindley. "Fotis Dulos Is Dead, Leaving Behind the Mystery of What Happened to Jennifer Farber Dulos." *Hartford Courant*, January 30, 2020.

Altimari, Dave, and Emily Brindley. "'If It Takes My Head to End This, So Be It.' Note Found with Fotis Dulos on Day of Suicide Attempt Proclaims His Innocence." *Hartford Courant*, January 31, 2020.

Altimari, Dave, Elizabeth Fawcett, Nicholas Rondinone, and Amanda Blanco. "Fotis Dulos Charged with the Murder of His Estranged Wife Jennifer Farber Dulos." *Hartford Courant*, January 7, 2020.

Altimari, Dave, and Josh Kovner. "In Court Motion, Fotis Dulos' Attorney Alleges There's a New Bill Indicating Jennifer Farber Dulos Saw a Doctor Nearly Two Months After She Disappeared." *Hartford Courant*, October 11, 2019.

Altimari, Dave, and Edmund H. Mahony. "North Carolina Woman Paid $147,000 to Help Fotis Dulos Post His Bond." *Hartford Courant*, January 29, 2020.

Altimari, Dave, and Nicholas Rondinone. "Judge Orders Fotis Dulos, Charged with Killing Jennifer Farber Dulos, to Strict Home Confinement amid Questions He Removed Items from Estranged Wife's Memorial." *Hartford Courant*, January 23, 2020.

———. "Michelle Troconis, Girlfriend of Fotis Dulos, Turns Herself In to Police on Additional Evidence Tampering Charge Connected to Disappearance of Jennifer Farber Dulos." *Hartford Courant*, September 5, 2019.

Altimari, Dave, Nicholas Rondinone, and Amanda Blanco. "Search Warrants Reveal a Horrific Crime Scene at the Home of Jennifer Farber Dulos." *Hartford Courant*, January 15, 2020.

Arnold, Amanda. "Unsolved Mysteries: What Happened to Jennifer Dulos, the Missing Connecticut Mom?" *New York*, September 6, 2019.

Associated Press. "Sister Defends Estranged Husband of Missing Mom of 5." July 2, 2019.

———. "Fotis Dulos, Accused of Killing His Missing Wife, Dies After Apparent Suicide Attempt." *USA Today*, January 30, 2020.

———. "Fotis Dulos Lawyers Banned from Discussing Case for 40 Years." July 14, 2021.

Auchter, Bernie. "Men Who Murder Their Families: What the Research Tells Us." *National Institute of Justice Journal*, May 25, 2010.

Backus, Lisa. "All of Fotis Dulos' Properties Now in Foreclosure." *CT Insider*, June 22, 2020.

———. "Attorney: Did 'Jailhouse Informant' Cut Deal on Domestic Violence Charges to Help Jennifer Dulos Case?" *Stamford Advocate*, December 14, 2021.

———. "Attorney: Kent Mawhinney's Deal on Domestic Charges Has No Impact on Jennifer Dulos Case, Prosecutor Says." *Stamford Advocate*, February 23, 2022.

———. "Attorney's Deal in Rape Case Pending 'Discussions' in Jennifer Dulos Homicide." *Stamford Advocate*, February 14, 2020.

———. "'Concerned' Fotis Dulos Called Bondsman Before Apparent Suicide Attempt." *CT Insider*, January 29, 2020.

———. "Ex-wife of Dulos Defendant Kent Mawhinney Claims He Abused Her for Years." *CT Insider*, June 17, 2020.

———. "Fotis Dulos Asked Friend to Make 'Alibi Call' Morning Jennifer Dulos Vanished, Search Warrant Shows." *Stamford Advocate*, July 31, 2022.

———. "Inside Fotis Dulos' Safe Deposit Box: Tiffany Ring, Rolex, Cartier Watches, Court Documents Reveal." *Stamford Advocate*, September 14, 2020.

———. "Jail Conditions Contributed to Fotis Dulos Suicide, Sister Says." *Stamford Advocate*, December 12, 2019.

———. "Jennifer Dulos' Mother Shows Strength amid 'Devastating Situation.'" *Stamford Advocate*, September 15, 2019.

———. "Judge in Dulos Divorce Calls for Change in Child Custody Disputes." *Stamford Advocate*, February 11, 2020.

———. "'Mawhinney's True Character' Revealed in New Documents, Attorney in Jennifer Dulos Case Says." *CT Insider*, March 3, 2022.

———. "Norm Pattis Kept $250K Retainer After Client Died in Jennifer Dulos Case." *CT Insider*, August 19, 2020.

———. "Prosecutor: New Canaan Was 'Epicenter' of Jennifer Dulos Homicide." *CT Insider*, July 17, 2020.

———. "Prosecutor 'Very Open-Minded' to Offer Deal to Find Jennifer Dulos." *Stamford Advocate*, February 14, 2021.

———. "State Seeks to Remove Attorney in Jennifer Dulos Case over Sweatshirt He Found with Worker's DNA." *Stamford Advocate*, October 12, 2022.

———. "'There Won't Be Much' Money Left for Dulos Children." *Stamford Advocate*, October 8, 2020.

———. "'Tremendous Amount of Legos' Focus of Debate in Fotis Dulos Estate." *Stamford Advocate*, February 4, 2021.

———. "Warrant: Fotis Dulos Asked for 'Alibi Call' Day Wife Vanished." *Stamford Advocate*, January 31, 2022.

———. "'Why Are They Withholding It?': Attorney in Jennifer Dulos Case Wants Psych Report." *Stamford Advocate*, November 18, 2020.

Backus, Lisa, and Pat Tomlinson. "Attorneys in Jennifer Dulos Case Meet in Private, Hearing Set for Wednesday." *Stamford Advocate*, November 29, 2022.

———. "Attorney in Jennifer Dulos Case: 'Inexcusable' Mishandling of Evidence Should Dismiss or Transfer Charges." *Stamford Advocate*, November 30, 2022.

Baker, KC. "How a Conn. Couple's 'Stereotypically Perfect' Marriage Went Sour Before Mom of 5 Disappeared." *People*, June 26, 2019.

Bhatia, Aatish, and Claire Cain Miller. "Explore How Income Influences Attendance at 139 Top Colleges." *New York Times*, September 11, 2023.

Bhatia, Aatish, Claire Cain Miller, Josh Katz, and Stuart Schmill. "Study of Elite College Admissions Data Suggests Being Very Rich Is Its Own Qualification." *New York Times*, July 24, 2023.

Binkovitz, Leah. "The 'Bone Finder' Uses Ground-Penetrating Radar to Find Lost Graves at Congressional." *Washington Post*, December 25, 2013.

Boyle, Louise. "Elderly Mother of Missing Connecticut Woman Is Seen in New York After Filing for Custody of Her Five Grandchildren—Lovingly Displayed on Her Phone Case—as Their Father Is Charged in Connection to Their Mom's Disappearance." *Daily Mail*, June 6, 2019.

Branch, Alfred. "Did Conditions in CT Jail Contribute to Fotis Dulos' Death?" *Patch*, February 4, 2021.

———. "Expensive Jewelry Reportedly in Fotis Dulos' Safe Deposit Box." *Patch*, September 15, 2020.

———. "Jennifer Dulos' Family Releases New Statement on Disappearance." *Patch*, May 24, 2020.

———. "Judge Ends Michelle Troconis' House Arrest in Jennifer Dulos Case." *Patch*, September 23, 2020.

———. "Michelle Troconis, Defendant in Dulos Case, Wins Removal of GPS Device." *Patch*, April 6, 2023.

———. "New Details on How Jennifer Dulos May Have Died: Warrant." *Patch*, September 4, 2020.

———. "New Theory Developed in Jennifer Dulos Case: Report." *Patch*, September 21, 2020.

Bregel, Sarah. "Motherhood Changes What Women Want in a Husband or Partner." *Fatherly*, December 23, 2018.

Brindley, Emily, and Dave Altimari. "'He Wanted to Do This!': Police Report Details Fotis Dulos' Last Hours in Farmington as He Prepared to Take His Own Life." *Hartford Courant*, May 23, 2020.

Burke, Cathy. "Montel's Wife Dumps His Duds." *New York Post*, April 11, 2000.

Business Insider. "Inside 10 of New York City's Most Exclusive Private Clubs." October 26, 2015.

Calhoun, Ada. "What We Mean When We Say Marriage Is 'Work.'" *New York*, January 22, 2018.

CBS New York. "Fotis Dulos Wishes Missing Wife Jennifer Dulos 'Happy Holidays' in Shocking Message at Civil Trial." December 4, 2019.

Chase Alumni Association. "In Memoriam: Hilliard Farber, 83, Headed Chase Manhattan's Bond Trading Desk." January 8, 2017.

Cleary, Tom. "Michelle Troconis: 5 Fast Facts You Need to Know." *Heavy.com*, March 15, 2021.

Cohen, Rich. "La Belle Simone." *New York*, November 8, 2013.

———. "Murder in Fairfield County." *Air Mail*, March 2, 2024.

———. "The View from Here." *Air Mail*, February 3, 2024.

Coscarelli, Joe, and Ben Sisario. "David Berman, Silver Jews Leader and Indie-Rock Poet, Dies at 52." *New York Times*, August 7, 2019.

Cromar, Ainslee. "'We Lost a Much Loved and Lovely Man to a Form of Mass Hysteria': Fotis Dulos' Family Releases Statement." *Boston.com*, February 4, 2020.

Danbury News-Times. "Westport Father Wins State's Longest-Ever Custody Case, 'a Tragedy for Everyone Involved.'" September 24, 2007.

DaRosa, Andrew. "Jennifer Dulos Disappearance Spotlighted on 'My Favorite Murder' Podcast." *CT Insider*, August 29, 2022.

Davis, Simon. "Meet the Guy Who Finds Forgotten Graves with a 'Bone Finder.'" *Vice*, January 26, 2015.

Dean, Dahlia. "Peeping Tom." *WWD*, May 22, 1995.

de Marneffe, Daphne. "The Secret to a Happy Marriage Is Knowing How to Fight." *Oprah Daily*, January 12, 2018.

DiChello, Taylor. "The Search for Jennifer Dulos Continues in Connecticut." Fox61, May 24, 2019.

Dillon, Nancy. "Murder Suspect Fotis Dulos Will Be Buried in Greece to Avoid 'Grave Desecration,' Lawyer Confirms." *New York Daily News*, February 4, 2020.

Dinan, Michael. "Accusations of Threats, Lying, Manipulation in Missing New Canaan Woman's Divorce Case." *New Canaanite*, May 29, 2019.

———. "After Dulos Case, New Canaan Police Investigators Seek More Video Surveillance Throughout Town." *New Canaanite*, January 23, 2020.

———. "Arrest Warrant: Friend of Fotis Dulos Connected to Grave Dug in Woods Two Months Before Murder." *New Canaanite*, January 8, 2020.

———. "Fotis Dulos Employee Emerges as Key Figure in Murder Case." *New Canaanite*, January 13, 2020.

———. "Lying in Wait: State Police Affidavit Points to Premeditation in Jennifer Dulos Case." *New Canaanite*, September 5, 2019.

Dulos, Jennifer. "Afternoon Dip." *Patch*, February 2, 2012.

———. "And God Created Washer/Dryers." *Patch*, May 6, 2012.

———. "Back to School-Yippee!" *Patch*, September 8, 2012.

———. "The Best Part of My Night." *Patch*, March 5, 2012.

———. "Blow Drying My Hair—Yes, This Is a Topic." *Patch*, January 16, 2012.

———. "Camp Monk." *Patch*, March 6, 2012.

———. "Carpool and Early Rising Musing." *Patch*, January 10, 2012.

———. "Christiane, My Caretaker." *Patch*, January 20, 2012.

———. "Crossed Off." *Patch*, March 14, 2012.

———. "The Family Bed." *Patch*, March 27, 2012.

———. "Goodbye, Charlotte Court." *Patch*, February 17, 2012.

———. "Happy Nothing." *Patch*, March 20, 2012.

———. "Impressions from Jan. 9 to Jan. 13." *Patch*, January 13, 2012.

———. "Lock and Key." *Patch*, December 11, 2012.

———. "More Sleep, No More." *Patch*, April 26, 2012.

———. "Morning Run." *Patch*, June 19, 2012.

———. "Movies." *Patch*, May 24, 2012.

———. "Nearly Six." *Patch*, February 24, 2012.

———. "New Year's Resolutions, How Am I Doing?" *Patch*, January 11, 2012.

———. "Nice Versus Kind." *Patch*, June 23, 2012.

———. "Party Time." *Patch*, October 5, 2012.

———. "Planning Central." *Patch*, April 10, 2012.

———. "Post Game Glow." *Patch*, February 6, 2012.

———. "Rainy Afternoon." *Patch*, October 4, 2012.

———. "Raising the Boys." *Patch*, January 27, 2012.

———. "Spreading the Word(s)." *Patch*, January 12, 2012.

———. "Surely, You're Not Escaping Winter That Easily." *Patch*, March 1, 2012.

———. "Watching My Butterfly Improve in Ballet." *Patch*, February 9, 2012.

———. "What We're Not Doing This (New) School Year." *Patch*, September 14, 2012.

———. "Yearning for Female Friends." *Patch*, February 22, 2012.

"Dulos' Sister in Greek Paper." Newsit World, January 2, 2020.

Dumas, Timothy. "Where Is She?" *New Canaan–Darien & Rowayton*, September/October 2020.

Duncan, Michelle. "Why One Fifth Avenue Is Still One of NYC's Most Star-Studded and Desirable Buildings." *Architectural Digest*, October 7, 2002.

Feldman, Kate. "Casey Anthony Opens Private Investigation Firm in Florida, Registered to Home of Former O. J. Simpson Investigator." *New York Daily News*, December 31, 2020.

Fenton, Reuven, and Bruce Golding. "Missing Connecticut Mom Said She Feared Her 'Volatile' Estranged Husband." *New York Post*, May 29, 2019.

Flowers, Tatiana. "Jennifer Dulos Divorce Shows Controversial Role of Court-Appointed Child Guardians." *Middletown Press*, July 27, 2019.

———. "Jennifer Dulos Facebook Page Demise Stirs Controversy." *Greenwich Time*, August 16, 2019.

Fortuna, Angela. "Three Years Since Disappearance of New Canaan Mother Jennifer Dulos." NBC Connecticut, May 23, 2022.

Fox61. "Attorney: Fotis Dulos 'Panicked,' Dumped Bloody Clothes After Finding Them." March 3, 2020.

———. "Drone Video Shows Police Investigating Dulos Case at Farmington Home Friday." June 7, 2019.

Friedmann, Meghan. "Man Claims He Found Knife, Bloodied Pillow in Hartford Trash." *New Haven Register*, August 3, 2019.

Fry, Ethan. "8 Lesser-Known Figures in the Jennifer Dulos Case." *The Hours*, May 22, 2020.

———. "Rena Dulos Defends Brother, Says She Was Once Close with Jennifer Dulos." *Stamford Advocate*, July 1, 2019.

Gardner, Ralph, Jr. "Requiem for a Writer: Friends and Family of the Late Robert Bingham Are Remembering Him This Week." *Wall Street Journal*, April 10, 2016.

Genzlinger, Neil. "That Litany of Complaints Is Attractive." *New York Times*, November 17, 2014.

Gidman, Jenn. "Twist in Missing Mom Case: A Man Named 'Fudge,' a Knife." *Newser*, September 10, 2019.

Gold, Michael. "Estranged Husband Disposed of Body of Missing Mother of 5, Police Say." *New York Times*, September 4, 2020.

———. "Fotis Dulos, Connecticut Man Accused of Killing Jennifer Dulos, Is Dead." *New York Times*, January 30, 2020.

———. "Inside the Turbulent Marriage of the Missing Connecticut Mother of 5." *New York Times*, June 5, 2019.

———. "Jennifer Dulos: 5 Revelations from the Missing Mother Murder Case." *New York Times*, January 28, 2020.

———. "Jennifer Dulos: How the Police Made a 'No-Body' Murder Case." *New York Times*, July 13, 2020.

———. "Jennifer Dulos Killing: Suspect May Have Dug Grave at Gun Club." *New York Times*, January 9, 2020.

———. "Missing Connecticut Mom: Husband's Girlfriend Accused of Inventing Alibi." *New York Times*, September 5, 2020.

———. "Mystery in a Wealthy Town: She Dropped Off Her Children, Then Went Missing." *New York Times*, May 3, 2019.

Gold, Michael, and Cheryl P. Weinstock. "Jennifer Dulos: Blood Found in Trash Matches That of Missing Connecticut Mother of 5." *New York Times*, June 3, 2019.

———. Jennifer Dulos's Husband Is Charged with Her Murder." *New York Times*, January 7, 2020.

Gold, Michael, and Neil Vigdor. "Fotis Dulos, Charged with Killing His Wife, Jennifer, Attempts Suicide." *New York Times*, January 28, 2020.

Gosselin, Kenneth R., and Josh Kovner. "Before Being Jailed in Connection with the Disappearance of Jennifer Farber Dulos, Her Estranged Husband, Fotis Dulos, Faced a Downward Spiral in His Business and Marriage." *Hartford Courant*, July 9, 2019.

Gray, Christopher. "Streetscapes: 1 Fifth Avenue; A Good Joke Not Well Retold." *New York Times*, October 4, 1992.

Grigoriadis, Vanessa. "Boy, Interrupted." *New York*, January 3, 2000.

———. "Fates and Furies." *Vanity Fair*, October 15, 2020.

———. "'Window-Shopping for a Life': With Accused Wife-Murderer Fotis Dulos on Life Support, the Grim End of a Perfect Couple." *Vanity Fair*, January 30, 2020.

Hagan, Ekua. "7 Kinds of Domestic Abuse, Including One That's Post-Divorce." *Psychology Today*, November 23, 2021.

Hartz, Taylor. "Nanny Details Contentious Relationship of Fotis Dulos and Jennifer Farber Dulos at Troconis Trial." *Hartford Courant*, January 17, 2024.

———. "Troconis Jury Hears from Parental Supervisor on Dulos' Visit with Kids Before Wife's Disappearance." *Hartford Courant*, February 1, 2024.

————. "Troconis Jury Sees Surveillance Videos from Hartford, Altered License Plates Pulled from Storm Drain." *Hartford Courant*, January 22, 2024.

Hill, Amelia. "The Fatal American." *The Observer*, June 30, 2001.

Hoffman, Chris. "Attorney Norm Pattis: Defender of the Despised." *CT Insider/ Connecticut Magazine*, February 18, 2020.

Hoffower, Hillary. "Step Inside 'Billionaire Mountain,' the Wealthy Aspen Enclave Where the Bezos and Dell Families Own Sprawling Mansions and Homes Go for as Much as $49 Million." *Business Insider*, August 26, 2019.

Hubbard, Kaia. "Here Are the States Where Your Marriage Won't Last." *U.S. News & World Report*, December 8, 2020.

Italiano, Laura. "Alleged Wife-Killer Fotis Dulos Had a 'Type'—Brainy, Pretty Brunettes." *New York Post*, January 31, 2020.

Jewish Telegraphic Agency. "Numerous Sport Clubs in New York Are Closed to Jews and Negroes." July 14, 1959.

Jones, Alex S. "The Fall of the House of Bingham." *New York Times*, January 19, 1986.

Kelley, Tina. "A Life of Comfort, Lived Hard; A Writer Is Remembered for His Promise and His Failings." *New York Times*, December 10, 1999.

Kibbe, Kayla. "When You Love Your Kids More Than Your Partner, Everyone Loses." *InsideHook*, May 10, 2019.

Kim, Leena. "The True Story Behind the Disappearance of Jennifer Dulos." *Town & Country*, June 5, 2021.

Klatte, Arline. "Young Playwrights Link Up to Create Their Own Company." *The Villager*, 1993/94.

Kluger, Jeffrey. "Here's What Happens in the Brain When People Kill." *Time*, April 10, 2015.

Kovner, Josh. "Chemistry and Calm, Then Loneliness and Turbulence in the Marriage of Missing New Canaan Mother Jennifer Farber Dulos." *Hartford Courant*, June 23, 2019.

————. "Fotis Dulos' First Marriage to Hilary Aldama Ended Quickly, Amicably." *Hartford Courant*, June 6, 2019.

————. "In 2010, Fotis Dulos' Mother, 77, Died After Being Struck by a Land Rover Driven by the Family's Nanny in Driveway of Avon Home." *Hartford Courant*, June 5, 2019.

————. "Michelle Troconis, Jet-Setting Businesswoman, Lived Openly with Fotis Dulos as He Defied Court Orders in Divorce with Missing Wife Jennifer." *Hartford Courant*, June 3, 2019.

Kuczynski, Alex. "The Eight-Day Week." *New York Observer*, March 10, 1997.

Lanese, Nicoletta. "Secrets in the Brains of People Who Have Committed Murder." *The Scientist*, November 1, 2019.

Leggate, James. "Fotis Dulos Connecticut Mansion Sells for $1.85M." *FoxBusiness*, April 8, 2021.

Leland, John. "An Elite School, a Boy's Suicide and a Question of Blame." *New York Times*, July 2, 2023.

Lerner, Jessica. "Mawhinney Is Suspended from Practicing Law." *Journal Inquirer*, June 20, 2022.

Levy, Ariel. "The Devil and Saint Ann's." *New York*, April 30, 2004.

Liebeson, Bess. "On the Trail of History in New Canaan." *New York Times*, October 1, 2000.

Livingston, Ikimulisa. "Hidden-Ball 'Trick' by Bonilla." *New York Post*, June 1, 2010.

Lorentzen, Christian. "Open City, Closed: Acclaimed Literary Journal Says Goodbye." *New York Observer*, March 2, 2011.

Loro, Anthony. "Fotis Dulos' Sister: 'Real Perpetrator Still at Large, Still a Threat to Public Safety.'" *YourContent News*, February 3, 2020.

Luperon, Alberto. "Co-Defendant in Alleged Murder of Jennifer Farber Dulos Is 'Jailhouse Informant.'" *Law & Crime*, December 7, 2020.

Luscombe, Belinda. "Why You Shouldn't Love Your Kids More Than Your Partner." *Time*, May 9, 2019.

Mahony, Edmund. "Judge Rules Fotis Dulos Estate Owes $2 Million to His Mother-in-Law." *Hartford Courant*, July 1, 2020.

———. "Gov. Lamont Blasts CT Chief State's Attorney Richard Colangelo: '. . . I Don't Hire Him. I Don't Fire Him. But If I Did He'd Be Gone.'" *Hartford Courant*, February 23, 2022.

———. "The Lawyer for Michelle Troconis Complained in Court Thursday That the Prosecution Has Been Slow in Providing Her Defense Team with Evidence They Intend to Use Against Her." *Hartford Courant*, September 14, 2023.

Maldonado, Zinnia. "Voicemails Left for Kent Mawhinney's Wife Days Before Jennifer Dulos Disappeared." Fox61, January 13, 2020.

Marchant, Robert. "Greenwich Police Charge 59-Year-Old 'Life Coach' with Illegally Practicing Law in Divorce Case." *Greenwich Time*, March 17, 2022.

Martin, Douglas. "Arthur Ortenberg, a Liz Claiborne Founder, Dies at 87." *New York Times*, February 5, 2014.

———. "Stanley Bosworth, Iconoclastic Head of Brooklyn School, Dies at 83." *New York Times*, August 11, 2011.

McFadden, Robert D. "Barry Bingham Jr., Louisville Publisher, Is Dead at 72." *New York Times*, April 4, 2006.

McNulty, Charles. "Narcissistic Courting." *Village Voice*, March 4, 1997.

———. "Writers' Bloc." *Village Voice*, January 26, 1993.

Mead, Rebecca. "The Wives of Others." *New Yorker*, April 9, 2007.

Miller, Joshua Rhett. "Jennifer Dulos' Family Still Feels 'Immeasurable Loss' 3 Years After Disappearance." *New York Post*, May 24, 2022.

Miller, Shannon. "Court Documents Reveal Dept. of Homeland Security's Involvement in Dulos Case." NBC Connecticut, August 4, 2022.

Montgomery, Paul L. "Hunt Pressed in New Canaan Killings." *New York Times*, December 12, 1970.

Moriarty, Erin. "'The Other Woman' in the Jennifer Dulos Case Tells Detectives, 'I Didn't Do It.'" CBS News, May 21, 2022.

Murdock, Zach. "Attorney Norm Pattis, Law Partner Barred from Speaking About Jennifer Farber Dulos Case for 40 Years Under Agreement to Settle Estate of Fotis Dulos." *Hartford Courant*, July 14, 2021.

——. "Family, Friends of Jennifer Farber Dulos Still Reeling from 'Nightmare' as Search Continues." *Hartford Courant*, June 21, 2019.

——. "Kent Mawhinney, Friend of Fotis Dulos, to Testify in Jennifer Farber Dulos Case, Prosecutors Say." *Hartford Courant*, February 2, 2021.

——. "Survivors of Domestic Violence Urge Connecticut Lawmakers to Pass Reforms Named for Jennifer Farber Dulos, Jennifer Magnano." *Hartford Courant*, March 24, 2021.

Murdock, Zach, and Nicholas Rondinone. "New State Police Arrest Warrant Details investigators' Theory of Jennifer Farber Dulos' Last Day as They Charge Estranged Husband, Fotis Dulos." *Hartford Courant*, September 4, 2019.

NBC News Connecticut. "Attorney Norm Pattis Reacts to Fotis Dulos' Suicide Attempt." January 28, 2020.

New Canaan Advertiser. "Missing New Canaan Woman Jennifer Dulos Case: Fotis Seen as 'Caring Father' While Coaching Water Skiing." July 8, 2019.

——. "Rena Dulos: Brother 'Astounded by the Accusations' in Missing New Canaan Woman Jennifer Dulos' Disappearance." July 2, 2019.

New York Times. "Body Identified as Mary Mount's; Connecticut Police Certain They Found Missing Girl." June 19, 1969.

——. "Chase Manhattan Accepts Finding by S.E.C. on Inadequate Controls." September 21, 1976.

Noodles, Larry. "Dulos Tied Up Jewish Wife with Zip Ties Before Murder." Larry Noodles.com, January 8, 2020.

O'Neill, Jesse. "Fotis Dulos' Lawyers Barred from Speaking About Murder Case for 40 Years." *New York Post*, July 14, 2021.

O'Neill, Tata, and Grace Duffield. "New Search in Jennifer Dulos Case Days Before Mawhinney to Appear in Judge's Chambers." *New Canaan Advertiser*, December 20, 2021.

O'Neill, Tata, and John Moritz. "Attorney: Troconis Prosecution Used to Justify 'Millions' Spent on Jennifer Dulos Search." *CT Insider*, December 3, 2021.

Owens, David. "State Makes Plea Offer to Kent Mawhinney, Fotis Dulos' Former Lawyer Implicated in the Killing of Jennifer Farber Dulos." *Hartford Courant*, February 14, 2020.

Pace, Eric. "William Levitt, 86, Pioneer of the Suburbs, Dies." *New York Times*, January 29, 1994.

Pinchbeck, Daniel. "Cast Your Magazine upon the Waters." *New York Times*, February 22, 1998.

——. "My Mother and Jack Kerouac." *Salon*, June 8, 2000.

Propper, David. "Michelle Troconis Trial Juror Dismissed for Telling Prosecutor 'We Love You' as Dulos Nanny Recalls Day Conn. Mom Vanished." *New York Post*, January 17, 2024.

Rand, Slade. "State Police Return to West Hartford Reservoirs to Search for Evidence in Disappearance of Jennifer Farber Dulos." *Hartford Courant*, September 12, 2019.

Rapkin, Mickey. "The Socialite Soprano and the Life Coach." *Town & Country*, January 20, 2016.

Ratliff, Jamie. "The CSP Central District Major Crime Squad's Crime Van Holds Everything Investigators Need to Process a Scene." NBC Connecticut, February 28, 2019.

———. "New Dateline Episode Sheds Light on Jennifer Dulos Case." NBC Connecticut, September 2, 2022.

Reakes, Kathy. "Man Charged in Connection to Death of Jennifer Dulos Accused of Trying to Cut Off GPS Device." *Newtown Daily Voice*, October 3, 2022.

Rondinone, Nicholas. "Family of Jennifer Farber Dulos Calls Claim That She Received Medical Treatment Months After Disappearance 'Absurd.'" *Hartford Courant*, October 14, 2019.

———. "Grandmother of Children of Missing Mom Jennifer Farber Dulos Says Her Daughter's Estranged Husband, Fotis Dulos, 'Uses His Children as Pawns' in Ongoing Custody Dispute, Recent Court Filings Say." *Hartford Courant*, August 29, 2021.

———. "In Lawsuit with Father-in-Law's Estate, Lawyer Claims Fotis Dulos Getting Help from Greece to Cover Cost of Criminal Defense." *Hartford Courant*, August 26, 2019.

———. "Kent Mawhinney, Accused Fotis Dulos Accomplice in Jennifer Farber Dulos Disappearance, Has Law License Suspended." *Hartford Courant*, January 29, 2020.

———. "Police Revealed New Theories and Evidence After Fotis Dulos and Michelle Troconis Were Arrested for a Second Time in Connection with the Jennifer Farber Dulos Case. Here's What We Learned." *Hartford Courant*, September 6, 2019.

———. "State Police Search Sprawling Farmington Home Once Owned by Fotis Dulos' Development Company." *Hartford Courant*, January 19, 2019.

Sanz-Garcia, Ana, Clara Gesteira, Jesus Sanz, and Maria Paz Garcia-Vera. "Prevalence of Psychopathy in the General Adult Population: A Systematic Review and Meta-Analysis." *Frontiers of Psychology*, August 3, 2021.

Schrader, Jessica. "Understanding the Effects of High-Conflict Divorce on Kids." *Psychology Today*, December 18, 2019.

Seabrook, John. "The Search for the Roots of Psychopathy." *New Yorker*, November 2, 2008.

Shapiro, Emily. "A Connecticut Mystery 1 Year Later: A Timeline of the Jennifer Dulos, Fotis Dulos Case." ABC News, May 21, 2020.

Shay, Jim. "Jennifer Dulos' Nanny Killed Mother-in-Law in Freak Accident." *Stamford Advocate*, June 6, 2019.

Skahill, Patrick. "After Decades of Burning Trash, MIRA Plant in Hartford Says It Will Close in July 2022." Connecticut Public Radio, December 2, 2020.

Smith, Courtney E. "*Gone Girl* Author 'Sickened' by Theory Invoking Her Book in Missing Mother Case." *Refinery2*, July 8, 2019.

Smith, Nicole. "Divorcing an Abusive Spouse: What to Do When Violence Is Part of the Equation." Survive Divorce, June 8, 2021.

Steinbuch, Yaron. "Fotis Dulos' 5 Kids Visited Him Before He Was Taken Off Life Support." *New York Post*, February 17, 2020.

Strickland, John. "What Makes a Killer?" How Stuff Works, September 13, 2010.

Tepfer, Daniel. "Clients Like Alex Jones, Fotis Dulos Court Disfavor for Attorney Norm Pattis." *CT Post*, June 22, 2019.

Tomlinson, Pat. "Kent Mawhinney, Charged in Jennifer Dulos Disappearance, Has Case Put on Trial List." *Stamford Advocate*, January 18, 2022.

———. "Michelle Troconis Said She'd Kill Jennifer Dulos 'When She Turns Up,' Pickup Truck Owner Testifies." *Stamford Advocate*, February 6, 2024.

———. "New Canaan Man Not Able to Stand Trial in Wife's Killing." *Stamford Advocate*, September 28, 2022.

———. "Owner of Truck Linked to Dulos Case Was Found 'Soaked in Sweat.'" *Stamford Advocate*, January 24, 2024.

———. "3 Takeaways from Day 4 in the Michelle Troconis Trial in Jennifer Dulos Disappearance." *Stamford Advocate*, January 17, 2024.

Tron, Gina. "Investigators Enlist Help of 'Bone Finder' as They Search Fotis Dulos' Former Property." Fox61, January 20, 2021.

———. "Investigators in Jennifer Dulos Case Believe Fotis Dulos May Have Shaved Head to Frame Employee." *New Haven Register*, September 21, 2020.

———. "Jennifer Dulos Became a 'Hermit' with 'Serious Psychological Problems,' Her Estranged Husband Now Claims." *Oxygen True Crime*, October 2, 2019.

———. "Judge Chides Fotis Dulos over Gag Order, Reminding Him It's 'Binding' After Recent Interview with Greek Blog." *Oxygen True Crime*, October 2, 2019.

Vander Hayden, Aly. "'This Is the Time to Come Forward': Former Prosecutor Discusses Finding Closure in Jennifer Dulos Case." *Oxygen True Crime*, October 5, 2020.

Vigdor, Neil. "'Revenge Suicide Hypothesis' Offered by Lawyer for Estranged Husband of Missing Woman." *New York Times*, June 2, 2019.

Vincent, Isabel. "Fotis Dulos Meticulously Planned His Suicide, Police Report Reveals." *New York Post*, May 23, 2020.

Wilkinson, Joseph. "Jennifer Farber Dulos Declared Legally Dead, More Than 4 Years After Disappearance." *New York Daily News*, January 9, 2024.

Williamson, Elizabeth. "Alex Jones Loses by Default in Remaining Sandy Hook Defamation Suits." *New York Times*, November 15, 2021.

Wines, Michael. "The Binghams of Louisville: Family Tragedy and Feuds Bring Down Media Empire." *Los Angeles Times*, January 19, 1986.

Wojtusiak, Vanessa. "Author of 'Gone Girl' Issues Statement Regarding Jennifer Dulos' Disappearance." News8, WTNH.com, July 5, 2019.

Wood, Alex. "Ex–Dulos Lawyer Avoids Rape Conviction, Sentenced for Violating Protective Order." *Journal Inquirer* (Manchester, Connecticut), June 20, 2020.

Woods, Amanda. "Fotis Dulos' Family Says He Was 'No Killer.'" *New York Post*, February 4, 2020.

DOCUMENTS

Note: I have not listed every document I have in my possession, or referred to; I have listed only those that are in the public record.

SEARCH WARRANTS: HOMES, VEHICLES, PHONES

Fotis Dulos arrest warrant: Evidence Tampering. June 1, 2019.

Fotis Dulos arrest warrant: Evidence Tampering. September 4, 2019.

Fotis Dulos arrest warrant: Count One, Murder; Count Two, Felony Murder; Count Three, Kidnapping in the First Degree. January 6, 2020.

Michelle Troconis arrest warrant: Evidence Tampering. June 1, 2019.

Michelle Troconis arrest warrant: Conspiracy Murder.

Kent Mawhinney arrest warrant: Conspiracy Murder.

STATE V. FOTIS DULOS, SC 20363

Judicial District of Stamford-Norwalk at Stamford Superior Court

Criminal; First Amendment; Whether Trial Court Properly Entered Gag Order Barring Defendant, Attorneys, Witnesses, and Law Enforcement from Making Public Statements "Posing Substantial Likelihood of Material Prejudice to This Case."

GLORIA FARBER, as Executor of the Estate of Hilliard Farber v. FORE GROUP, INC., and FOTIS DULOS.

GLORIA FARBER, as Executor of the Estate of Hilliard Farber v. FORE GROUP, INC. et al.

Restraining order ex parte, June 20, 2017.

Ex parte order for emergency custody, June 20, 2017.

Defendant's reply, June 26, 2017.

Defendant's amended reply, June 26, 2017.

Order of protection, June 28, 2017.

JDNO notice—order re: application for relief from abuse, July 11, 2017.

Order—Restraining order issued after hearing, July 25, 2017.

Judger Heller on Second Application for Emergency Custody filed by Jennifer Dulos, March 1, 2018.

COURT TRANSCRIPT TESTIMONY

Jennifer Dulos v. Fotis Dulos at Stamford, June 27, 2017.

Jennifer Dulos v. Fotis Dulos at Stamford, June 28, 2017.

Jennifer Dulos v. Fotis Dulos at Stamford, July 11, 2017.

Jennifer Dulos v. Fotis Dulos at Stamford, January 24, 2018.

Jennifer Dulos v. Fotis Dulos at Stamford, January 31, 2018.

Jennifer Dulos v. Fotis Dulos at Stamford, February 27, 2018.

Jennifer Dulos v. Fotis Dulos at Stamford, March 2, 2018.

Jennifer Dulos v. Fotis Dulos at Stamford, March 5, 2018.

Jennifer Dulos v. Fotis Dulos at Stamford, March 19, 2018.

Jennifer Dulos v. Fotis Dulos at Stamford, March 27, 2018.

Jennifer Dulos v. Fotis Dulos at Stamford, April 24, 2018.

Jennifer Dulos v. Fotis Dulos at Stamford, April 26, 2018.

Jennifer Dulos v. Fotis Dulos at Stamford, June 5, 2018.

Jennifer Dulos v. Fotis Dulos at Stamford, June 8, 2018.
Jennifer Dulos v. Fotis Dulos at Stamford, June 10, 2018.
Jennifer Dulos v. Fotis Dulos at Stamford, July 12, 2018.
Jennifer Dulos v. Fotis Dulos at Stamford, July 13, 2018.
Jennifer Dulos v. Fotis Dulos at Stamford, July 27, 2018.
Jennifer Dulos v. Fotis Dulos at Stamford, July 30, 2018.
Jennifer Dulos v. Fotis Dulos at Stamford, August 28, 2018.
Jennifer Dulos v. Fotis Dulos at Stamford, September 18, 2018.
Jennifer Dulos v. Fotis Dulos at Stamford, September 21, 2018.
Jennifer Dulos v. Fotis Dulos at Stamford, October 3, 2018.
Jennifer Dulos v. Fotis Dulos at Stamford, October 9, 2018.
Jennifer Dulos v. Fotis Dulos at Stamford, October 31, 2018.
Jennifer Dulos v. Fotis Dulos at Stamford, December 11, 2018.
Jennifer Dulos v. Fotis Dulos at Stamford, April 16, 2019.

VIDEO LINKS

"Body Language Analysis of Fotis Dulos Interview, Suspected in Wife's Disappearance." Dr. Judy Ho, December 5, 2019. YouTube, www.youtube.com/watch?v=aqHXLv_fano.

"Court Appearance: Fotis Dulos Faces Judge." WFSB 3, June 3, 2019. YouTube, www.youtube.com/watch?v=4D0oSfNuGSw.

"Court Appearance: Michelle Troconis and Fotis Dulos." WFSB 3, June 22, 2019. YouTube, www.youtube.com/watch?v=-H2V3JDHxBU.

"Court Arraignments: Fotis Dulos, Michelle Troconis and Kent Mawhinney Face a Judge." WFSB 3, January 8, 2020. YouTube, www.youtube.com/watch?v=3dkHj_vont0.

"Courtroom Video: Fotis Dulos Appears in Stamford Superior Court." WFSB 3, August 9, 2019. YouTube, www.youtube.com/watch?v=dc1F3HQ-CxA.

"Courtroom Video": Michelle Troconis sentencing, including victim impact statements and statements from Troconis's friends and family. Court TV on YouTube, May 31, 2024. www.youtube.com/watch?v=wS-X4CDME8U.

"Excavator Brought to Property Linked to Fotis Dulos." NBC Connecticut TV, January 20, 2021. www.nbcconnecticut.com/news/local/excavator-brought-to-property-linked-to-fotis-dulos/2406339/.

"Exclusive Interview: Attorney Norm Pattis Reacts to Fotis Dulos's Suicide Attempt." NBC Connecticut, January 28, 2020. www.nbcconnecticut.com/news/local/exclusive-interview-attorney-norm-pattis-reacts-to-fotis-dulos-suicide-attempt/2216114/.

"Exclusive: One-on-One Interview with Fotis Dulos Attorney, Norm Pattis, One Year After Jennifer's Disappearance." Fox61 [Ben Goldman, interviewer], May 22, 2020. www.fox61.com/article/news/crime/interview-with-fotis-dulos-attorney-norm-pattis/520-0a004c22-27af-4124-b476-78025aec017a.

"Face the State: Attorney for Fotis Dulos, Rich Rochlin." WFSB 3, July 11, 2019. YouTube, www.youtube.com/watch?v=SAlP00s1OcM.

"Fotis Dulos Arraignment on Murder Charges." Law&Crime Network, January 8, 2020. YouTube, www.youtube.com/watch?v=5RF00QtMUKs.

"Fotis Dulos: I Know What I've Done and What I Haven't Done—the Truth Is Going to Come Out." NBC 4 New York, July 2, 2019. www.nbcnewyork.com/news /local/fotis-dulos-interview-i-know-what-ive-done-and-what-i-havent-done /1515929/.

"Fotis Dulos in Court Asking to Dismiss Charges." Law&Crime Network, October 7, 2019. YouTube, www.youtube.com/watch?v=g5CIzDyjDbg.

"Fox61 Exclusive: State Police Final Interview Before Gag Order in Jennifer Dulos Case." Fox61, September 12, 2019. YouTube, www.youtube.com/watch?v =cYTrQWPp8kA.

"Full Interview: Attorney for Jennifer Dulos' Family [Richard Weinstein] Addresses Case." WFSB 3, September 11, 2019. YouTube, www.youtube.com/watch?v =d54uFRnPvuY.

Holcombe, Madeleine, and Brian Vitagliano. "Newly Released Videos Show Fotis Dulos Disposing of Evidence the Day His Estranged Wife Disappeared, Attorney Says." CNN, August 25, 2020. www.cnn.com/2020/08/25/us/fotis-dulos -video-disposing-evidence-michelle-troconis/index.html.

"'I Didn't Do It' | New Video Released of Michelle Troconis Interrogation by Police." Fox61, February 3, 2021. YouTube, www.youtube.com/watch?v=8R7sGYDFCnE.

"Jennifer Dulos Case: Missing Mom's Estranged Husband's First Interview." NBC New York I-Team [Sarah Wallace, interviewer], July 12, 2019. YouTube, www .youtube.com/watch?v=GjbQjePZbF8.

"Michelle Troconis Motion Hearing." Law&Crime Network, February 3, 2021. YouTube, www.youtube.com/watch?v=Rqi47_TVoVU.

"Michelle Troconis Pleads Not Guilty to Conspiracy to Commit Murder (Jennifer Dulos Disappearance)." Law&Crime Network, February 7, 2020. YouTube, www.youtube.com/watch?v=YcwB6wBvKOg.

Moriarty, Erin. "Video Shows "the Other Woman" [Michelle Troconis] in Missing Mom Jennifer Dulos Case Being Grilled by Cops." CBS News, May 19, 2022. www.cbsnews.com/news/jennifer-dulos-case-michelle-troconis-video/.

———. "What Does the Other Woman Know? The Disappearance of Jennifer Dulos." CBS News, February 13, 2021. www.cbsnews.com/video/what-does-the -other-woman-know-the-disappearance-of-jennifer-dulos/#x.

"New Video Released in Investigation into Disappearance of Jennifer Dulos." ABC 7, August 24, 2020. abc7ny.com/jennifer-dulos-connecticut-fotis-video /6387061/.

"Video: Friend of Jennifer Dulos [Carrie Luft] Speaks to Dr. Oz." WFSB 3, September 19, 2019. YouTube, www.youtube.com/watch?v=7WgkapLKrxs.

Acknowledgments

Dozens of people helped me research and write this book. In addition to the detectives, lawyers, and officials who spoke on and off the record, and the professionals who were kind enough to share their insights and time, I would like to give special thanks to Timothy Dumas, who read an early version of this book for accuracy, helped with his knowledge of the case (which he covered as a journalist), and shared his knowledge of Fairfield County and the Stamford Superior Court; Lisa Nkonoki, who toured me around Farmington and helped me understand the dynamics of the high-profile Fairfield County divorce; Eduardo Machado, who shared his memories of Jennifer and introduced me to other members of the Playwrights Collective; Janet Renard, the copy editor, who made this book better; Tom Beller, another early reader; Rich Rochlin and Eric Broder, who helped from the legal side; Jessica Medoff, my wife, a former prosecutor who fact-checked and helped in areas of criminal law; my father, Herb Cohen, aka Handsomo, who taught me "to care, but not that much"; my sister, the Babe Ruth of Asset Forfeiture, Sharon Levin; and my brother, Steven Cohen, a former federal prosecutor who offered legal advice gratis. Thanks also to D. J. Paul, Hugh Warrender, Colette Burson, Kate Robin, Tim Cunningham, Daniel Rybicky, the staff at the Rose Collection of the New York

Public Library, Warren St. John and Alfred Branch at *Patch*, Dave Altimari at *CT Mirror*, David Lipsky, Graydon Carter, Alessandra Stanley, Michael Hainey, George Pendle, George Kalogerakis, Vanessa Grigoriadis, Dan Kirschen, and Jonathan Galassi, whose unrelenting cry was "more detail."